To A fellow Red Willet Xxo

MY YOUTH
MY KOP

Peter Etherington

First published 2002 by the author, Peter Etherington, in association with Countyvise Limited.

Copyright © 2002 Peter Etherington

The right of Peter Etherington to be identified as the author of this work has been asserted by him in accordance with the Copyright, Design and Patents Act 1988.

British Library Cataloguing in Publication Data.
A Catalogue record for this book is available from the British Library.

ISBN 1 901231 33 X

Countyvise Limited, 14 Appin Road, Birkenhead CH41 9HH
Printed by Birkenhead Press Limited, 14 Appin Road, Birkenhead CH41 9HH

This book is dedicated to the memory of Bernie Carroll.

ACKNOWLEDGEMENTS

First of all I would like to say a great big thankyou to everybody who bought my first book, "One boy and his Kop" for making it the rip-roaring success it was. Sales of that book not only allowed me to finance this book but also made a significant contribution to the following charities: Zoe's Place Baby Hospice; Hillsborough Justice Campaign; Claire House Children's Hospice; West Lancashire Community Hospice; Wigan and Leigh Hospice and the British Heart Foundation. I thank you all on behalf of those charities.

The old beer-addled brain cells are now rearranging themselves so Brian Pead's, "A Complete History of Liverpool Football Club" was once again an invaluable source of reference.

Alan Edge: what can I say about this man that I haven't said before? Well, quite a lot actually but I'll content myself with thanking him for once again supporting and assisting me.

The striking front cover of "One Boy and his Kop" was responsible I feel for many sales. Tim Kelly produced that cover and I'm hoping his design for this book will have the same affect. Tim is also responsible for the design of my website www.oneboyandhiskop.co.uk Thanks Tim.

Thanks go to the editors of the various LFC fanzines and websites for their continued support of "One boy and his Kop" and "MY YOUTH - MY KOP." John Pearman of Red All Over The Land might be a crotchety old bugger but he's not half useful when you need help.

Finally, I would like to thank the three most important people in my life for putting up with me. I know I can be a moaning old get at times but without my three children: Stevo, Little and Jelly Bean or Steven, Evelyn and Angela to give them their Sunday names I would be nothing. Thanks kids.

CONTENTS

FOREWORD

By Alan Edge (author of "Faith of our Fathers")

As we Liverpudlians plough our lone furrows along life's highways and byways, our collars turned up against the wind and the rain and anything else our mini-odysseys might care to pit us against, have any of you ever taken the time out to stop and wonder about the sudden upsurge in the number of Eddie Stobart trucks on the roads today? Likewise, as you gaze heavenwards towards that endless troubled sky wrapped so densely round us, have you ever pondered why suddenly it seems littered with twice as many jumbo jets as before?

If you're one of those for whom the answer to such imponderables as these generates as much excitement as the news of Vegard Heggem's latest crock amongst LFC's crack medical team then I suggest you read no further. If, however, you are more of an intrepid soul, with the inquisitive grey matter of a three-year-old, then you might just care to read on.

In late Spring my daughter was on holiday in Tunisia. Part of the deal involved a trip to the desert oasis of Tozeur. On arriving at this isolated nirvana she was greeted by those run-of-the-mill oasis sights any of us oasis virgins might expect - lush copses of date palm trees, vast expanses of leafy shade, giant man-eating spiders, mountains of camel dung and a central duck pond. Intriguingly, however, was the rather untypical oasis scene that confronted her. It was the sight of a group of Arab nomads huddled together, as if as one, all enraptured by their English-fluent mainstay reading out loud his copy of our very own Peter Evo's version of the Koran, "One Boy And His Kop."

Nor does this meandering tale stop there.

My son who, at the very same time, was completing the

field work element of his combined degree in advanced yoga and ice fishing amidst the frozen wastes of the Alaskan Tundra had, incredibly, chanced upon a bevy of fur-lined Eskimos also frantically devouring a copy of Peter's book. Coincidences beyond belief, I am sure you'll agree.

Now I shall bore you no further with the mechanics of selling sand to the Arabs or snow to the Eskimos. Such feats, of course, will lie forever beyond the scope of mere mortals such as ourselves. I will say, however, that when an ordinary Scouser such as Peter Etherington can so captivate such diverse ethnic groups with his everyday tales of footy deeds and escapades in pursuit of his beloved Liverpool Football Club then, manifestly, we are faced with something special in our midst. Not to mention the fact that we have also - quite possibly - unearthed a plausible solution to the mystery of all those Eddie Stobart lorries and jumbo jets pinballing the distant corners of the globe laden with copies of Peter's new enterprise, "MY YOUTH - MY KOP."

My fellow Liverpudlians, I give you the second instalment in the life and times of a Liverpudlian whose celebration of what it means to be an ordinary footy fan - a Scouse one at that - is a joy to behold. A veritable oasis of enchantment.

CHAPTER ONE

THE LANGUAGE BARRIER

Life in Skem was hard at first. We just couldn't settle. We seemed to be spending more time back in Liverpool than we did in the land of roundabouts. Going from the busy urban sprawl of Bootle and Litherland to the relatively quiet pastures of countryside Skem was not suiting us at all. Yes, there were plenty of Scousers in Skem, which after all was built (the New Town anyway) as an overspill for Liverpool. Kirkby, which itself was originally supposed to be an overspill town, was now overspilling into Skem. There was also the very big obstacle of the language barrier. It really was like stepping into another country. Don't get me wrong, the people were fine, it was just that they spoke this weird dialect.

"Toreet Cliff!"

"Toreet Dave!"

I was in the local ironmongers, Garner's, looking to mong a bit of iron and also acquire a couple of door numbers for our new home.

"Excuse mate. 'Ave yer got a couple of number fours?"

"Toreet lad! Arse thee fettlin'?"

What!

"Cliff, arse geetin' two number fours for yon mon?"

What the fuckin' 'ell were these spacemen on about?

It seemed what they were saying was, in Scousespeak, "All right mate. 'Ow're yer doin'?" and, "Cliff, 'ave yer got two number fours for this lad?"

"Er, I'll 'ave an 'ammer too please mate."

"Cliff, fetch yon mon thommer too."

"Does young 'un want claw or ball?"

Er, excuse me. I am 'ere yer know. Yer could ask me. I can speak, even if it is a different language than you two.

"A claw 'ammer please."

"Eh up. Weather's set fair ter middlin' isn't it young 'un?"

"Er, yeah mate."

What the fuck was this madman going on about?

Just one more thing and then I could escape.

"Got any turps mate?"

"Does want video turps or cassette turps?"

Okay I made that last bit up but it was with a sense of relief I left the shop with my two number fours and thommer, sorry, hammer!

The neighbours were as bad too. We were sitting in the living room of Frank and Linda acquainting ourselves with our next door neighbours.

"Does want a drink?"

Oh, that's nice I thought, we're gonna get a bevy. Yeah, a nice cold bottle of Newcy Brown will go down very well on this beautifully warm spring day.

"Yeah, go 'ead Frank. That'd be nice."

Five minutes later me and Ev were sitting, looking aghast at each other with a steaming hot cup of tea each. Words, if we could have exchanged them anyway would have been superfluous, the looks said it all: "This isn't a drink. This is a fuckin' cup of tea!"

Worse was to come!

"I've geetin' your little 'un some toffees."

Ah, isn't that nice?

Linda then produced a bag of Jelly Tots and gave them to said little 'un. Even our little Stevie knew that Jelly Tots weren't toffees - they were jellies!

And they all had mad names! Snoz, Jonty, Esso, Hamburger, Storm, Twisty, Lollipop and Red Eyes. Where did they get these names? Who gave them to their unfortunate recipients? I might as well have been on another planet! Which was exactly what my Dad thought as not once did he ever set foot in Skem. Mam was very reluctant too but she did at least make the occasional visit. Even Granny Martha honoured us with a state visit on one memorable occasion (more of that later) but Dad was firmly super-glued to his fireside armchair. Of course Skem was 15 miles away in the days before the M58 so I couldn't reasonably expect a family who regarded a day at Seaforth Sands as a foreign holiday to come traipsing through the countryside avoiding the sheep and cows that blocked the stagecoach paths.

A week or so after moving to Skem my Granny Evo died. She'd had a good innings I suppose and was cracking on, I think, about 90 when she passed away. It was still sad though and even sadder to see what it did to my Dad. I'd liked going to Granny Evo's when I was a kid. There was always a shilling or two for me when I visited her little flat in Douglas Place. Granny Evo was looked after by my Dad's half-brother Uncle Teddy. I didn't particularly get on with Uncle Teddy. I think he resented me going there. He was okay in a sort of "put up with him" kind of way. To compensate for that though was the fact that Auntie Rosie and Uncle Jimmy Boyle lived in Douglas Place too. Uncle Jimmy, as I've described earlier, was a total Liverpool fanatic, as were my cousins Terry, Kevin, Paul and Rose Marie. I'd made arrangements to take the day off work to attend the funeral on the 7th June. I went to Mam's straight from work the day before so I wouldn't miss the kick-off of the Poland v England World Cup qualifier. When I arrived at Mam's all hell broke loose. Granny Evo's funeral had been that day and not the day after as I thought. Dad went off his head accusing me of not giving a fuck, which really upset me. There was no reasoning with him though that I had my dates mixed up. He was very drunk, very angry, very upset and very violent. Mam and the kids Mark, Collette and Price were very frightened. The way Dad was carrying on somebody was going to get very badly hurt. He had to be stopped. I stopped him. I wasn't very proud of it but it had to be done. I felt disrespectful towards Dad. I really loved him and it felt like I didn't love him any more because of what happened. It's a thing that should never happen between a father and son but it had and there was nothing that could be done about it now.

"Clowns to the left of me, jokers to the right, here I am, stuck in the middle with you."

Oh thanks very much Stealer's fuckin' Wheel! Thanks for fuckin' reminding me that I was well and fuckin' truly stuck in this God-forsaken fuckin' one horse town! I was very soon going to lose my job at Walter Holmes too the way I was going on. I had to get the six o'clock (in the morning!) bus from the Derby Arms to make sure I got to the Black Bull for the 61 to Seaforth. The twenty-minute walk then to Beech Road got me to work just in time. An eight hour working day turned into a thirteen hour day overall as I arrived home at seven o'clock. That was when I had the money for the bus fare, which wasn't very often. Hitchhiking was a pain in the arse when I had to do it to get to work. I'd thumb it anywhere to watch the Reds but it was a drag to get to work. I could get to Leeds by thumb about an hour and a half after setting off but Skem to Litherland was invariably a two to three hour journey. So it was that I was on a final warning after one memorable week where the earliest I got in to work was 9 o'clock on the Wednesday. I was going to have to get a job in Skem and get one fast otherwise I was gonna join the Skem dole queue; that is if they had a dole office! The only joy in all this was little Stevie running into my arms to greet me when I got home from work. The little fella really did love it. He had a big fat garden to play in. Well it was more like the Amazon jungle but you know what I mean. Percy Thrower I was not!

"Who the fuck's Percy Thrower Evo?" I hear you ask. Percy Thrower was the 1970's version of Alan Titchmarsh although just a tad more irritating! There was no Charlie Dimmock type (Tommy Smith Footy Studs) to brighten up Percy's wittering about roses and lobelias either.

"San Miguel Senor?"
"Fuck off Manuel!"
"Por favor?"
"Por favor my fuckin' arse!"

This twat of a Spanish beach waiter was doing my 'ead in! Little
Stevie was happily playing in the sand with a group of other kids.
I was lying on a sun-lounger. Ev had just finished Ambre
Solairing me to within an inch of my life and was now slowly,
beautifully, surreptitiously tossing me off under the towel I had
draped over the Evo donga. Ev was on the vinegar stroke and my
little white mice were about to burst forth. I just did not need
Manuel, his music of the fuckin' mountains nor his poxy fuckin'
San Miguel at this moment!
"Eez free Sir."
"Oh well that's fuckin' different then isn't it! Giz one."
No problem anyway; the hand job would turn into a bonkfest
later as I intended ravaging Ev's beautiful body.
"Sangria for the senorita?"
"Yeah and keep yer fuckin' eyes off 'er tits!"
"Come on Peter. We'll take these to our room. I'll put Stevie in
the cot and then I'm gonna take you to heaven and back."
"Come on Stevie. 'Urry up son. Time for bo-bos!"
Once Stevie had been sung to sleep with his favourite lullaby,
"You'll Never Walk Alone" Ev set about divesting me of my love
fat - a pleasure that Manuel had so cruelly denied me earlier.
"I love you. I love you," I whispered as I kissed her tender body,
stopping just short of her little honeypot.
"Lower, lower," she whimpered.
"I LOVE YOU. I LOVE YOU," I croaked in my best Barry White
voice.
Ev was straddling me. Her beautiful globes, chocolate digestives,
TSFS and all were jutting out in front of me in all their glory. For
some strange reason though they seemed to be just ever so
slightly out of reach as if my arms weren't quite long enough to
twiddle those knobs you could get Radio Luxembourg on. My
tumescent member was aching to be enveloped between those
silky smooth honeypot walls.
Mad that isn't it? You never get your end away in your dreams!
Something always stops you short. If you don't wake up yourself

some twat will always do it for you. Said twat on this occasion was the bastard bus conductor! Buses were still operating with a driver and a conductor in those days.

"Eh mate, come on, wake up!"

"Wha' wha'. Ev I love yer. Tommy Smith, Tommy Smith!"

"What? I know who Tommy Smith is but who the fuck's Ev? Come on mate, the bus 'as broke down. We need a push."

"Fuck off!"

"What d'yer mean fuck off? We need a push. Yer wanna get 'ome don't yer?"

"Yeah, I fuckin' do but I'm not pushin' any fuckin' bus!"

"Come on mate, these women are gonna push. Surely you can?"

The bus was absolutely chocker block, downstairs and upstairs as well as it turned out (they still had double-deckers in those days too). All heads were turned (average age about 124) towards the protracted negotiations. Problem was I was a stubborn bastard as well as being knackered, the bus conductor was a twat and Henry Kissinger couldn't make it having far more pressing matters to attend in the Middle East.

"I don't give a fuck! These women 'aven' been up since five o'clock this fuckin' mornin' an' worked a full fuckin' day gettin' covered in shite and sawdust! Go an' find a phone an' get another bus to come out."

"We're in fuckin' Bickerstaffe mate! Yer won't find a phone within two miles of 'ere!"

"Bickerstaffe? Where the fuck's Bickerstaffe?"

"Exactly!"

The bus cuntductor did have a point - we were in the middle of nowhere (Dusty Springfield - real name Mary O'Hara - 1967) but I was fucked if I was gonna push a fuckin' bus!

"'Ave yer got a large pole mate?"

"What for?"

"So yer can secrete yerself into the darkest, smallest corner yer can find and fuck yerself very slowly to within an inch of yer miserable little life."

"Go 'ead, get off the fuckin' bus!"

"What am I supposed to do? Yer said yerself we're miles from fuckin' anywhere!"

"I know! Just get off yer fuckin' little twat!"

"Ah fuck off Reg Varney!"

Reg Varney played the character of Stan in the very popular TV sitcom of the time, "On the Buses". Quite why it was so popular I haven't got a fuckin' clue, as it was surely the worst programme ever to flicker into the nation's living rooms. Reg Varney actually played the driver but I couldn't remember the name of the conductor so Reg would have to do.

"Yeah, go 'ead fuck off yer little bastard!"

Charming language from the coffin dodgers! I thought old people weren't supposed to swear?

"Fuck off yer owld twats! Yer won't be 'ome in time to get yer fuckin' pensions!"

Half an hour later I was beginning to regret my rashness, as I was still nowhere near home. I'd just passed Four Lane Ends, which was what passed for a landmark in this shithole of a place, when the great unpushable approached. Ah good; they'd managed to get it going. I'd put my hand out and stop it. Things would be a bit awkward for a minute or two on there but I'd paid my fare so was entitled to go all the way to the Derby Arms. The bus not slowing down was not a good sign. Neither was the fact the driver had one hand on the steering wheel while two fingers of the other hand told me exactly his thoughts on my possible return to the bus. Similarly, as the bus passed me, Reg and the coffin dodgers were also expressing their thoughts to the young Evo in the time-honoured way. Well fuck the lot of yer! I had my own way of expressing my views to those who so blighted my life: belt undone, zip down, jeans lowered, skids lowered, turn round and cheeks spread as far as I could possibly get them so the Evo arsehole was in full view of the similar arseholes on the bus! One all I call that! A dishonourable draw.

"Where've yer been? It's nearly eight o'clock!"

"Oh I've been lying on a beach in Majorca Ev."
I suppose that was true really - well at least in my dreams.
"Fuck off funny arse!"
"Well where the fuck d'yer think I've been Ev? I'm covered in fuckin' sawdust and shite, I've got wood chippings in me arse and I've got more fuckin wood splinters in me 'ands than Jesus fuckin' Christ so take a flyin' fuckin' guess at work!"
I loved her to fuckin' bits but she really did do me fuckin' 'ead in at times!
"Well where've yer been after that?"
"Yer wouldn't believe me if I told yer Ev."
"Well go on, try me."
"The bus broke down."
"Yer fuckin' liar!"
"Well why the fuckin' 'ell ask me then if yer don't fuckin' believe the answer I give yer! Yer might as well make yer own fuckin' answer up. Go on then, where've I been?"
"Yer've been to yer Ma's 'aven' yer? Then yer went to your Pauline's and 'ad yer tea there didn't yer?"
"For fuck sake Ev, no I didn't go to me Ma's or get fed at our Po's. I just wish to fuck I 'ad! I've 'ad fuck all to eat since dinnertime!"
Ev did have a point I suppose in that because, as I said, we couldn't settle I did spend quite a bit of time at my Mam's. The lads in work used to call me The Spaceman - I was always going to Ma's. Think about it. On the other hand she had no point at all about me going to our Po's. Ev had this sort of dread, hatred if you like, of me getting fed at our Pauline's. I did sometimes but always ate my dinner up like a good boy when I got home. I suppose maybe this irrational fear was brought about by the fact our Pauline made the best curry this side of Bombay whilst Ev struggled with a boiled egg! Well maybe she wasn't that bad but Ev was more Tommy Smith than Delia Smith - which is, I suppose, a bit of an insult too to Tommy Smith as apparently he was, maybe still is, quite a good cook. I can never mention Tommy Smith without thoughts of Ev's beautiful raspberry ripples pouring into my head, making my heart pound and my

loins ache! Which reminds me of a marvellous scene from the classic sitcom Porridge. It went something like:

FLETCHER (RONNIE BARKER): "Men without women get a stirring in their loins."

GODBER (RICHARD BECKINSALE): "Where's your loins Fletch?"

FLETCHER: "Well Lenny, you know when you're lying awake at night thinking of your lovely girlfriend Denise?"

GODBER: "Yes Fletch!"

FLETCHER: "Well you know where you get a stirring?"

GODBER: "Yes Fletch I do!"

FLETCHER: "Well that's your loins!"

Meanwhile, back at the row:

"Well, yer've missed Coronation Street now!"

"Oh fuckin' 'ell what am I gonna do? I've missed Coronation Street. My life's never gonna be the same again. Fuck Coronation Street, I'm fuckin' starvin'! Where's me tea?"

"In the oven but it'll be burnt now. It's been in there for an hour and a half!"

"Oh well that'll make a change won't it."

"Well, yer've only yerself to blame!"

"Fuck off will yer Ev. Yer'd give a fuckin' aspirin a 'eadache!"

I dragged the charred remnants of congealed sausage, egg and chips (a "meal" I was to become very used to over the years) from the incinerator (sorry oven - Ev seemed to think that everything had to be cooked or kept warm at a temperature just slightly below that of the Sun) and got stuck royally in.

"Did yer enjoy that?"

"Yeah Ev it was lovely," I lied through my now blackened teeth

It wasn't worth telling her the truth as I'd had enough grief for one day through telling the truth but Ev wasn't finished with me yet.

"Come on Peter, why were yer so late 'ome?"

"I've told yer Ev, the bus broke down an' I had to walk 'ome from Bickerstaffe."

"Where's Bickerstaffe?"

"Exactly!"

"Fazackerley? That's where I had our Steven. God, that's a long way. Yer walked all the way from there?"

"Yeah Ev."

"Ah God, no wonder yer knackered. I'm sorry Peter. It's just that sometimes I think yer've got another woman."

"Another woman! Yer fuckin' jokin' aren't yer? I've fuckin' got enough with one!"

Ev cried.

"Oh come 'ere Ev. I was only messin'. I love you. You're the only woman I want or will ever want. Besides, you take so much out of me in bed I'd 'ave nothin' left for any other woman."

Ev smiled.

"I love you too Peter. I'll make it up to you when we go to bed."

We watched "The Family" together. "The Family" was the first of the "fly-on-the-wall" documentary genre - a genre that has since spawned some great programmes and some absolute dross. "The Family" followed the Wilkins family from Reading during the trials and tribulations of their everyday lives. It was a great programme but I could never help thinking following the Evo family would have made far better television. Ev loved it and would never have missed a minute of it. I was falling asleep well before the end so dragged my weary body up the wooden hill to bed. I was asleep as soon as my head hit the pillow.

The familiar stirring in my loins was being caused by Ev ever so gently caressing my turgid acorn into a raging oak tree. I woke up. This time it was no dream. My lovely wife was indeed doing what she was so brilliant at.

"Peter, I'm sorry for moanin' at yer before. Come on, I'm wearin' yer favourites."

That was enough to bring me fully awake (and fully erect for that matter).

Manuel was nowhere to be seen. Perhaps he'd fucked off into the mountains to play his music. Our rickety old bed that had been passed down through two generations was no Majorca beach but sometimes reality is so much better than dreams isn't it?

CHAPTER TWO

FLYING TOOLS

"Evo, where's yer weddin' ring?"
I looked down at third finger left hand (Martha Reeves and The Vandellas 1967 - covered by The Pearls 1972). Peter Vac-Vac (so called because he operated the Vac-Vac wood-treating tank) was indeed right - there was no wedding ring.
"Fuckin' 'ell no, she's gonna kill me!"
The only two possible places it could be were the two places I'd been working that day; with Vac-Vac or in the Sin Bin. The Sin Bin was the sawdust collection room and was appropriately named as all the bad boys were sent to work in there. It was a right fuckin' shithole of a place being as it was infested with rats. It also fuckin' stunk to high heaven of piss - stale piss at that. The regular incumbent (who fuckin' loved it in there) Lonely, was a dirty, lazy bastard who couldn't be arsed using the toilet to piss like any even half-decent human being and would just piss all over the sawdust sacks. I'd been working in the Sin Bin for about a month. I was now seen to be a permanent fixture as Lonely's "mate" seeing as the split between Peter Etherington Esq., and Walter Holme Builders was imminent. By this time I was either late or absent more times than I was actually there.
"Lonely, 'ave yer seen me weddin' ring?"
"Don't fuckin' call me Lonely! Me name's Peter."
I could only just about make out Lonely mumbling this as he had a very distorted mouth which gave the impression he had two peaches either side of his gob. Vac-Vac did a brilliant impression of him. We called him Lonely because he was a dead ringer for the scruffy, little odious character in the TV series Callan and besides, he never talked to any fucker. My guess was that as he'd been gone for two hours, stunk of Bentox, Buckfast, Stingo, Double Diamond and Gauntlet bitter, he'd found the ring, took it over to the Railway and flogged it to some no-mark in there for a couple of quid.

"Come on Lonely. For fuck sake, just tell me, who d'yer sell the ring to? Me missus'll fuckin' kill me if I go 'ome without it!"
"I 'aven' fuckin' seen it. Now fuck off before I piss all over yer!" mumbled Lonely/Marlon Brando.
What could I do? I was fucked! I had to get out of the Sin Bin anyway as I was nearly puking up from the smell. Overpowering even Lonely's piss and the smell of all the other shite he'd been drinking was the stench of Gauntlet. I kid you not, that was the worst ale ever brewed on this earth! I'm sure the Railway used to attach a pipe directly to the Leeds/Liverpool canal under the Lift Bridge and just siphon it straight into the Gauntlet pump. I think they used to get the devil down to bless it or something. Double Diamond was okay though. That was a sort of pale ale type bevy on draught. Very nice if you like that sort of thing but I couldn't stomach more than a couple of pints of it.

I cried on the bus home. Not just because I was absolutely shittin' meself over what Evelyn was gonna do but also because I was genuinely upset that I'd lost the wedding ring she'd bought me. Okay it was only a fairly cheap, thin, 9-carat effort but we'd only been married just over two years and soft arse me had gone and lost it.

Ev was laying the stair carpet when I got home. I made the almost fatal mistake of telling her I'd lost the ring while she had a claw hammer in her hand.
"Ev, I've lost me weddin' ring."
No questions asked. No discussion. No screaming banshees (not yet anyway). Ev was sitting about five steps up the stairs and flung the hammer straight at me. Honestly, another eighth of an inch to the left and you wouldn't be reading this now. The hammer scraped my ear before it thudded into the wall behind me and bounced back, boomerang style, almost into Ev's hand. I was taking no chances - I bounded the steps, legged it past Ev and locked myself in the bog.
"Yer fuckin' stupid bastard! Where the fuckin' 'ell did yer lose the ring?"

"I don't fuckin' know! If I knew that I'd 'ave the fuckin' thing now wouldn't I?"
I was dead brave behind the bog door. It was a good job the lock was fairly strong as by now Ev was trying to kick down the door. I couldn't blame her I suppose - what a stupid twat I was for losing the ring in the first place. Poor little Stevie, not yet two years old, must have been wondering what the fuck he'd let himself in for having this pair of mad arses for parents. An hour later and I thought it might be quite safe to emerge from my self-imposed solitary confinement in the bog. That was a mistake! Five minutes or so of grappling, scratching, biting and hair pulling ensued, and Ev had a go too, before I was allowed the dubious pleasure of sitting down to my congealed egg, sausage and chips.

And then there was the little pussycat! Now don't get me wrong, I'll never do them any harm but I'm NOT an animal lover. I'm just not a pet man. I've had a few pets and they've all either let me down or fucked off on me but more of that later.
"Mister, d'yer want this kitten? Me Mum said we've gorra get rid of it."
I felt sorry for the two little kids and their kitten standing at the door but I was fucked if I was gonna have a house full of fleas.
"Nah, yer okay kids. Go and ask somebody else."
"Ah, poo poo lat!"
Little Stevie had spoken!
"Come on Peter, let's 'ave it. It's a lovely little thing. Ah, look at its eyes."
Ev had spoken! I was outnumbered two to one but I wasn't gonna let this go without a fight.
"No Ev, they stink! There'll be piss 'n' fleas all over the place."
"No there won't I'll look after it proper."
"Ah poo poo lat, poo poo lat!"
Further resistance was useless. The poo poo lat, sorry pussycat, was handed over and Smokey (after Mr. Robinson - finest soul singer ever) was welcomed (sic) into the Evo household. But I had a cunning plan!

Ev, like my Ma, was a creature of habit. I told Ev I liked pilchard sarnies, so, like my Ma before her, she would be making me pilchard Reg Varney's to take to work for all eternity.

"I've left yer butties on the sideboard. Make sure yer put the cat out before yer come to bed." Ev shouted down from the bathroom.

"Yeah, no problem Ev."

Hehehehehe! Smokey was on his way out!

"There ya go Mr. Robinson lad", I whispered, "nice meal there for yer mate."

"Ev, come and 'ave a look what this fuckin' cat's done!" I shouted up to my beloved the next morning. Smokey was lying on the couch having had a good night's kip after filling his belly with my pilchards. Even the greaseproof bread wrapper had been licked clean. Nice one Smokey!

"Oh my God. It's ate yer carryin' out!"

"Yeah, I fuckin' know. What am I gonna do? It's too late to make any more an' I've only got me bus fare. I'll 'ave fuck all to eat all day 'cos of that fuckin' cat!"

"Ah, I'm sorry Peter. Why didn't yer put it out last night anyway?"

"I forgot. Ev, it's gonna 'ave to go. Either Smokey goes or I go!"

The cheeky bitch actually thought about it for a minute!

"Yeah I know. I'll see if Mary wants it."

"Okay, nice one. I'm off to work. See ya. See ya Smokey."

I gave Smokey a nice little goodbye pat before making my way to the Derby Arms to thumb a lift to work. Mission accomplished and I was fucked if I was gonna go all day with nothing to eat because of some cat! Smokey got a good deal out of it though - his belly was full and he was off to Mary's where he would be royally fed. Everyone was happy! Yer can't ask for more than that!

Ev's penchant for throwing things at me was to be further exercised after another massive row. She really was very good at it. If "Throwing sharp, dangerous objects at your husband's head" had been an Olympic event Ev would have the Gold every time - no doubt!

"Peter, go the shop for me and get twenty Sovereign."

"Ah, I'm knackered Ev. I've just got home from work. You go."

"I can't; Corry'll be on in a minute."

"Fuck Corry!"

"Yer never do nothin' in this 'ouse you!"

Ev didn't know about the flagrant use of double negatives.

"Well what do I do then?"

"Nothin'! That's what I said."

"No, you said I never do nothin' in this 'ouse. So if I don't do nothin' I must do at least do somethin'."

"What the fuck are you on about?"

"Well it's either "I do nothin'" or "I don't do anythin'". To say I don't do nothin' means that I must at least do somethin'."

"Stop takin' the fuckin' piss!"

"I'm not takin' the fuckin' piss. Yer takin' the piss outta yerself. Yer using a double negative."

"What the fuck's a double negative?"

It was then that I pushed her just that little bit too far.

"The use of double negatives is far too prevalent in today's English language."

"Fuck you and yer double fuckin' negatives!" Ev screamed, just before picking a screwdriver from the sideboard and half turning to hurl it at my head. It couldn't be a little, sort of blunt screwdriver either could it? It had to be a big, fat, fuck off one, sharp as yer fuckin' like! And it couldn't be the plassy handle that hit me full on the forehead either could it? It had to be the fuckin' business end that smashed into and sliced open my forehead just above my left eye. I slumped off the couch and could immediately feel myself fainting.

"Oh Peter, Peter, I'm sorry! Are yer alright?" I could vaguely hear just before I passed out.

When I came round I was lying on the tiled floor; my face resting in the pool of blood that had streamed from the gash over my eye.

Ev and Stevie were nowhere to be seen. It turned out later that she had just picked the little fella up and legged it over to the Derby Arms to get the bus to her Ma's. I managed to stumble my way to next door to seek assistance from Linda. The cut didn't turn out to be too bad after all - a lot of blood made the cut seem far worse than it actually was. I was determined to milk it though as I was now under the tender ministrations of Linda, which I was quite enjoying, especially as she did have the most marvellous pair of boobies! I was lying on the couch as she tended to me which gave me the most wonderful view of her pendulous breasts, sitting there proudly like a pair of Big Ben's bells. I didn't have Ev beside me that night, as I knew by then she was at her Ma's, but I did have something to think about to keep my loins tingling!

Ev and Stevie still weren't back when I got up for work the next morning so I decided to jib it and go watch the movie that was currently making all the headlines; "Enter the Dragon" starring Bruce Lee. It was to be my first visit to the all singing, all dancing, state of the art shopping centre; The Concourse or the Conny as it was to be forever known, where the Oscar cinema was housed. I was sort of enjoying my newfound freedom as I sauntered my way down to the Conny.

"Enter the Dragon" had been recommended to me by Steve Best who was the brother of a girl, Lesley, Ev had made mates with. Steve was, still is, an absolute loon but what a guy. I know I can use the odd swear word but every other word out of Ste's mouth was F! He talked that fast he sounded like Stanley Unwin on speed.
"Eh Peter, yer wanna fuckin' go 'n' watch that fuckin' film yer know Enter the fuckin' Dragon. Fuckin' great is it yer know. Yer wanna see that fuckin' Bruce Lee, fast as fuckin' 'ell 'e is. Ee arr, d'yer want me to show yer some of the fuckin' kicks and punches 'e does? Fuckin' brilliant 'e is!"
"Err, no thanks Ste. I saw the mess yer made of that lad."

Ste had indeed made a horrible mess of a lad who'd upset Lesley. Ste was a boxer and knew just exactly where to hit so there was no way I was gonna let him be a Bruce Lee wannabe on me. "Ack, ack, ack, ack, ack, ack, ack!" That was Ste laughing. Yeah, I know - sounds like a Tommy gun!

Everything that Ste had told me about Enter the Dragon and Bruce Lee was correct. The film was brilliant in an all-action kind of way. It would never win any Oscars but by God it was exciting. I had never in my life seen anybody move as fast as Bruce Lee. Pity the poor chap was now dead! Anyway, I came out of the Oscar determined to take up the martial art Kung Fu; if I could be arsed that was. It wasn't to be long before I would have to use the techniques the late Mr. Lee had taught me on screen.

The scene outside the Oscar replicated the film. It was fuckin' mad! There were lads all over the place kicking and punching fuck out of each other - for real! A group of about six lads approached me. "Eh lad, where're yer from?" "I'm from Bootle. Why where the fuck are you from and what the fuck's it gotta do with you anyway?" I was tactful like that you see. I knew I was gonna get a hiding so I might as well front them. "'E means where d'yer live soft arse!" "Down there, Church Farm." "Well we're the Tanhouse Riot Squad!" By now the six of them had me surrounded like Red Indians around a wagon train. Get the first one in Evo lad! The one behind me was getting it first. I thrust my elbow out behind me as hard as I could; his scream told me I'd made good connection. I then butted the lad in front of me before falling under a hail of roundhouse kicks, Kung Fu punches and everything else the TRS could hit me with.

Having finally escaped from Bruce and his mob I limped my way down towards Church Farm. Another gang of four or five lads were waiting by the subway.
"Where're yer from lad?"
Fuckin 'ell not again!
"Look I've just been kicked to fuck up there by some fuckin' loons called the Tanhouse Riot Squad. If youse are gonna do the same just fuckin' get it over with but I'll take two of yer fuckers down with me. I live 'ere - Church Farm."
"Ah, no you're alright mate, we live 'ere too. They're always coming down 'ere to fight with us."
"Well, I just wish some fucker'd told me. I got fuckin' battered up there!"
"I know you don't I? Don't yer work in that wood yard in Litherland?"
"Yeah, you're the lad who comes to take the sawdust away aren't yer?"
"Yeah, Charlie O'Rourke's me name."
That was the first meeting in a now near thirty year friendship with Charlie. What Charlie doesn't know about music, especially Soul and Tamla Motown isn't worth knowing.

By the time I got home the feeling of freedom I'd had earlier in the day before setting off for the pictures was now well dissipated. I was totally pissed off! I was aching all over, especially where Ev had screwdrivered me - there was a coggy on my head as big as a size 5 Mitre. The biggest pain though was in my heart - I was missing my wife and child. I wanted them back. Having not yet mastered the art of cooking I was even missing Ev's congealed egg, sausage and chips!
OOH OOH BABY I WANT YOU BACK!
Never mind; footy season starts tomorrow. First game at home against Stoke. **YIPPEE!**

CHAPTER THREE

SETTLING DOWN

Shanks was convinced that his team of League Champions were going to sweep all before them this season - so convinced in fact that he signed only one new player; a raw, gawky kid from Halifax called Alan Waddle. Shanks, it must be said, hadn't been entirely happy with John Toshack last season despite the fact Tosh had formed a lethal, legendary, almost telepathic partnership with Kevin Keegan. That "experiment" on Kick Off where Tosh and Kev royally (and quite deservedly) took the piss out of Gerald Sinstad was truly hilarious. Poor old Gerald must have thought he had Kreskin and Uri Geller in the studio rather than Tosh and Kev. Tosh had been alternated, mostly in away games, with Phil Boersma, to give more mobility but all reports suggested that "Duck" was a Tosh clone. Ah well, Shanks knew best. The opening day 1-0 win was fairly easy if a little scrappy. Steve Heighway scored a rare headed goal against a Stoke side who didn't look that interested. Back to Ma's after the match for tea and interrogation.

"Where's Ev and the baby?"

"At 'ome Mam."

"Why didn't they come down?"

"She 'ad too much to do Mam - washin' an' all that."

"'Ow're yer settlin' then in Skem?"

"Ah great Mam. Sound's a bell, honest."

"Yer sure? I'm sure I saw Evelyn in the Strand this mornin'."

Oh shit! I couldn't be telling Ma that me bird had fucked off and took the baby with her. Besides, Ev would be back tonight so no prob and what Ma didn't know wouldn't hurt her.

The return of.........**LILY EYES!**

Oh, fuckin' 'ell no!

"Yer lyin' Peter. I always know when yer lyin'."

"Oh okay Mam, we just 'ad a bit of a row. She's been at 'er Ma's for a couple of days. She'll be back today. She's probably already

back in Skem now. Does me Dad know?"
"No, not yet. It's best 'e doesn't know either. 'E's in the Walnut.
Get 'er back an' stick at it. She's a good girl Ev. Yer've got the
baby to think of too."
"I know. I love them both Mam. It's 'orrible without them.
They'll be back today though I'm sure."
"What's all those cuts and scrapes on yer face?"
"I got jumped by a gang of lads yesterday Mam."
"Did Ev do any of them?"
"Don't be soft!
I stayed to watch Match of the Day and caught the last bus back
to Skem. I'd lost my keys jumping up and down in the match
when Stevie had scored but no prob - my beloved would be at
home to welcome me with open arms and congealed egg, sausage
and chips.

The house was in darkness as were most of the houses in Willow
Hey seeing as by this time it was nearly midnight. They must
have gone to bed. Ev wouldn't be happy at me knocking her up
(ooh er missus) but I'm sure she wanted me back in her bed as
much as I wanted her.
Knock, knock.
No answer.
Come on Ev, it's pissin' down 'ere!
Knock, knock, knock!
Still no answer.
"Ev, open the fuckin' door will yer, it's pissin' down!"
No answer.
KNOCK, KNOCK, KNOCK, KNOCK, KNOCK!
"Ee arr mate, what's all that noise?"
"Fuck off!"
Fuckin' ell! She wasn't at home. Must still be at 'er Ma's. What
the fuckin' 'ell was wrong with 'er? We'd only 'ad a bit of a row
and it was 'er who'd screwdrivered me. There was no need to stay
away for the best part of three fuckin' days! I was well fucked!
The kicking I'd taken yesterday from the TRS was now well and

truly kicking in, so to speak. My head was fuckin' bangin' from the screwdriver induced coggy (I think I must have brain damage or something). I was also fuckin' starvin'! Ma's tea of pig's belly and boiled spuds (don't ask) was six hours ago. I'd kill for Ev's congealed egg, chips and sausage now! It wasn't to be though. I was cold, wet, tired, hungry, battered and bruised. It took me back to my return from Highbury fifteen months ago. This time though there was to be no carnal delight at the end of it. This time I was going to sleep on a rain-soaked street like some fuckin' owld tramp. I was about to settle down for the night on the bench in the play square twenty yards or so away from the door. I couldn't break a window or kick a door in as Ev would go fuckin' spare when she did eventually come home and probably fuck right back off again! Just then some fuckin' massive bloke appeared from around the corner.

"Did you tell me to fuck off before?" Giant Haystacks was seriously troubled.

"No mate, not me. There was some fuckin' loon screamin' and shoutin' at that door there though."

"I'll kill the little twat if I find him!"

"Well I'm just off 'ome now mate. 'Ope yer find 'im. Cheeky gets round 'ere aren't they?"

I wandered aimlessly about while Haystacks returned to his stable. I was about to return to my bench when at last I had a stroke of luck. I found an empty flat! I was gonna have to be Bobby the Burglar to get in like but at least I would be under cover. **I LOVE THE SOUND OF BREAKING GLASS!** (Nick Lowe - 1978).

Shit! The whole of Skem must have heard that! I'd have Haystacks coming to piledriver me any minute now! The flat was completely empty. This was a step up from the street - only a minor step up mind but a step up all the same. I thought I was gonna shiver to death. The tiled floors were too cold to sleep on so the bog was to be my bed for the night. Not easy sleeping sitting on a bog but that's how it was to be. What I'd have given for a nice warm blanket. Ah! The Footy Echo!

HEIGHWAY HEADER SINKS SAD STOKE!
The Footy Echo in those days was broadsheet so plenty of covers for me. Oh deep fuckin' joy!
LIFE WAS SHIT!

I awoke what seemed an eternity later about five minutes away from double pneumonia and stiff as a board. I didn't have a watch but it was still dark so I guessed four o'clock ish. It was still pissin' down outside but I was gonna have to go for a walk and get some food in my belly from somewhere or I was gonna die. I could hear a faint whirring from somewhere not too distant. I followed the noise. Fuck me it was a milk float. Fuckin' milkies are early in Skem aren't they? On a Sunday morning too! I followed Mick the Milky as he did his deliveries. Two bottles of milk, a block of cheese, six eggs and a carton of yoghurt. That'd do me. I'm 'avin' them off! I found an old carrier bag blowing in the wind (gotta be a song there somewhere - probably by Leonard Cohen or Bob Dylan) and placed my booty inside.

I was about to turn into Church Farm when I heard a motor behind me. I turned to see the most welcoming sign of a police car. A cell was preferable to the cold bog and I might just even get some brekky rather than the milk and cheese I was set on enjoying back at Tramp Towers.
"What are thee up to yon mon?"
Fuck me - Skemplod. That's all I need!
"I'm locked out. Any chance of locking me up for the night?"
"Nay lad!"
"Come on, I'm freezin' 'ere."
"We can't just lock thee up for nowt."
"It won't be for nothin' - I've just done something. I've broke a window to get into an empty flat and I've just robbed this gear off a doorstep."
"Nah then yon mon, don't be silly. Tha's geetin' them from twenty-four hour garage."
There's a twenty-four hour garage in Skem? Fuck me. That's

handy. Not at the moment though 'cos I didn't have a penny to my name!

"Ee arr, come on, lock me up. Yer'd be quick enough to lock me up if I'd done nothin' wrong. Great isn't it? When I wanna get locked up I can't! What time is it anyway?"

"It's nearly four o'clock. Nah get thee sen 'ome to thee Mam."

Fuckin' cheeky woolyback twat!

Cheese, yoghurt and milk wasn't the best meal in the world but it did at least fill my empty belly. I decided that I was gonna hitch hike to Ev's Ma's in the morning to try talk her round to coming home. Only problem was I was actually going to have to face her Ma who I hadn't spoken to for six months. Kitty had made tentative attempts to patch things up, especially when we got our own place in Skem but me, being the stubborn bastard I was back then, steadfastly refused. Knobhead! I was sadly to live to regret that.

"Wher're thee goin' yon mon?"

"Wher're you?"

"Bootle."

"That'll do."

The wonderful smell of freshly baked bread permeated the air as I sat beside the driver of the Warburton's van on his way to do deliveries in Liverpool from Wigan.

"Tha looks rough lad. What's tha bin up to?"

"Ah, it's a long story mate. Yer probably wouldn't believe me if I told yer."

"You a Liverpooler?"

Now I was very grateful to this generous Wigan gentleman for giving me a lift but I hated the way the wools called Scousers Liverpoolers. If he said it again I was gonna knock the pie-eating twat out!

"Er, yeah mate."

"Aye, I saw thee programme. You fettlin' the game yesterday?"

"Yeah mate."

"Aye, I'm a United supporter me sen."
"Are yer mate?"
Just drive yer stupid Wigan twat. I'm fuckin' knackered 'ere. I can't be arsed with you bangin' on!
"Whereabouts in Bootle yer goin' mate?"
"First drop's Linacre Lane."
Fuck me, that was handy. I'd get out there and walk the fifteen minutes or so to Kitty's.
"What time is it mate?"
"Six o'clock."
Fuckin' 'ell, six o'clock! No chance of goin' to Kitty's yet. I was just gonna have to hope somebody was up at me Ma's. As well as a gang of loaves there were also a shedful of cakes in the back of the van. Wigan Warby must have seen me eyeing up the chocolate eclairs.
"Eh up lad, 'ave a cake. Tha looks as if thee could do wi' it!"
"Ah ta mate!"
I didn't need any second asking. Memories of Mrs. Roberts' marvellous cakes came flooding back to me as the chocolate éclair slid effortlessly down my neck. I was warming to this nice old fella now and was feeling a bit shitty for thinking bad of him. I was though deffo gonna rob one of his loaves before I got out.
"My grandson's a Liverpool supporter."
"Is 'e mate? Some sense in the family then."
"Eh up lad, we're 'ere."
"Ta for the lift mate. See ya."
"'Ang on lad. Can I 'ave tha programme for little 'un?"
"Course yer can mate. I'll swap yer for a thick sliced loaf."
I put the loaf in the carrier bag with the box of eggs I still had.

The rain had mercifully stopped and given way to bright sunshine. It looked as if this Sunday would be a blazingly hot August day. There was a light on when I got to Ma's. I thought there might be as Dad had taken to sleeping downstairs in front of the fire a lot these days as his circulation was bad. I was though gonna have to concoct a story as to why I was there. I knocked gently on the door.

"Hiya son. I've been expectin' you."

"'Ave yer Dad? 'Ow come? And at half-six in the mornin'.'"

As ever at Ma's, no matter what the weather, the fire was blazing up the grate. Bootle had long since been declared a smokeless zone. The only hard fuel supposed to be burned was coke. Dad said you couldn't get a good fire from coke and there was no way he was gonna use the gas fire contraption that the Council had provided so he was still doing business with Charlie Clarke on a regular basis.

"Just get yerself in 'ere and get a warm. Yer look bloody awful."

One cup of stewed tea later and I was ready for the Dad Gestapo to kick into action.

"Yer away from Evelyn again aren't yer?"

"Yeah, well rather she's away from me. 'Ow d'yer know?"

"I saw Kitty in the Saltbox last night. She told me."

Guy Fawkesed by Kitty - fuckin' marvellous!

The whole thing just got on top of me so I cried and blubbered all to my Dad. Well not quite all - I didn't mention the screwdriver. When the Great Flood of Bootle finally stopped I realised I was starving again.

"Dad, I'm starvin'. I just bought these eggs and bread from the shop. Is it okay if I make myself some egg on toast?"

"Giz them 'ere. I'll do it for yer. 'Ave yer 'ad any kip?"

"Only an hour or two Dad."

"Well get this scran inside yer, go an' 'ave a kip and then get yerself along to Kitty's and get yer wife and son back."

"Okay, ta Dad. Can yer lend us a quid so we can get the bus 'ome? I'm skint."

Well fed, well rested and a few bob in my sky rocket, I was ready to take on the world - even Kitty!

"Ev, come on. Come back to Skem. I want yer. I need yer. I miss yer and I miss our Ste."

"No Peter, it's 'orrible, I don't like it."

"Well I don't like it much either but we're just gonna 'ave to put up with it. We've got no chance of gettin a house around 'ere, especially now we've got one in Skem, and we can't move back in 'ere with yer Ma. Remember as well - you were the one who wanted to move to Skem in the first place."

"You wouldn't move back in 'ere anyway - you 'ate me Mum."

"Don't be stupid, I don't 'ate 'er, we just don't get on. We're Son-in-Law and Mother-in-Law. That's what Sons-in-Law and Mothers-in-Law do! Come on love. If we wanna be together we're gonna 'ave to go back. Come on, it'll be better when I get a job up there. I won't be travellin' up and down 'ere to work everyday so we'll get on better."

I eventually managed to talk my darling wife into coming home with my little precious Steven.

"What 'appened to yer 'ead anyway?"

"I got battered by some lads at the Conny."

"No yer didn't. Yer've been fightin' at the match 'aven' yer?"

Oh no, 'ere we go again!

"Yeah Ev, sorry, I was."

"I wish yer'd stop all that fightin' at the match. Yer've got responsibilities now."

"Okay Ev, I will."

"I'm not askin' yer to stop goin' the match, just to stop fightin' when yer there."

"Well that's just as well 'cos the only way I'm gonna stop goin' the match is when they put me six feet under in a wooden overcoat!"

"I 'aven' got much in for tea. Will egg, sausage and chips do?"

"Only if it's congealed."

"What d'yer mean?"

"Nothin', I'm only messin'. That's absolutely wonderful. Thanks love."

EV IS BACK!

Stevie was glad to be back in his own cot. I could tell that by the way he was calling flies cows. Something he picked up from his Mum who would shout "Cow" at flies. Strange creatures women aren't they?

"I'm sorry for 'ittin' yer with the screwdriver Peter."

"It's okay Ev. It didn't 'urt much anyway. Fuckin' good shot though wasn't it?"

We were both pissin' ourselves laughin'!

"Come on, let's go to bed. I'll make it up to yer. I bought some new knickers in the Strand."

WAAAAHHHHAAAYYYYYYY!!!!!!!!!!!!!!!!!!!!!!

THE BEST PART OF BREAKIN' UP IS WHEN YOU'RE MAKIN' UP!

CHAPTER FOUR

GUILT AND GRIEF

A midweek defeat at Coventry was followed by a trip to Leicester. I always liked going to Filbert Street as there was always a cracking atmosphere. Only problem was it was red hot under the low roof in the small end behind the goal we were in. Tosh, in his first game of the season, gave us the lead but Leicester equalised. Leicester fans were gaining an increasing reputation as bad boys and so it proved after the game, as we had to dodge a hail of bricks and bottles being thrown from side streets before even reaching the main battleground of a park. Once in the park, which we had to cross to reach the station, an almighty battle ensued. Fortunately I was with John Dever who, whilst always shittin' himself at the prospect of getting a good hiding, invariably managed to avoid trouble. I was quite happy about this as the wounds from my battles with the TRS and Ev were only just healing.

Successive home wins against Derby and Chelsea set us up for the return with Derby at the Baseball Ground. The Baseball Ground was probably the worst pitch first class football has ever been played on; it made Orrell Pleasure look like Wembley! No excuses though for our 1-3 defeat - Derby played us off the park and were still quite a good side even though they hadn't really built on their League Championship success of a couple of seasons earlier.

The daunting (for us fans) trip to Birmingham was next. I'd nearly been knifed at St. Andrews last season so was taking no chances this time. Luckily for me I was on my own this time. I just took my place behind the goal and kept a pretty low profile, even though I was in amongst our supporters, what few of them there were as most Reds had decided against getting their heads kicked in here for the second season running. I didn't trust those nasty bastards after last season when they were in all parts of the ground looking to perform major surgery on any Scouser they could find! Brian Hall shot and scored but not many Kopites roared to give us a 1-1 draw. Phil Thompson had taken the step up from the FA Youth Cup Final side of two seasons earlier and was now firmly established in the first team. He was joined for this game by one of his teammates in that FA Youth Cup run: Derek Brownbill. Great things were expected of Derek after starring in the Youth team but he never really lived up to those expectations. Mind you, Derek was in good company as nobody else from that team ever really made it either: Thommo must have been something special, which indeed he was, even if he could have smoked a ciggy in the shower!

The next game at home against Tottenham was a cracker, as most games with the Lilywhites were. I really liked Tottenham as a team; it was just their fans that were nauseating. My arse had never been the same since a good kicking there four years earlier. Anyway, back to the footy. We were 1-2 down with just fifteen minutes to go, Pat Jennings having performed his usual heroics at Anfield. Pat was mine, and I'm sure, most Reds second favourite opposition goalkeeper of all time behind Gordon Banks. My third favourite is Gordon West but whisper that to the Evertonians! Anyway, there was the big Irishman throwing himself this way and that, keeping out everything we could throw at him until we were awarded a penalty. Pat had saved two penalties against us in the previous season's match at Anfield so we weren't holding our breath on scoring this one - well we were I suppose. Up stepped Alec Lindsay to despatch the penalty with the sweetest left foot most Reds have ever seen. Shanks said that Alec could open a tin of peas with his left foot, which was just as well because apparently Alec wasn't overblessed with brains and might have had trouble opening a tin of peas with a tin opener! 2-2 - game on! The Kop was great in these situations, roaring the players on, driving them forward when to all intents and purposes they had nothing left to give. It usually paid off too and this time was no exception. Mr. Dependable - The Silent Knight - Chris Lawler could always be depended on in these situations. Chris didn't let us down. He'd scored our first and sent the place barmy when he netted his second with virtually the last kick of the game. The 3-2 win reminded me of the classic victory against Everton in November 1970 - oh what memories!

I was feeling pretty good when I got to my Mam's. Ev was supposed to be there too with our Ste.
"Where's Evelyn?"
"I don't know Peter, she 'asn't arrived yet."
"Well she said she was going to 'er Mum's an' would meet me here with Steven at half-five."
Ev arrived at seven o'clock and had obviously been crying.
"What's the matter Ev?"
"Me Mum's in hospital. I've just been to see 'er."
"Why, what's up?"
"They think she's got a chest infection or somethin' or it might be TB. She couldn't breathe properly today so we called an ambulance for 'er and they've kept 'er in."
"Is she gonna be okay?"
"Yeah, they think so. They said she'll probably be in for a few days while they do tests."
I'd fallen out with Kitty but I hoped she'd be better soon, not only for her sake but for Ev's too who was clearly really upset by it. I hated seeing Ev like this. I'd give her shit sometimes about turning on the waterworks too easily, prick that I was, but it upset me too to see her like this.
"Come on Ev, she'll be okay."
"Yeah, I suppose so."

Just when it seemed as if we were settling down in Skem Ev had to be going up and down to Liverpool to visit Kitty in hospital. I'd go straight to Mam's after work and meet Ev after she'd been to visit Kitty so we could get the bus home together.
"Come in and see me Mum with me Peter."

"No, I can't. It'd be too awkward. We 'aven' spoke to each other for six months."

"Come on, she wants to see yer. She likes yer you know."

"I'll go in with yer at the weekend."

I quite liked Kitty too but fact was we just couldn't get on. I suppose on my part it was the fact I couldn't handle her being as nice as pie to me one minute and then at my throat or talking about me behind my back the next. I suppose I should have realised that is just life and that's what Mothers-in-Law are like. For Kitty's part maybe it was that she was a bit jealous because I'd taken her little girl away from her. Whatever it was the chemistry didn't match and we hadn't spoken since February, when for the second time Kitty had lashed me out of her house (we were living there) and I had to go stay at Ma's for three months before moving to Skem. Kitty was actually quite right to lash me as I'd been a prick to Ev but you don't realise these things when you're young. Sometimes even fully-grown adults aren't grown up.

"Peter, don't go the match. Come with me to see me Mum."

"I can't Ev. We're playing Man United at Old Trafford and the coach is booked."

"Please, she wants to see yer."

"Look, I'll lose the coach money if I don't go and John Dever's expecting me. I'll go in on Monday with yer."

"Promise?"

"Yeah, promise, honest."

We didn't chance going in the Scoreboard End again after last year's shennanigans at Old Trafford. We opted instead for the comparative safety of the United Road Paddock. Whatever Scousers were inside Old Trafford must have been well spread out, as when the Stretford End hordes made their usual charge across the pitch to the Scoreboard End they found nobody to fight with.

"Scousers where are you?"

We're in 'ere, safe as fuckin 'ouses and laughin' our fuckin' 'eads off at youse yer manc twats!
The game was shite; we drew 0-0 and got away from Old Trafford without so much as a bad look at us. **HAPPY DAYS!**

I was awoken on the Monday morning, just before I was due to get up for work anyway, by a knock on the door.
"Who the fuck's that at this hour of the mornin'?"
I looked at Ev's face and she seemed to know.
I opened the front door.
"Hiya Pete."
It was Ev's brother John, red-eyed and tearful. Ev had heard her brother's voice and was halfway down the stairs.
"What's the matter?"
"Ev me Mum's dead. She died a couple of hours ago."
Ev broke down screaming and crying. I felt so sorry for her but there was nothing I could do other than to try and comfort her. John was in his van so took Ev and Steven down to Litherland. I stayed at home with the excuse that I had some work to do in the house. Truth was I was too much of a shithouse to face the family of a woman who had just died and I had not spoken to for eight months. **GOBSHITE!**
Why hadn't I just patched things up with Kitty when I had the chance? Why had I been so fuckin' stubborn? Why didn't I go to visit her in hospital? Again, my only excuse, if any, is the ignorance of youth. All I know is that for nearly thirty years that has played on my mind. I've always felt guilty about it but it's something I have to live with.

Kitty's body was taken on the Wednesday to lay in the front room of 49 Hinton Street until her burial on the Friday. Things went on while Kitty's body was laying at rest that really upset Ev but which she couldn't say too much about. It also didn't go down very well with Ev that I'd chosen to go the match on the Wednesday rather than stay with her. We'd made hard work a fortnight earlier in Luxembourg of getting a 1-1 draw against

Jeunesse D'Esch, actually being a goal down before Brian Hall equalised. We also made hard work of the second leg winning with an own goal and the clincher from Tosh.

The mood at Kitty's funeral on the Friday wasn't helped by me once again being a prick. I did my usual trick when I couldn't handle something of disappearing, leaving Ev to cope with her grief without the support of her husband; not that I was very good at giving support in those situations anyway. I thought I was right at the time by taking the view that it wasn't right to have a bevy at somebody's funeral. We were there, after all, to mourn the deceased not to enjoy ourselves by having ale. My stance on that subject has since drastically changed. I now realise that we are at a funeral to celebrate a life not to mourn a death. If only I'd had the same attitude then as now.

Steven's second birthday on October 8th and Ev's 21st three days later should have been causes for great celebrations but Ev just couldn't bring herself to snap out of her grief. I was doing my best to help her but it was to no avail; it was just going to take time.

By a strange quirk of fate Eddie Physick and his wife June were living on the same Church Farm estate as us. I felt like telling Eddie it was all his fault anyway as it was on his couch that young Steven was conceived! Eddie worked in Thorn's making colour TV tubes and got me an interview there. I also had an interview at Courtauld's but got neither job, which is just as well seeing as both factories were shut down within a couple of years. I'd also applied for a job in a place called Grimwood Heating Elements but had heard nothing from them since so I was more than surprised when a letter arrived telling me to attend an interview there on Monday 15th October. I really hoped I would get the job, as I was desperate to jump from Walter Holme's before I was pushed. I really was skating on thin ice now with my timekeeping and attendance and whilst it was a pain in the arse getting up and down to Litherland every day the last thing I wanted was to be on the dole. We were settling down again now in Skem - being out of work would just set us back once more.

If such things as CV's had been around then mine wouldn't have been very impressive. I'd had seven jobs in five years since I'd left school, all of them very menial that virtually anybody could do. The job description at Grimwood's said that some electrical work would be required. Well I might have been many things but I was certainly no fuckin' spark! I attended the interview more in hope than expectation. Please God, let me get the job!
"Hmmm, Peter, you don't seem to have any gaps in your employment record."
I was being interviewed by a guy called Graham Calland. I learnt later that he was an ex-copper and a bent one at that - allegedly!
"Yes Mr. Calland. I've had three jobs." Lying through my teeth!
"It's just that people who can supposedly account for every single day of their working lives have normally been in prison for those times."
Ee arr, fuckin' 'ang on 'ere arse'ole! I might be 'avin yer on and I can be a bit of a prick sure enough but I'm no fuckin' criminal!
"No Mr. Calland. I've never been in trouble with the police."
"Well you do know we'll be checking on that."
Oh shit! Fuck off with yer fuckin' suspicious ex-copper's mind will yer. I only want a fuckin' job. I don't wanna guard the Crown fuckin' Jewels or somethin' for fuck sake!
"No problem Mr. Calland."
"Yes, well we'll also be sending for references from previous employers including your current one."
Oh well I'm fucked then aren't I? Thanks for the interview, sorry to waste yer time, now stick yer fuckin' job right up where the sun don't shine!
"That's fine Mr. Calland. I'm sure Mr. Hughes at Walter Holme will give me a very good reference."
"In that case Peter, when can you start?"
Fuck me, the daft twat's givin' me the job!

"Have I got the job Mr. Calland?"

"Yes Peter, you have got the job. I repeat - when can you start?"

Fuckin' 'appy days! You lot must be fuckin' desperate!

"I'll have to give a week's notice when I go to work tomorrow Mr. Calland so I can start next Tuesday."

"Very well, but if unsuitable references arrive after you start you'll be out on your ear."

Well I should make it to the end of the first week then at least.

"No problem Mr. Calland. I'm sure my references will all be glowing."

"Very well. We work a double-day, two-shift system: 6:30 - 2:30 and 2:30 - 10:30. Report to Mr. Clarke in Number One factory at 2:30 next Tuesday."

Fuckin' 'ell that's appy isn't it? A sleep in as well! Mind you it's gonna be a bit of a pig getting' up for earlies an' I'm gonna 'ave to do jiggery pokery for midweek games when I'm on afternoons but otherwise ace. Ta mate, you're a good 'un!

"Thank you Mr. Calland."

Bobby Bendy didn't hear me as he was already on the phone - probably to Bill Hughes.

I was planning my campaign of serious suckholing to Bill Hughes tomorrow. I wouldn't need an excuse for being off; I'd just tell him that I'd been for a job in Skem, got it and would he be so kind as to lie his arse off and give me a glowing reference should Grimwood's ask for one. The situation was to be taken out of my hands.

I clocked on at 8:30, which although half-an-hour late was half-an-hour before I was normally clocking on, when I was actually in work that was, these days.

"You are a waste of fuckin' skin! There's people out there desperate for a job an' your fuckin' round bein' late and off! Well I've fuckin' 'ad enough! When yer 'ere yer okay, yer a decent worker, but yer never fuckin' 'ere and yer could be the best worker in the fuckin' world but yer not when yer not 'ere. I might as well

bring a fuckin' tramp in from the scrappy. YER SACKED! Yer fuckin' finished Friday. I'll 'ave yer cards, wages and yer P45 ready for yer then!"
WOW! Fuckin' 'ell, did this man 'ave a cob on or what? Of course he was right - I'd been a fuckin' arsehole. It had been hard for me though having to rely on thumbing lifts or worse, the vagaries of public transport, to get from Skem to Litherland and back every working day (well some days) for the past five months. I didn't want to part on bad terms. Besides, the new job might still depend on me getting a decent reference from Bill.
"Yeah, I'm sorry for fuckin' yer around lately Bill. I was off yesterday cos I went for a job interview in Skem. I got it. I start next Tuesday. I suppose a reference is out of the question?"
"Fuck off!" Bill shouted from halfway down the yard.
Lonely had been watching all this and was pissin' himself (not that he ever did anything else) laughing.
"You can fuck off too yer fuckin' smelly owld twat! I've been fuckin' dyin' to tell you exactly what I thought of yer. Yer robbed me fuckin' weddin' ring and yer've been rippin' me off for fuckin' months with the money yer get for the sawdust. Now go 'ead, fuck off outta me sight before I rip yer fuckin' smelly 'ead off yer pissy shoulders!"
That was me with a cob on!

I did basically fuck all for the rest of the week except say ta ra to all the lads there. Even though I'd had seven jobs in five years this was comfortably my longest spell in any of them - eighteen months, so I was going to miss the lads I'd become attached to. Some of the tradesmen were a pain in the arse but most of them were okay. The likes of the Lloyd brothers - Jackie and Jimmy who for years led the singing in the Kop. Then there was the resident barber - Billy Turpin. Billy had looked after my hair to such a degree that I now sported a boss feather cut and all for just a couple of bob. Billy was a bit of a God Squad man so it was bloody hilarious the first time I, or anybody else for that matter, heard him swear. Billy was playing in goal for Everton Red

Triangle in a Cup Final at Bootle Stadium. I was standing behind the goal watching while an opposition player took a free kick from about 35 yards. The free kick, which Billy didn't have a hope in hell of seeing, thundered toward and fairly whistled past him. Billy stood transfixed with his eyes still towards the pitch.
"Peter, where did that go?"
"Look behind yer Billy."
"Fuckin' 'ell!"
Funny as fuck!
Then there was a joiner called John Hankin who was also a superb amateur footballer. I saw John once on a quagmire of a pitch at Buckley Hill cover every blade of mud! Brilliant!
Billy Wade, a painter, was also a boss footballer having played at a very good amateur level for Marine and some excellent Sunday League teams.
All my fellow labourers were sound as a pound. One guy (no pun intended) Kenny Guy was a drummer in a band. I'm not sure he ever made it past the local circuit type of thing but he had about five coloured guys in the band too. They all came to see Kenny in work one day and looked as if they'd all just stepped out of a Shaft film. I think they went on to become The Real Thing. Yes, I was gonna miss them all - even Lonely I suppose but a brand new adventure awaited me at Grimwood's, if I could get a reference.

"Billy, can I 'ave me wages and cards and that?"
"Yeah, ee arr. That Grimwood's 'ave been on to me for a reference. I lied like fuck and said you were sound's a bell."
"Thanks Billy. I'm sorry for arsin' yer around."
"Okay. Good Luck and try sort yerself out now."
My handshake of appreciation to this man was genuine. Good bosses are hard to come by - Billy was certainly one of them.

CHAPTER FIVE

JOBS, JAPES AND JALOPIES

Buoyed by the expectancy of starting my new job I was well up for the trip to Leeds. Before the match Don Revie was being presented with a Manager of the Month award and quite deservedly so. Revie was not everybody's cup of tea but he was certainly a very good manager. Revie, like his very good friend Shankly, knew exactly how to get the best out of what were, to begin with, very ordinary players and turn them into very good ones. Unfortunately for Revie and Norman Hunter "Mr. Bites Yer Legs" had made a catastrophic mistake in England's midweek match against Poland at Wembley, virtually gifting Poland their goal in the 1-1 draw that saw England fail to qualify for the 1974 World Cup. All through the award ceremony us Reds in the Cowshed end chanted "Hunter for Poland." Not very nice I suppose, even Shanks was gesturing for us to be quiet, but it was funny. Revie, Hunter and Mick Jones, scorer of the only goal, had the last laugh though as Leeds notched up another victory on their remorseless march to the title.

"Our John's gettin' married on December 1st."
I didn't need to check the fixture list - I knew we were playing West Ham at home that day.
"Is 'e Ev? That's nice."
"Don't say you're not goin'."
"Okay I won't say it."
"Are yer goin' then?"
"No."
"Why not?"
"Well you tell me the only reason I'd miss your John's weddin'."
"Yer goin' the match?"
"In one!"
"Oh, come on Peter, Yer've gorra go!"
"I 'aven' gorra go and I'm not goin'. I'll go in the night after the

match. Yeah, I'll look forward to that an' 'avin' a bevy an' that with your John but I'm not goin' durin' the day. I'm not missin' the match."

Christ, deja vu or what? I'd been here before over my wedding and the meeting of parents.

"Our John'll 'ave a cob on."

"Your John won't 'ave a cob on. 'E knows I won't miss the match. 'E'll be okay. I'll talk to 'im."

"Yer not fair!"

I left the last word to Ev. She had seemed to accept it so I left well alone while there were a cluster of sharp objects to hand.

"John, I won't be able to go to yer weddin'."

"I know Pete, Liverpool are playin' West Ham at 'ome. No problem mate as long as yer there in the night."

"Don't worry John I will be, wild 'orses wouldn't stop me. Your Evelyn thought yer'd 'ave a cob on."

"Ah, tell our Gipper to fuck off!"

For some strange reason that I never, ever did find out John used to call his sister Gipper.

"You tell 'er to fuck off! When I tell 'er to fuck off I normally get somethin' dead 'eavy and sharp 'urled at me 'ead!"

"Yeah, I know! She twatted me once with 'er 'igh 'eel cos I called 'er a witch!"

Hmm…must remember never to call 'er a witch.

First day at Grimwood's was brilliant. I just knew I was gonna settle here. The factory was very noisy but absolutely chocker block with machines, people and very importantly loads of fit women. Not that I would ever have strayed with any of them of course as, fit though they were, none of them could match up to what I had at home, no woman could, but there was no harm in looking and thinking. I was welcomed to the factory by the shift manager, Eddie Clarke. I had some battle royals with Eddie over the years, mostly over my timekeeping, but one thing you had to say about Eddie was that he was consistent; no side, no favourites

- he treated everybody with equal contempt.
Then there was Ernie Statter. Ernie was a smashing old chap
from Wigan.
"Eh up young 'un. My name's Ernie."
"Hiya Ernie. I'm Peter."
"'As tha just moved up 'ere wi' Mam."
"What?"
"Does tha live at 'om wi' Mam?"
Mary rescued me. Mary was my archetypal fantasy of an older
woman. She was in her mid-forties, blonde, busty and a divorcee.
Mary had kept herself very well and looking young. She was as
Scouse as the Liver Buildings too. On top of all that she really
was a very nice woman. AND WHAT BOOBS!
"Ernie's askin' d'yer still live at 'ome with yer Mam."
"No I do not! I'm twenty years of age and a married man with a
son aged two!" I answered most indignantly.
"Aye, I'm sorry son. I thowt tha were only baht sixteen."
I understood that! I liked this Ernie geezer!
JOKE TIME!
Wiganer takes his cat to the vet.
Wiganer says to vet, "Yon cat's poorly."
Vet says, "Is it a tom?"
Wiganer says, "No, I've browt it wi' me."
COAT TIME!

Another character was Terry. Now, not to put too fine a point on
this and to put it mildly, Terry was a little bit camp. When he
came over to welcome me to Grimwood's I thought Larry
Grayson had just arrived!
"Oh hello. You seem like a nice boy!"
"Errr.....alright mate yeah."
"My name's Terry."
When he held his hand out to me I didn't know whether to shake
it or kiss it!
"Errr... yeah, I'm Peter."
"Do you think you'll like it here Peter."

"Well, yeah, it's been alright so far. The people are okay."
"Oh they are but some of them are right bitches - and they're the men!"
Terry went into this big, mad, camp laugh. I didn't care what he was or was his predilections were, Terry was alright.
"Are you wed Peter?"
"Yeah, I've been married for two and a half years and I've got a son aged two."
"Oh, you naughty boy!"
I just fell about laughing at this. So did Terry.
"You have to be careful in here though not to snag yourself on anything. You wouldn't believe the number of pairs of tights I've laddered in here! Mind my tights!"
Nutcase but sound as a pound. Terry was what he was and was quite comfortable with it. In fact he didn't give a shit what anybody thought about him or what he was. His philosophy was that if anybody had a problem with him that's exactly what it was - their problem, not his. All this in an age when it wasn't fashionable to have that philosophy.

Our European Cup hopes ended at the hands of the crack Yugoslav side Red Star Belgrade. They won both legs by a 2-1 scoreline; most of the damage being done by a lad called Jankovik who scored in both legs.

John's wedding to Carol went off quite well considering I wasn't there, probably BECAUSE I wasn't there! The world didn't fall apart or anything like Ev thought it would seeing as I wasn't there and was at my beloved Anfield instead. Alan Waddle made his debut against West Ham in a 1-0 win and had a sensational game doing everything but score in a marvellous performance on a skating rink of a pitch. Okay, he was gangly and looked awkward, wasn't the greatest footballer in the world and had a touch like a baby elephant. What you couldn't fault "Duck" for though was effort. He was running everywhere and raining shots in on goal. We laughed at his antics when he fell about but Alan looked like he could become a crowd favourite for years to come. Duck's greatest moment of his Liverpool career was to come the following week; more of that later (he he). The win against the 'Appy 'Ammers (my arse) put me right in the mood for a good bevy at John's night time do. I wasn't disappointed. It was a great do, everybody enjoying themselves, singing and dancing and generally having a ball; exactly the way weddings should be. There wasn't even the traditional "Scouse wedding fight" although me and Ev did come close. By the end of the night though she'd forgiven me my heinous crime of missing the wedding to go the match and the even worse, terrible crime, a hanging offence surely (I know, don't call you Shirley) of....wait for it.....**LOOKING AT A WOMAN!** Terrible man I am! Should be bloody horsewhipped! Fancy looking at a woman! And me a man as well! A married man at that! Bloody awful! What's the world coming to? Seriously though - what's this "Scouse wedding fight" thing all about? As far as I'm concerned it's just a myth that's been perpetuated down the years by the anti-Scouse brigade. Okay, I don't mind the likes of Harry Enfield taking the piss but there are some people who actually believe it! I've been to dozens of weddings and never once seen a fight: a minor skirmish here and there but never a full-blown fight. Everybody's too busy enjoying themselves to be arsed fighting. I love weddings - just as long as they're not my own!

A miracle occurred at Anfield on December 4th 1973 - Ian Callaghan scored! Not only did he score; he scored again and again! A hat trick for Cally - that's nice isn't it?
Altogether now:
IT'S CALLY, IT'S CALLY, IT'S CALLY DA DA DA DA DA DA!
I don't think even Cally himself could believe he'd scored three times. He rarely scored three times in a season let alone in one game! The unfortunate team on the end of Cally's goal blast were Hull City in a League Cup 4th Round replay. Pity there were only 17,000 people there to see it. The low attendance was due

to midweek games having to kick off in the afternoon. A floodlight ban had been imposed by the due to be defunct Edward Heath led Tory government because of industrial action by power and mine workers. I'd done jiggery pokery to get the day off work to go the match. Some of the excuses I gave to get shift changes or days off would have to be heard to be believed, which they weren't, if you see what I mean. In the end everybody, bosses included, sussed that I was a Red and that nothing on earth would keep me from a home match. To be honest though they were mostly very good in letting me go the match; as long as I did a shift or made my time up there wasn't normally a problem.

So to Goodison four days later for the annual battle against our beloved blue brethren. Mike Lyons scored what looked like a perfectly good goal with a towering header only for it to be ruled out for offside. Mike never did have the best of luck against us. We won the game with a goal by....guess who.....**ALAN WADDLE**! Go 'ead! Alan couldn't trap a bag of cement but bloody 'ell he was a Red hero for ever after flicking that goal in. This was to be, or so we thought, the beginning of a great career for Duck but in fact it was the only goal he ever scored for us. Tosh saw him off as he did with so many of his supposed replacements. Anyway, for now, Alan was our hero. The term "clown" to describe a shite footballer had been popularised by Brian Clough who used it against Jan Tomasezwki (392 on a Scrabble board) the Polish goalkeeper who had virtually single-handedly denied England victory in the World Cup qualifier at Wembley. Jan had made some great saves but had also had a bit of luck with some unorthodox stops. Clough had snidily (that's a surprise isn't it?), contemptuously dismissed Tomawhatsits as a clown. So it was that after getting all the usual shite from the Evertonians on the bus back to my Ma's about how they were cheated (although they did have a point about Lyons' goal) and how they should have had seventeen penalties and Waddle's goal was offside one of them came out with the coup de grace:
"That fuckin' Waddle's a clown!"

My riposte was perfect:
"Well I didn't see you fuckin' lot laughin'!"
1-0 TO THE REDS AND 1-0 TO EVO!
Mind you it was all banter and nothing really nasty, out of order
or violent about it. That's changed a bit now but not as much as
some people would have you believe.

Back at Mam's Ev and Stevie were already there.
"Peter, I've got a surprise for yer."
"'Ave yer Ev, what's that?"
"Dad, Dad, look, look!"
The little fella was very excited. What was this all about?
"Don't get a cob on will yer Peter."
"What is it for Christ's sake?"
I might have said "for fuck sake" if Mam hadn't been there but I
didn't swear in front of me Ma 'til I was 35. I was a good lad yer
see!
"Ee arr look."
With that Ev opened this box and out popped a cute little, brown-
eyed puppy's head. Even my ice-cold heart (where pets were
concerned) melted.
"It's one of our Linda's dog's pups. Can we 'ave it Peter?"
"Yeah, of course we're 'avin it! We'll call it Dixie."
Dixie Dean was one of my all-time great footballing heroes. Of
course I'd never seen him play but I'd read loads of books about
him, one of which I'd just finished, and he had really captured my
imagination so Dixie was going to be the Evo family's pet's name.
Altogether now!
AAAAAAAAHHHHHHHHHH!

Workin' 'appily away, no problems, not a care in the world. Me
and Ev gettin' on great. Ste happy. Lookin' forward to Christmas
a couple of weeks away. Reds doin' well. Singin' "Merry
Christmas" by Slade which was surely gonna be the Chrimbo
Number One. Bang bang, knock that element in! Hammer,
hammer, bang, bang. Fuckin' 'ell, what's that I can see? Fuckin'

'ell look at that! Oh my God! Sadie working on the machine next to me, VERY short black leather skirt on, bending over every time she pulls the handle of the machine; about every ten seconds. Fuckin' 'ell look at those little, skimpy black knicks (Ev's got a pair like that) and lovely arse cheeks (them too). Oh my God! Donga nearly banging elements in for me instead of hammer. Christ, I'd shag that!

NEED TO GO AND GIVE IT THE FIVE FINGER SHUFFLE!

Just 'ave a couple more looks first. Go 'ead girl! Go 'ead Sadie - fuckin' sound that! Wonder if you're doin' it on purpose? Probably are! Don't give a fuck though - makin' me 'appy! One more bang of the 'ammer.

OW! FUCKIN' 'ELL!

Just twatted my thumb instead of the element.

THROB, THROB, THROB!

That was my thumb as well as my donga!

I was off work for a month, which was no bad thing after I got over the initial pain and discomfort as it meant I'd get sick pay from the SS and holiday pay from work - a little scam Dad had taught me. Gettin' some of the money back you'd put in for years in tax and National Insurance he called it. Quite bloody right too! I mean, I never asked to go in that scheme - I was just put into it. That other scheme's a good 'un too isn't it? That one where yer get a dodgy sick note, pretend yer've got somethin' wrong with yer for the rest of yer life and then sit on yer arse for ever gettin' loads of money every week for doin' jack shit! I know loads of people on that scheme and they annoy the fuckin' shit outta me! I've every sympathy with people who are genuinely ill and can't work and those who genuinely WANT to work but can't find a job. There are too many though who just DON'T WANT to fuckin' work and want every fucker who is working to pay for them and their lifestyle, which incidentally doesn't mean not being able to 'ave a bevy, a bet, a toke and wear designer clothes. I've worked with lads who've had one leg, no legs and crippling back problems but they work because they WANT to.

"Where're *you* goin? It's seven o'clock in the mornin'."
Ev always could tell the time.
"To Wolves."
"Where's Wolves?"
"Yer know, Wolverhampton."
"No, I don't know. Where's Wolverhampton?"
"In the Midlands."
"Where's the Midlands?"
"Oh for fuck sake Ev! Where d'yer fuckin' *think* the Midlands are? In the middle of the fuckin' country of course!"
"Oh alright! Fuckin' 'ell cobby arse! When did yer decide this anyway?"
"About five minutes ago when I woke up."
"Yer can't go, we've 'aven' got no money."
I decided against reminding Ev of her continual use of bad grammar in that she was using a double negative in view of the fact I didn't want a screwdriver in my head again.
"I can go an' I am goin'. I'm gonna thumb it."
"'Ow come yer goin' so early?"
"The kick-off's at two o'clock."
"'Ow come? I thought matches in the week kicked-off in the night?"
"Well in case yer 'adn't noticed Ev there's a national power emergency at the moment. There's a ban on floodlights so midweek games 'ave to kick off in the afternoon."
"Oh yeah, I seen that in the paper."
Saw Ev - saw. I saw. I have seen.
"Is that why the telly finishes at ten o'clock now?"
Fuckin' 'ell Ev, abarr as quick as a 44 up the Valley you girl aren't yer!
"Yeah, well spotted Ev!"
"See, I'm not thick yer know!"
Well that's a fuckin' matter of opinion!
"I know yer not Ev."
"'Ow come yer wanna go to....where is it....Wolves anyway?"
"Well, I'm off work so I thought I might as well."

"Why don't yer come shoppin' with me instead?"
GET TO FUCK!
"I thought yer said we 'ad no money?"
"We 'aven't. I'm goin' to St. Helens to spend the Provvy cheque."
"Well tell me what it was like cos I ain't goin'!"
Fuckin' 'ell it was bad enough goin' to Wooly Wigan without sampling the dubious delights of St. Helens.
"Okay. What time will yer be 'ome?"
"Fuckin' 'ell I 'aven' gone yet! Giz a fuckin' chance. I don't know, abarr eight or nine o'clock I suppose. Depends on whether I can bunk on a coach or not on the way 'ome."
"D'yer 'ave to leave so early?"
"Yeah, I'm not sure of the way so I wanna give meself plenty of time in case I struggle for lifts and that."
"Are yer sure? Another hour won't make no difference will it?"
With that Ev pulled back the bedclothes. **BW'S!** Fuckin' 'ell, go 'ead! I never could resist BW's! They could make me forget even Ev's flagrant misuse of the English language. Ev wouldn't have known a double negative if it had jumped up and bit her on the tit!
"No, I don't suppose it will. Come 'ere!"

At midday I was beginning to regret not only my extra hour of carnal lust (well no, not really; I never regret that) but also the whole daft idea of thumbin' it to Wolves in the first place. I don't know why, it might just be me and I'm not the greatest one for directions and finding my way anywhere anyway, but Wolverhampton always seems a massively difficult place to get to by road. It was just two hours before kick-off and I was stuck in a road in the middle of nowhere (Dusty again) having been dropped there by a lorry driver. I'd stood there, thumb frozen, for an hour. I had no colours on so had at least a chance of a lift. Good news was there were plenty of Wolves supporters going in that direction. Bad news was there was no sign of any of them stopping for me. Maybe I just *looked* like a Scouser. My luck wasn't all bad. I found myself ensconced in a nice warm car with three Wolves supporters - a middle-aged man and his couple of late-teens sons. They were all sound lads, especially the boys. I couldn't understand a word any of them were saying but I got the fact they were sound lads from the way they didn't want to beat me up. I did hope it wasn't one of them whose scarf I'd robbed at Molineux three years earlier.

As for the match itself - shite! John Richards, a great striker, scored the only goal to see us out of the League Cup. No chance of a lift back on a coach either due to the fact there weren't any! Well, none that I could see anyway. There couldn't have been more than a hundred or so Reds at Molineux that afternoon. I made my way to the station to try and bunk the train home but bad Wolves lads were snarlin' everywhere so I decided to give that a wide berth and get the thumb out again. I honestly thought I would never get home. I got to Sandbach services at midnight and fell asleep in the café. I was awoken by the same lorry driver who had given me a lift the day before.

"Eh lad, come on, wake up. It's five o'clock in the mornin'! I gave you a lift yesterday didn't I?"

"Err...yeah... s'right yeah. Five o'clock? Fuckin' 'ell she's gonna kill me!"

"Who's gonna kill yer? Yer Mam?"

"No, me missus!"

"Yer never fuckin' married are yer?"

Why the fuck didn't people ever believe I was married? I know I looked younger than my twenty years but I wasn't exactly Jimmy Clitheroe!

"Yeah, I am mate and she *is* gonna fuckin' kill me!"

"Where d'yer live?"

"Skem."

"I'm goin' to Wigan. That any good to yer?"

"Yeah, that's great mate. Thanks a lot."

I'm not sure that he was actually going to Wigan. I think he was going somewhat out of his way to get me somewhere near home but probably felt sorry for me. In any case I was very grateful for the lift. By now, I'd had a bellyful (or rather not, I was absolutely starvin') of thumbin' so I was gonna bunk the first bus back to Skem no matter what!

"Ee arr mate, I'm skint. Can I give me name and address in?"
"Nay tha' fuckin' can't! Fuck off!"
"Ah go 'ead mate please. I've been on the road all night."
"Well just get thee sen upstairs an' keep tha fuckin' 'ead down. If checker's geetin' on I don't know fuck all baht thee!"
Hmmm....it wasn't worth explaining to Reg Varney (Wigan version) the finer points of double negatives so I just headed for the seclusion of the upper deck. I waved goodbye to our cheery bus conductor as I alighted (why did they call it that?) when I reached the Derby Arms.
"Cheers mate. Thanks a lot."
"Fuck off!" was his friendly riposte.

I fell into my bed exactly twenty four hours after leaving it.
"Where the fuck 'ave *you* been?"
"Oh please Ev, not now, I'm fuckin' knackered!"
"I thought yer said yer'd be 'ome at eight or nine o'clock last night?"
"Well I couldn't get lifts an' I fell asleep at the services. Please Ev, just let me go asleep I'm fucked!"
"Well I'm not am I?"
"What d'yer mean?"
"What d'yer *think* I mean? I've been lying awake waitin' for yer all night!"
"Oh I see. Okay then. Another hour won't make any difference will it?"
"No it won't an' it better 'ad be a bloody hour!"

OH, I WISH IT COULD BE CHRISTMAS EVERY DAY! SO HERE IT IS MERRY CHRISTMAS, EVERYBODY'S HAVIN' FUN!
Christmas '73 was great! Nice watch and a Benny off Ev. Mr.

Sherman was still sticking to his traditional button down collar style, which I found quite appealing in the face of the penny-round and flyaway revolution. I did have some of those too though. I had a Peter Werth shirt with a collar that big it would have got me to an away match with a good wind under me! I bought Ev perfume (Tramp: she liked that. Stop laughin' at the back!) and some VERY skimpy underwear, which was as much a present for me as it was for my darling spouse. Reds had won seven and drew two of the last seven League games. Off to Burnley on Boxing Day; no problem there. Thousands of Reds at Turf Moor; we were bound to win!

"Christ Dave, 'ow many turkey sarnies yer got there mate?"
I tried not to swear in front of David Jones, as he was a little bit posh. Dave's Reg Varney's could have fed the Third World for a year or me for a week! Chitty Chitty Bang Bang (Dave's 1954 Ford Pop) was cranked up, filled up and ready to make the three-hour journey to Burnley. Only an hour in a proper car but Dave's chugger was incapable of going any faster than 30mph. Whatever could go wrong that day went wrong including us getting beat of course! We even got some hassle from the normally hassleless Burnley fans. Leighton James it was who tore us apart that day. James was a right gobshite who after one match (it might have been this one) spat at Tommy Smith in the tunnel. As James was like shit off a shovel Tommy had no chance of catching him. James though was lightning quick, Matthewesque in the dribble, a brilliant crosser of the ball and had a great shot. All in all, almost the complete footballer so there was no need for him to be such an annoying little shit although he was to be forgiven for ALL his indiscretions by the Kop a few years later. All will be revealed in the fullness of time! Back to this game - Tommy Smith had regained his place in the team at right-back after an injury to Chris Lawler. There were rumours of unrest between Smithy and Shanks and that Tommy was on his way, either on loan or permanently, to Stoke. Tommy was to go on to play quite well in his new position but not in this

game. James absolutely tore him to shreds. The Turf Moor pitch
that day was made for fast wingers like James. Tommy would
have kicked him I'm sure if he could have got near enough to the
Welsh Wanker (I mean Wizard). An equaliser six minutes from
time by Peter Cormack seemed to have given us the point I
thought we deserved. We were still celebrating when Ray
Hankin won it for Burnley with a last minute winner.
"Fuckin' spawny Burnley bastards!"
No, it wasn't me! It was David (never swear) Jones. Christ,
things MUST be bad!

Right, which daft twat came up with the fuckin' brilliant idea of
playin' football on New Year's Day? Okay, great idea that NYD
was now officially declared a public holiday and we didn't have
to go to work (not that many people went to work when it
WASN'T a holiday anyway) but we shouldn't be asked to go and
watch a game of football in the freezin' fuckin' cold, being pushed
around by 40,000 people. Okay, I didn't mind this normally, in
fact used to quite revel in it, but not on a day when my head's the
size of Birkenhead and my guts are jumping like a crowd of 13
year old girls at a David Cassidy concert! Peter Cormack scored
for the third successive game (having notched the only goal of the
game at Stamford Bridge three days earlier) to equalise Keith
Weller's goal. Weller was the only one who had anything like the
right idea. Okay, he got called "a fuckin' big puff" by the Kop
because he was wearing a pair of his tart's white tights but at least
he was a warm fuckin' big puff! Ev had a pair of white tights just
like them. I was thinking I should have worn them myself 'til I
remembered that my bollocks would have been freezing seeing as
Ev's tights were crotchless (he he he)!

My return to work after my "enforced" extended Christmas break
was to a three-day week. Oh that's okay isn't it? I only work two
now! Mr. Heath (God love him) had decided that industry should
only work three days to save energy during the current fuel and
power crisis. This meant that hundreds of thousands more people

would be registering as unemployed for the days on which they could not work. Laughing Ted had also decreed that TV should shut down at ten o'clock in another bid to save energy. He did have some strange ideas did Mr. Heath. As it turned out the three-day week was to benefit me and most others in Grimwood's. There was no restriction on the number of hours that factories could stay open during the three days so it was decided that we would work three twelve-hour shifts. For four hours of each of these shifts we would be paid overtime rate, which was nice! Shifts were 06:30 - 18:30 and 18:30 - 06:30. We would work these shifts until the power crisis was resolved which would be when the Happy Sailor finally gave way to Harold Wilson in the General Election due on the last day of February. It was mad: Grimwood's was booming while the rest of the country was in crisis! These working arrangements suited almost everybody, including myself, as we would also get three days dole because it was proved that we had worked a sufficient number of Saturdays in the previous months for that to count as a working day. So, all in all, we would be working 36 hours instead of 37.5 but would be getting quite a few bob more than normal; the overtime payments and the three days dole money putting us well in pocket. Laughing! Keep Ted in I say! It was during this period that I first crossed swords with Tricky Dicky. Dicky was the night-shift foreman, a Wiganer, and hated Scousers. I was in the canteen one night having overstayed my allotted ten-minute break.

"Eh up Peter. Arse thee fettlin'?"

"Err.. yeah, I'm fine thanks Dicky. I was on me way out, honest."

"Nay, don't be frettin'. 'Ere, get thee sen a cup of tay."

"Err...right, okay Dicky, thanks."

"I don't like Liverpoolers yer know."

Grrrrrrrrrr! That bloody word again!

"I know Dicky, I've 'eard. So why're yer buyin' me a cup of tea an' bein' nice to me? I'm a Scouser."

"I know, but tha's okay. Tha's a good worker. All t'others are bloody lazy gets who don't wanna work!"

"Ah, that's not fair Dicky. Most of us are sound an' there's loads of Wiganers an' Skemmers 'ere who are far lazier than Scousers." With that, Dicky's mood changed.

"Reet, come on nah, let's 'ave thee. Tha's 'ad long enough."

"Yeah, okay Dicky. On me way mate. Thanks for the tea. I'll buy yer one back later."

"Nah, tha's okay Peter. Keep tha money in pocket. Tha needs it more than I do."

He didn't seem too bad Dicky. Tales of him being a two-faced, snivellin', snidey, connivin', snot-gobblin', turdburglin' little twat had obviously been grossly exaggerated.

"Peter, come into my office a minute."

Oh shit! Eddie Clarke didn't look a happy man. What the fuck 'ad I done this time?

"I'm gonna 'ave to give yer a warnin'."

"Why? I 'aven' been late this week 'ave I?"

"No, but Dicky's reported yer."

"Reported me? Reported me for what? I 'aven' done anythin'!"

"'E said you 'ad twenty minutes for one of yer ten-minute breaks last night."

"Yeah, that's 'cos 'e bought me a cup of tea an' was gabbin' to me for another ten minutes after I was on me way ourra the canny!"

"Well, 'e's asked me to give yer a warnin'. I wasn't there, don't know what wen' on, so I'll 'ave to take 'is word for it. Sorry about that Peter."

"Okay Ed, no problem."

I went in search of Dicky.

"'Ee arr Dicky! What's the Denis Law 'ere mate?"

"Tha wha'?"

"You know! Yer reported me to Eddie and I've just 'ad a bloody warnin' now!"

"Don't tha cuss at me or I'll be reportin' thee agin!"

"Yeah, but it was you who bought me the cup of tea an' then sat there gabbin' to me for ten minutes while I drank it!"

"Well I didn't bloody ask thee to sup the bloody thing. It's yon fault. Nah geet back to bloody work. Bloody Scousers are all the same!"

Fuck off yer fuckin' two-faced, snivellin', snidey, connivin', snot-gobblin', turdburglin' little twat!

"Christ, no wonder they call you Tricky!"

Harsh lesson learned!

Moral of the story is: **NEVER TRUST A WIGANER BEARING A CUP OF TEA!** Well, not if he's nicknamed Tricky anyway.

CHAPTER SIX

A CUP FULL OF RELIGION

FA Cup 3rd Round day is brilliant. You can always count on shocks, upsets and the odd giant-killing act, which is fine as long as your particular giant club is not the one being killed! Previously unknown players can become the name on every football fan's lips in the country. Peter Kitchen was very nearly one of those.

We'd been drawn at home to Doncaster Rovers. The game had been hyped up quite a bit due to Kevin Keegan being a Donny lad. There'd be no problem though as Donny were riding the crest of a slump at the bottom of the Fourth Division while we...well... we were us. When Donny boy Keegan scored as early as the third minute we stood back and waited for the goal feast to arrive. Dave Rylands, centre-half from the '72 FA Youth Cup Final side was in the starting line-up for what turned out to be his only first-team appearance for Liverpool. Poor Dave was being given a torrid time by centre-forward Peter Kitchen. Kitchen it was who equalised. Still no problem though we thought as there was plenty of time to go - still in the first half. A massive rethink was underway though when winger Brendan O'Callaghan gave Donny a half-time lead. Kim Book, so badly embarrassed by George Best's six goals past him in an FA Cup tie four years earlier when playing for Northampton, was keeping out all we could throw at him. Donny's favourite son gave us the equaliser just before the hour mark but the Belle Vue men weren't finished yet. Kitchen, a smashing little player, was everywhere and always looking for the ball. His shoot on sight policy nearly paid dividends when a wonderful shot from him hit the bar late in the game, nearly giving Rovers the win they probably deserved. That's how close we came to seeing the following day's headline: **KITCHEN SINKS 'POOL AND SENDS THEM DOWN THE DRAIN!**

It wasn't funny though; we'd nearly gone out of the FA Cup and I could do without any more of that thank you very much! The replay three days later was a much tamer affair; goals from Heighway and Cormack giving us a fairly comfortable victory.

Another cracker against Birmingham followed. Whilst not quite in the same vein as the 4-3 the season before a rare Phil Thompson goal added to Keegan's two gave us a 3-2 win.

An absolutely dire game at the Victoria Ground was about to end in defeat. Standing in the open end the previous season on a warm Easter Monday at the Stoke Glamfest was fun. It was a different story on a freezing cold January afternoon this time round however. If the GlamReds had been wearing their make-up on this day it would have been running all over their faces from the cold-induced tears! Who should save our bacon in the very last minute, saving us from an ignominious 0-1 defeat? None other than Tommy Smith who might well have been playing for Stoke had his proposed transfer gone through earlier in the season. I never was one for wrapping up well against the elements despite the fact I hate either extreme of heat, hot or cold. My hands and feet were like blocks of ice, my legs as stiff as my donga (which incidentally had shrivelled to acorn size) during a good night with Ev as I shuffled my way back towards the warm haven of the coach. I was in no mood for any shennanigans with the Stoke boys so when three of them approached me with their polite request for me to furnish them with the correct time they were met with:
"OH FUCK OFF!"
They were so taken aback they just did as they were told and fucked off, probably to seek out some other hapless victim. If you were said hapless victim then I'm sorry but I just couldn't be arsed having it with them that particular day.

Our FA Cup 4th Round tie went pretty much the same as the previous round. Carlisle United, a good side on their way to promotion from the Second Division, did well to hold us to a scoreless draw at Anfield. Shanks paired Tosh and Phil Boersma up front with Keegan dropping a little deeper. The experiment flopped in the first game but paid rich dividends in the replay, both players scoring in an easy 2-0 victory.

Tiger Feet by Mud was at Number One. Little two-year-old Stevie absolutely loved this song! It was so funny to hear him say, "Here Tiger Feet! Here Tiger Feet!" whenever it was played on radio or telly. It was even funnier seeing him doing all the actions that Mud did with the hands on the hips and rocking from side to side. I think this might have shaped his rock 'n' roll future although the "Drainpipe, drainpipe" (well that's what it sounds like to me anyway) lyrics of Napalm Death are a far cry from the "That's right, that's right, that's right, that's right I really love your tiger light" innocence of Mud. Pity kids have to grow up isn't it?

Another last minute goal from Peter Cormack gave us a 1-0 win over Norwich. People were looking for the secret of our being able to score last minute goals to secure vital wins and draws. Of course there was no secret. Shanks had just instilled into the players a never-say-die spirit and that a game of football lasted from first whistle to last.

Our FA Cup 5th Round tie was an inestimably more comfortable affair than the previous two rounds. A very good Ipswich team were comprehensively outplayed in a 2-0 win at Anfield with goals from Little Bamber and Mighty Mouse. Man of the match though was undoubtedly Tommy Smith. After initially struggling in his new right-back role Tommy was now positively revelling in it. Ipswich's dangerous left-winger Lambert didn't get a kick. Well he did but not of the ball if you see what I mean!

Two 1-0 home wins on the bounce against Southampton and Burnley; very late goals again from Boersma and Toshack respectively set us up for the latest game in our FA Cup adventure. Wolves won the League Cup beating Manchester City 2-1 on the same day we beat Burnley. I was especially made up for the bloke and his two sons that had given me a lift on such a miserable day three months earlier. As League Cup Final tickets were so much easier to get hold of than FA Cup Final tickets they were probably there. Nice one lads!

Bristol City had beaten Leeds at Elland Road in a replay the previous round so our 6th Round tie at Ashton Gate looked pretty difficult. For some strange reason I can remember Ernie Hunt's underpants playing some part in the victory at Leeds but for the life of me I can't quite remember what! Ernie's magic thundercrackers failed him this time though; Tosh scoring in a fairly comfortable 1-0 victory.

The games against Leeds were always eagerly anticipated now even more so than the clashes against Manchester United who were struggling mightily at the bottom of the First Division. 56,000 packed into Anfield to see the two great sides from Liverpool and Leeds do battle. Leeds had set a new record by going 29 games unbeaten from the start of the season before going down 2-3 at Stoke. We were eight points adrift of Don Revie's men but had two games in hand so although we'd have a chance if we took both points it was also imperative we did so. Steve Heighway scored the only goal of a great game, and I mean a really great game. Those games against Leeds in that era really were something to behold. The atmosphere at Anfield and Elland Road was ever electric with the Kop seeming to save something really special for those games. The games were heightened by the mutual respect which Shanks and Don Revie had for each other. The players too, with the obvious exception of Tommy Smith and Allan Clarke, also had massive respect for each other. Although no quarter was ever asked or given the games were played in the right spirit with hardly a booking and certainly not a sending-off that I can remember in sight.

The League game at Molineux was a totally different affair than the League Cup tie there in December. As it looked a distinct possibility that we could achieve the double there were about ten thousand Reds in the South Bank. Where were all these twats when I was freezin' me bollocks off here in December? Brian Hall scored the only goal of the game but I best remember it as hearing this song for the first time:

THOSE WERE THE DAYS MY FRIEND
WE TOOK THE STRETFORD END
WE TOOK THE SHED, THE NORTH BANK HIGHBURY
WE TOOK THE GEORDIES TOO
WE FOUGHT FOR LIVERPOOL
WE ARE THE KOP OF LIVERPOOL FC!

We had too but those days were long gone. As the song says: Those were the days. The transported Kop was absolutely bouncing as news came through on trannies of Leeds astonishing 1-4 defeat at home to Burnley. We were giving it a real go now for the League and with the FA Cup semi-final a week away why shouldn't we be thinking in terms of the double?

Our second trip to Old Trafford that season was for the FA Cup semi-final against Leicester. Dave's jalopy was once more fired up and off we jolly well went. They're not very friendly those Man United supporters are they? Their own team were playing at Chelsea but they turned up in their droves to give us untold agro both before and after the match. Still, we wouldn't have to put up with them for much longer. The match itself was a bit of a non-event. The bright springtime mood of the weather had seemed to permeate the players and both sets of supporters. The nearest anybody came to scoring was when Keegan hit the bar. A huge cheer went up when it was announced that Red Rum had won it's second successive Grand National. My Dad would be well pissed by now as I knew he had a few bob on Rummy. Dad loved a bet and had many favourite horses such as Arkle, Nicholas Silver and Nijinsky but Rummy was his all time favourite. The biggest cheer of the day though was reserved for the news that Leeds had lost again, this time 1-3 at West Ham. After their wonderful 29 game unbeaten start to the League season Leeds had since taken only four points from six games. They had seemingly fallen apart and surely the Championship was going to be ours!

"Jack, can I swap shifts tomorrow please? Me Granny's in 'ospital. I wanna go an' see 'er."
Jack Huyton was my shift foreman. He was a man of advancing years shall we say but pretty kindly so was bound to let me swap.
"Who are Liverpool playin'?"
"They're playin' Leicester at Villa Park in the semi-final replay Jack but I'm not goin', honest. I'm goin' to see me Granny."
"Tha's a lyin' little tuss. Tha's goin' match isn't tha?"
"Well alright yeah but can I swap Jack."
"Aye, we're areet now! Aye, go on then but don't never say I never do nowt for thee!"
*Fuckin' 'ell Jack, I'm not even gonna **begin** to work that one out. Must be at **least** a quadruple negative!*
"Ah thanks a lot Jack. I will, I mean I won't....I think....whatever!"

The display at Villa Park was one of our best of the season. We were the better side in the first half but had to settle for going in at half-time with no goals scored. It was no more than we deserved when Brian Hall put us into the lead just a minute after the restart. Totally against the run of play Leicester's brilliant winger, Len Glover, equalised with a fine goal. There was no better player in the country at the time than Kevin Keegan and he it was who put us back into a deserved lead with an absolute cracker. Tosh wrapped the whole thing up four minutes from time. The scenes on the pitch at the end were amazing! We were on the old open Witton Lane Terrace and seemingly the whole of that end emptied to celebrate on the pitch. Kevin Keegan especially was being carried shoulder high all over the place. We then all moved toward the Leicester fans in the Holte End but not to mock or bait them but to applaud them. The Leicester fans reciprocated this great act of sportsmanship. It was good to see respect between two sets of fans. It was a very happy Evo that boarded the Sunniways coach for home (well to me Ma's anyway). I floated rather than walked from town to Bootle before making my way back to Skem by magic carpet, I mean bus, the following morning. I loved it in Skem by now, was well settled with a good job and everything but this toing and froing to town for away games was becoming a real pain in the arse. What d'yer mean I didn't 'ave to go? **DON'T BE FUCKIN' STUPID!**

Since the defeat at Burnley on Boxing Day we had remained unbeaten in eleven games, dropping only three points. We added to this by beating QPR at Anfield with an Alec Lindsay penalty and a comical own goal by Terry Mancini. "Henry" as Terry was known after the famous conductor (don't mention conductors! It's okay Evo; this one's an orchestra conductor, not a bus conductor) was one of the game's real characters of the era. A harmless looking cross suddenly bounced off Henry's wonderfully bald pate and flew past the startled Phil Parkes in the R's goal! The Kop took the piss as only the Kop could and even Henry joined in the fun by conducting (that word again) the singing, which was quite appropriate I suppose don't you think?

The games were coming thick and fast now (but nobody moaned) so two days later we were to play Sheffield United in a rearranged game at Bramhall Lane. I got the special for this one which was full of mean scallies. That was just as well as there was a large "reception committee" of Blades, quite literally, waiting for us when we arrived. After the long walk from the station we settled ourselves into the Cricketers Arms until more "fun and games" ensued and the Police forced us out and into the ground. Leeds were top with 54 points from 37 games while we had 50 from 34. A win here would do us nicely. Not to be. We lost 0-1 and it would now be a struggle to catch Leeds as they had virtually an extra point by virtue of their vastly superior goal difference. The Easter period was going to be crucial.

Another Jalopy Jaunt to Maine Road on Good Friday. Why didn't David go to the midweek aways where I was risking life and limb to get home? We looked well on the way to a much-needed victory when Peter Cormack put us ahead in the first-half only for our lead to be cancelled out by Frannie Lee (no, not from the penalty-spot). As in the previous season we opted for the safety of the Platt Lane Stand. Also, as in the previous season, the stand was invaded by Kippax boys about ten minutes before the end. We did well to make it safely back to Jolly Jalopy. Now on the subject of Good Friday:

I don't know, I'm up the fuckin' wall with it all! I used to fuckin' hate that Lent bollocks at school! As if it wasn't bad enough being force-fed that pancake shite at school dinner on Shrove Tuesday, (Mardi Gras), a French invention by the way (wouldn't you just know it) we then had to suffer the indignity the next day of some religious weirdo using his thumb (what else had he used it for I ask?) to put a fuckin' cross on our foreheads with ash! We had to leave the fucker on all day as well - couldn't get a wash 'til the next morning! Not that I used to get a wash more than once a day anyway - more like once a week. I used to get a bath once a year on my birthday whether I needed it or not! Then what happens for the next forty days? We have to give up something we like! For forty fuckin' days! Never mind; the day after Ash Wednesday's Maundy Thursday isn't it? That's when poor kids get some of the Queen's hard-earned dosh (ha ha). One piece for each year of her life isn't it? Might be our turn this year! Nah, no fuckin' chance - Betty wouldn't come to Bootle! Nah - Maundy Thursday's the day before Good Friday isn't it? BAD Friday - FISH Friday maybe but certainly not fuckin' GOOD Friday, but more of that later.

Anyway, what's Saturday done to the fuckin' Catholic Church or anybody else for that matter? I mean, you've got Shrove Tuesday, Ash Wednesday, Maundy Thursday, Good Friday, Easter Sunday and even fuckin' Easter Monday when Jesus rose from the dead after being done in three days earlier. Yeah, rose from the dead my arse! How the fuck can anybody rise from the fuckin' dead? Anyway, if he had he would surely have gone and done that fuckin' snide Judas in wouldn't he? Snitching twat. And that fuckin' Peter or Simon or whatever the fuck he called himself - he'd have got twatted surely.

"Nah, I don't fuckin' know no Jesus! Who the fuck's 'e? Nay, nay and thrice nay!"

Fairy stories the fuckin' lot of them!

Old JC (well, fairly young JC actually - he was only supposed to be 33 wasn't he? But how does any fucker know?) was doing a Reggie Perrin methinks!

So why the fuck haven't we got anything to do with Saturday? Not fuckin' fair if you ask me. Should report that fuckin' Catholic Church to the Commission for Equal Opportunities for Days, or something.

Anyway, back to Lent. I've gotta be honest, there were only three things I really, I mean really, liked when I was a kid: footy, sweets and wanking. Now there was no chance, as you can imagine, of me giving up footy! There was an equally similar chance of me giving up wanking seeing as I was doing it at least three times a day from the age of about eleven thinking about my Ma's mate Jane (read all about it in OBAHK). So there was only my sweets left.

For one ninth of every year I had to forgo the delicious delights of Chocolate Eclairs, Bon Bons, Mars Bars, Milky Ways and other such heavenly pleasures. Now I ask you - is that fair? And what was the fuckin' point anyway? To prove that I was a good Catholic boy? If I was that I wouldn't have been pulling my pud at every given opportunity would I? Oh no - the Catholic Church frowned upon such heinous crimes as they did anything that brought you even the merest smidgen of pleasure! What was I to do - leave all my little tadpoles safely inside their sac 'til my bollocks exploded like some great creamy white volcano?

Funny when the greatest religious freak of all time, Canon Wilcox, asked Miggy, aged just ten at the time mind you, what he had given up for Lent.

"Ciggies", Miggy replied.

Ten seconds later poor little Miggy lay battered and bruised on the floor as the fuckin' madman screamed at him, "HEATHEN!"

Anyway, I digress (but isn't digression good for the soul - the writer's soul in any case?), back to that ash shite. Where did they get the ash? From some palm shit or something that had been forced into your hands by the religious weirdo nearly a year earlier. I mean, I didn't want the fucker anyway, didn't ask for it, but then they had the cheek to take the fucker back off me, burn it and make a cross on my head with the ashes! What was that all about?

More digression, back to the sweeties. Okay, I used to cheat a bit. I 'd ram as much Cough Candy and Victory V's down my neck as I could with the excuse (please forgive me God) that it was for medicinal purposes. The same was true for Stickylite sticks, Aniseed Balls (there's a joke there somewhere - think about it) and Licquorice (twat of a word to spell). Not that any of that cut much ice with my owld fella when he caught me with á bag of Cough Candy about two days into Lent. I got the leathering (literally) he considered I so richly deserved seeing as I was breaking one of the Catholic Church's golden rules. Of course, he was very religious wasn't he? Used to go to Mass every Sunday didn't he? My arse!

Talking, as we were, of licqourice (how long ago was that?) I remember being told, by Mr. Costigan in a Religious Instruction lesson, the facts of life. He clearly defined the role a woman's clitoris played in her anatomy. Trouble was I misheard him and thought for years that all girls had a piece of licqourice (told you it was a twat of a word to spell) stuck at the top of their fanny. Funny when I lost my cherry at the ripe old age of sixteen to be searching through Evelyn's undergrowth, after successfully working my way inside her milky white thighs, for that piece of licqourice. I mean, what size was it? Was it a Pomfret Cake or was it that tiny little one, millions of which you used to get in a little plassy box? I didn't know - all I was looking for was this bit of licqourice that would give my darling Evelyn such untold joy should I rub it for a few seconds. I absolutely shit myself when I finally discovered it after many hours of searching. Not a piece of licqourice in sight, just this flappy little buttony thing. Couldn't get the bloody thing to work though. There I was pulling, flicking and messing with not a sign of the supposed ecstasy Ev was supposed to be in.

"Lick it!"

"You're fuckin' 'avin' a laugh aren't yer? It fuckin' stinks down 'ere! Smells like a fuckin' cod's 'ead it does! It's fuckin' bad enough lookin', never mind lickin'!"

My first sight of a fanny was indeed a frightening, traumatic moment! Like a big, red, angry, hairy gob! Fuckin' 'orrible! And the smell! Jesus Christ (how did he get in here?) it fuckin' stunk! It did actually smell like a cod's head. Mind you, it was Friday.

Ah, never mind; let's try her Tommy Smith's Footy Studs. I twiddled with them that much I got Radio Luxembourg in the end! Women's anatomy still baffles me to this day. I still haven't worked out how to work that liquorice - I mean clitoris!

Anyway, back to the plot - if there ever was one.

Fish Friday.

What was Fish Friday? Every fuckin' Friday in Catholic school. Couldn't eat meat. You'd die if you did. Jesus died on the cross on a Friday so we couldn't eat meat.

What?

What the fuck was that to do with anything? No wonder for years I fuckin' hated fish - being force-fed it every Friday. Even the Chinese chippies wouldn't serve you a meat pie on a Friday. What the fuck did it have to with them? I sneaked a bit of Corned Beef out of the pantry one Friday, got caught by my Ma and got absolutely fuckin' battered for it! My Ma was as equally religious as my Dad. Oh yeah, and she was a Protestant so what in God's name (whatever it was) did it have to with her? Maybe she was a closet Chinawoman.

So what happens just seven days before the end of my enforced forty-day sweet fast? I get that fuckin' palm thing shoved between my unwilling hands again! Good job I hadn't had a wank that morning! Or had I? The religious weirdo was shoving the body of Christ (my arse) into my licqourice stained gob when I "accidentally" (hehe) bit his fingers. You couldn't eat before you had your "body of Christ" either as to do so would mean certain death. You HAD to have your cannibalistic feast too as not to do so would also spell your untimely demise. The freak got his own back for my chomping his fingers by shoving his half-chewed digits so far down my throat that I nearly puked. Good job he hadn't had a wank that morning! Or had he? No, of course not! Priests don't wank! They're much too holy for that! Their little tadpoles just disperse naturally around their body! Anyway, should they need to crack one off all they've got to do is think of the Virgin Mary and their dirty thoughts will disappear. Funny, that used to MAKE me give it the five-finger shuffle! I must confess to once having a tug looking at a picture of VM. Come on, she was a very pretty young lady! I'm not having that virgin bollocks though. How can you be a virgin and have a baby? Methinks young Mary was having a little dabble where she shouldn't have while Joseph was out making coffee tables for the local Jerusalem Julies!
"Er, Joseph, I'm pregnant."
"Yer can't be. I 'aven't shagged yer yet."
"Er, I know, but it's er, this thing called er, the Immaculate Contraption. No, the Immaculate Conception. That's it yeah, the Immaculate Conception! It's where yer 'ave a baby without ever getting shagged."
"Well 'ow come none of the other girls round 'ere 'aven' 'ad the Immaculate Contraception?"

"The Immaculate CONCEPTION Joseph."
"Yeah, whatever. Well, come on, 'ow come?"
"Don't know Joseph. I must 'ave been picked special like."
"Well, 'ang on. I've seen that John the Baptist geezer round 'ere a bit."
"Ah, 'e's just a friend Joseph, honest. Anyway, I can't get shagged by anyone ever can I? I'm dead pure aren't I?"
MY FUCKIN' BIG, FAT, HAIRY ARSE!
Not to worry anyway, I'll be getting the ashes of that palm thing on my head again next year. Oh deep, fuckin', unconfined joy!

And then there's the greatest misnomer of all: **GOOD FRIDAY!**
GOOD Friday?
I call it fuckin' **BAD** Friday! Not only can you not have a nice steak (one of the great joys of life) but you can't even get a bevy at a decent time of day or night either. Pubs open at 12 - close at 3. Open again at 7 - close at 10:30. Why? Did Jesus get snotted before 12 or between the hours of 3 and 7? Who knows? I certainly don't! How do we know for certain what time he went to Mount Olive (sorry, that's another joke) I mean Mount Calvary? Mad isn't it.

It just might all make sense one day but I very much doubt it. One thing I do know - the Catholic Church has a fuckin' lot to answer for!

CHAPTER SEVEN
I'M NOT GOIN' TO WEMBLEY (AGAIN)!

I was keen to go to Portman Road but the Jolly Jalopy would have struggled to make it to Northwich never mind Ipswich. I didn't have enough money for a coach or train so I decided to make do with listening to the radio and watching the highlights on MOTD. The 1-1 draw kept us in with a shout but we were losing ground now.

We got back on track with a great 4-0 win against Man City. All the goals came in the first half so it was time to take the piss with City kicking into the Kop in the second half. Denis Law being ex-Man U obviously came in for loads. Denis was to retire after the summer's World Cup. He'd had a great career and had often been courted by Shanks after playing for the great man at Huddersfield. Denis though made his fame and fortune down the other end of the East Lancs and good luck to him. The most flak in this match though was reserved for Frannie Lee. Frannie of course was known as a diver. I'm not sure this reputation was wholly deserved but he did seem to get a lot of penalties, scoring something like 13 in the '71-'72 season. After one extravagant, shall we say, "fall" Frannie was baited by the Kop with "Frannie is a diver" to the tune of that classic hit of the day by the wonderfully gifted singer/songwriter Mike Batt, "Remember you're a Womble." Oh how we loved to see Great Uncle Bulgaria and co cavorting around the stage singing such a superb song on Top of the Pops. Worse was to come for our barrel-chested villain though. Frannie missed an absolute sitter that my Granny would have scored. "Frannie is a Womble!" Frannie took it in good part though even though he must have been severely pissed off by then. A photographer's long lens camera was used to simulate a machine gun as Frannie sprayed the Kop with pretend bullets. Denis and Frannie were two of the great characters in the game at a time when characters abounded. There were some great Cup

Final songs doing the rounds in the Kop; one I especially liked
was to the tune of the conga:
Let's all go to Wembley, lets all go to Wembley
Da da da da. Da da da da!
Toshack, Heighway, Keegan
The best you've ever seen 'em
Da da da da. Da da da da!

My favourite though, and I don't know where it came from or
who made it up was to the tune of an old song in tribute to the
Beatles, Oh Beatles we love you:
Shankly is our hero; he showed us how to play.
The mighty Reds of Europe are out to win today
He made a team of champions, with every man a king
And every game we love to win and this is what we sing...
WE LOVE YOU LIVERPOOL WE DO
WE LOVE YOU LIVERPOOL WE DO
WE LOVE YOU LIVERPOOL WE DO
OH LIVERPOOL WE LOVE YOU!

We've won the League, we've won the Cup,
We're masters of the game
And just to prove how good we are
We'll do it once again.
We've got another team to beat and so we've gorra try
'Cos we're the best in all the land
And that's the reason why...
WE LOVE YOU LIVERPOOL WE DO
WE LOVE YOU LIVERPOOL WE DO
WE LOVE YOU LIVERPOOL WE DO
OH LIVERPOOL WE LOVE YOU!

Clemence is our goalie, the best there is around
And Keegan is the greatest that Shankly ever found.
Heighway is our favourite; a wizard of the game
And here's the mighty Toshack to do it once again.

WE LOVE YOU LIVERPOOL WE DO
WE LOVE YOU LIVERPOOL WE DO
WE LOVE YOU LIVERPOOL WE DO
OH LIVERPOOL WE LOVE YOU!

What a song!

All hope of the title was virtually lost in the next match at home to our lovely blue neighbours. We did everything but score in a goalless draw but in fact Everton came closest to winning it when Bob Latchford, their big-money signing from Birmingham, hit the post. As news came through of Leeds' 3-2 win at home to Ipswich it meant that we would then have to win all our remaining three games, at home to Arsenal and away at West Ham and Tottenham, whilst hoping Leeds lost their last game at QPR; an unlikely scenario. Everton had more or less decided the destiny of the League title that day (not that they were involved themselves of course) and how the Evertonians danced!

The final nail in the coffin was hammered in by, ironically as it turned out, Arsenal's Ray Kennedy. Ray was a fine player but I hated him that night for scoring the only goal of the game. I felt so sick I wanted to puke. I went back to Mam's where Ev and Stevie were waiting for me.
"What d'yer reckon son?"
"Just not quite good enough this season Dad but we'll win it next."
"Oh never mind, yer'll win the Cup. The Cup's better than the League."
Dad looked at me and I looked at Dad. Ev's piece of homespun philosophy had not gone down too well with either of us. Why do women say the most stupid things at the most stupid times?
"Yeah, I remember when they won the Cup that time when our Peter was a lad and we were all dancin' round 'ere and 'avin parties and that. It was great wasn't it Peter?"
Dad's look said it all. If it could have been translated to words it

would have said, "You strangle your wife and I'll strangle mine." Instead of committing wifeicide or whatever it's called Dad and me decided to concentrate on the possibility of me getting a Cup Final ticket.

"Any chance of a ticket son?"

"Nah, no chance Dad. I've tried everywhere."

"Well, I've told yer 'aven' I; you go all these matches all over the country an' they're not arsed whether yer get a Cup Final ticket or not."

"I know Dad but yer need a season ticket to even 'ave at least a chance of gettin' one an' there's more chance of me gettin' a Cup Final ticket than a season ticket!"

"I don't think the Queen's goin' this year. Write to 'er an' ask 'er if she's not can yer 'ave 'er ticket."

That made me chuckle.

"No, but Tarby and Cilla and all their cronies'll be there though won't they? They go to loads of matches though don't they? I'm fed up Dad, I really am."

"Oh it's better watchin' it on the telly anyway. Yer see more an' yer don't 'ave to pay all that money."

I loved my Ma very much but I was deffo gonna kill 'er if she didn't shut up!

Cup Final day in the Evo household Skem was superb but I was still gutted I wasn't at Wembley. There was though no use brooding over it; I'd just have to get on with it and make the most of watching it on the telly. It had to be on the BBC of course! BBC had by far and away the best coverage and the best commentator. David Coleman was now the BBC's "Voice of the Cup Final". It wasn't quite all over for Kenneth Wolstenholme, possibly the best and most famous football commentator the world has ever known, he was to make a comeback in later years, but the Coal Man was definitely Number One at the Beeb. ITV's Brian Moore was a fine commentator too but not a patch on Coleman. 44 Willow Hey was bedecked inside and out with all kinds of red and white regalia for the day but it seemed not many other people on Church Farm were of a similar disposition. I missed the atmosphere of Bootle where for sure the parties would be in full swing before and after the match.

Even watching on the telly the mood felt right. Reds seemed to be slightly both outnumbering and outsinging the Geordies. Newcastle players seemed nervous as they walked out in ridiculous coloured tracksuits; something like purple and yellow they were. Our players though looked confident and relaxed as well as gloriously turned out in red tracksuit tops.

The first half was a pretty staid affair with the better chances falling to us. Larry Lloyd and Phil Thompson were coping very well with the Magpies strike force of John Tudor and Malcolm Macdonald. Macdonald had been full of himself in the build up to the match with graphic details of exactly what Newcastle, he in particular, were going to do to us. Hardly worth us bothering turning up he said! Well it's a bloody good job we did isn't it? Supermac was indeed a very good striker but he must have wished he hadn't opened his mouth as Thommo not only had him in his arse pocket but also stitched it up too!

Alec Lindsay scored a cracker six minutes into the second half only for it to be ruled out for offside against another player. We didn't have to wait long though for the jumpin' 'n' jivin' to start. Tommy Smith, having a brilliant game in his right-back role, crossed and Keegan slammed the ball into the Newcastle net. Cue wild celebrations at Wembley and Willow Hey. Our Ste, as my little sister Collette had nine years earlier, watched in bewilderment as I cavorted around the room. It all got a bit too much for the little fella so he decided sleep would be the best option, took himself off up to his room and spent the rest of the Cup Final in the company of the Wombles and Smash men on his bedroom wall.

Heighway's goal fifteen minutes from time following an excellent header from Tosh virtually sealed the match. As me and Ev were locked in an embrace jumping around the room that familiar warm feeling stirred my loins. With the little fella safely tucked up in the land of nod and the game all but won I half thought about flirting the beautiful one upstairs for a quick frolic. Shanks insisted though that a game lasts for ninety minutes and you must keep going until the final whistle so I wasn't going to argue with the great man. How right Bill turned out to be as a brilliant passing move, Liverpool at their very best, ended with Tommy Smith scampering Thompsonesque down the wing and delivering a perfect low cross for Keegan to tap in from a couple of yards. That was the cue for a classic piece of commentary from our man Coleman:

"Keegan two. Heighway one. Liverpool three. Newcastle none!" Okay, not quite in the same League as Kenneth's masterpiece eight years earlier but great all the same.

"Supermac is only good when it's rainin'!"
I didn't feel in the least bit sorry for Macdonald. He was quite rightly getting everything he deserved from the Red Army. On the other hand I did feel very sorry for a young Kirkby lad, Terry McDermott, who had been the best Newcastle player on the pitch. Terry cut a forlorn figure as he trooped away from Wembley. Terry's only consolation, if any, was that by the end of the day he had the shirt of the Man of the Match (for me anyway): Phil Thompson, his Kirkby buddy. Dignity in victory is as important as dignity in defeat; proven when the Newcastle players were applauded off the pitch by the Reds as our men were still doing their lap of honour.

Right, game over, celebrations done, coverage finished, David Coleman off for a cup of tea, Pink Panther on the telly (why was the Pink Panther always on the telly after the Cup Final?); cue Evo joke:
Where does the Pink Panther come from?
I don't know Evo. Where does the Pink Panther come from?

73

Durham, Durham, Durham, Durham, Durham, Durham, Durham.
All that done, little Ste in bed, time for a frolic! YIPPEEEEE!
Even Shanks couldn't deny me that!

After celebrating in the grand style me and Ev went for liquid
celebrations in the Derby Arms where not only all the Liverpool
songs were belted out but also the hits of the day: Seasons in the
Sun; Waterloo (which had just reached Number One that day)
and last but not least Tiger Feet! Go 'ead! I still ended the day
crying though.
"What's the matter Peter?"
"I shoulda been there! I shoulda fuckin' been there!" I blubbered.
I shed real, proper, sobbing tears in my confused and emotional
state.
"I know love. I know."
Maybe, just maybe, she was finally beginning to understand. I
wasn't holding my breath though.

I made sure I was in town for the homecoming celebrations the
following day. It was a very poor second best to actually being at
Wembley the day before but it was still superb anyway. I was
jealous of all the lads swapping tales of the weekend and how the
Geordies had been marvellous and very loyal supporters. We'd
even cheekily nicked their own Blaydon Races song to gently
take the piss:
**"Oh me lads, you shoulda seen 'em runnin'.
Runnin' down the Wembley Way without the FA Cup!"**

I did something very stupid the following Wednesday: I went to
Tottenham! This, for once, was just one of those away games I
really shouldn't have gone to. There was no need to, nothing at
stake. No good reason to imperil myself at the hands of the
Tottenham hordes. You'd think I'd have known better wouldn't
you? But no, I ignored the fact I'd had major trouble on both of
my previous visits to White Hart Lane and decided to go. You see
it was a sort of act of defiance on my part. My thinking was, I

couldn't get a ticket for the Cup Final and I'd show some of the part-time twats who did that I was a PROPER supporter! I had enough money to go, could go as there was no problem getting the day off work, so I bloody well was goin' AND bugger the bloody lot of them! It wasn't one of my better decisions. There weren't many Reds at Tottenham. Well there wouldn't be would there? No, they'd all spent up the previous weekend! I didn't mind the lads who went the match on a regular basis getting tickets, the fact I didn't get one was just tough shit. It really did annoy the shit right out of me though when I saw people whom I knew hadn't been the match for years getting a ticket. I made the journey by train with not a single Red in sight. I kept the lowest of low profiles in the Paxton Road end, living in constant fear of gettin' sussed by the bad lads and gettin' my 'ead kicked in! Yeah, the Paxton Road lads would probably go for the head whereas the Park Lane lads five years previously had gone for the arse (ooh err missus!). I don't think my arse has ever recovered from that kicking! The few other Reds inside White Hart Lane that night were keeping it as firmly shut as I was. Steve Heighway's goal that gave us a 1-1 draw was greeted with hardly a ripple. I just gave it a little Chris Lawler. The usual berserk scenes of mayhem were happening on Seven Sisters Road after the match. The Reds that had been sussed were getting legged and kicked all over the place. I fluked it by dodging down a few side streets, managing to reach the station and then Euston with my arse and my head intact.

Town was chocker block with Celtic supporters on the afternoon of our last match of the season, against the Bhoys in Ron Yeats testimonial match. The ABC cinema was chocker block with St. John's Ambulance personnel. Not that the Celtic supporters were causing any trouble to the patrons of the ABC but because "The Exorcist" was showing there. The supernatural horror classic might be considered old hat now but then it was so shocking and scary that people watching it were fainting in their droves. I loved it; thought it was brilliant. Ev wasn't so impressed. Although she wasn't one of the hundreds across the country that fainted watching it she was deeply affected; so much so that she was a complete nervous wreck.

"Peter, don't go the match tonight."

"I've got to Ev. It's Ron Yeats testimonial."

"Please, I don't wanna go 'ome on me own. I'm dead scared."

"Well you go to your Linda's, pick our Ste up and stay with 'er while I'm at the match. Get to the Black Bull for ten o'clock and I'll be on the bus from the match. I'll meet yer on it. You'll be okay."

Celts supporters took up the entire Anny Road end. The few that did venture into the Kop were summarily booted out. It was a great pity really given the rapport that now exists between both sets of fans but that's how it was then. The crowd of 30,000+ made it a great night for Big Rowdy. Ron himself donned a Celtic shirt. When Bobby Charlton made a guest appearance for Celtic he was cheered to the rafters by the Celtic fans; not so much by us! Walton Breck Road was a pretty scary place to be after the match as the Celtic fans stormed along it but I made it safely to the Halfway House to catch the bus. I duly met Ev and little Ste at the Black Bull. The poor girl was terrified! She slept with the light on that night and for many nights after.

The 1973-'74 season had been a good one for us. We'd been denied retaining our League title only by a very good team. We had made Anfield the usual fortress; conceding only four points on our own patch. It was the away record that needed drastic improvement. Eleven draws away from home is not good enough to win the League, certainly not in that particular season. After the early round scares we'd won the Cup in some style. The team that Shanks had started assembling four years earlier was now somewhere near it's peak; a League Championship and an FA Cup were testimony to that. Yes, with a few additions and minor adjustments Bill Shankly was going to lead our great club to glory for many years to come!

CHAPTER EIGHT

WEMBLEY AND WOMEN

July 12th 1974:
I was listening to Radio Merseyside news just before leaving for my afternoon shift.
"Bill Shankly has resigned as Manager of Liverpool Football Club."
I could hardly take the newsreader's words in. I was listening in a daze to a recording of Shanks press conference at Anfield.
"It is with great regret myself and the Board of Directors at Liverpool Football Club have accepted Mr. Shankly's resignation. We would like to place on record our appreciation of Mr. Shankly's fifteen years of excellent service to Liverpool Football Club."
Chairman John Smith might just as well have been talking from the Sea of Tranquility rather than the Anfield boardroom for all the sense his words were making to me.
IT JUST COULDN'T BE TRUE!
Why would Shanks resign? Why would the greatest manager in the history of the game want to leave his beloved Anfield? He was one of us - he couldn't leave! It was like me saying, "I'm not going the match anymore." It just doesn't happen! What's happened?
HE HASN'T DONE ANYTHING WRONG!
Managers who look like their gonna get the sack 'cos they're shit resign, not highly successful managers who have won trophies galore and will continue to do so for many years to come. Tears were rolling down my face as I turned the telly on for confirmation of the sensational news. The screen was filled by some obnoxious manc prick taking great delight at breaking the news to Scousers in town. He seemed to be revelling in the astonished, disbelieving reaction, especially by clearly upset young lads. The horrible realisation finally sunk in when people at work were discussing who Shanks successor would be. Various names were bandied about including that of Brian Clough. I

certainly didn't want him! If the club were going to look outside
for a Manager my own personal choice would have been Celtic's
Jock Stein. Nobody had given much thought to the club
promoting from within but really that was the logical move and
one which the club quite rightly made. Bob Paisley, although at
first reluctant was going to be our new Manager. It was a good
appointment in that if Shanks was going to change his mind and
take the twelve months holiday that the club had suggested then
there could be no better temporary appointment. The club though
couldn't afford to be second-guessed. It became clear that Bill's
mind was made up and there was no going back. Maybe he later
regretted it but the deed was now done and that was that. Nobody
has ever really got to the bottom of why Bill did the very
unShankly thing of quitting. Maybe he wanted to spend more
time with his family; after all LFC had been virtually his whole
life for the past fifteen years. Whatever it was Bill wasn't really
saying. Emlyn Hughes claimed that he came the closest to
knowing when he was round at the Shankly home one day. Bill,
Emlyn claims, was about to tell him when there was a knock at
the door. Bill went to answer it and the moment had gone. Bill
would never divulge the information now. I've no reason to
disbelieve Emlyn either as Shanks saw in Crazy Horse his soul
mate: a man as passionate about football in general and Liverpool
Football Club in particular as he was. There were difficult times
in the first few weeks of the transition as Bill very often used to
turn up for training. His very presence had a somewhat unsettling
effect as you can imagine. Bob and his staff had a job to get on
with of keeping Liverpool Football Club at the very pinnacle of
English and hopefully European football. Bill's presence might
have been seen as something of an intrusion; certainly Shanks
seemed to be rather more welcome at Everton's Bellfield, which
he lived nearer to anyway, than he was at Melwood. It was quite
easy though for Everton; it wasn't their problem. No, we just all
had to accept that the great Shanks was no longer Manager of
Liverpool Football Club. Somebody else might have been doing
his job, after all no one man, not even Shanks, was bigger than
Liverpool Football Club, but he'd never be replaced.

I was about to be hit with another bombshell. Well, not really a bombshell as it had been planned. Ev had missed her period and was off to the doctor's for the Gravindex test. Good old G confirmed that there was indeed to be an addition to the Evo family. Nice one - a little bruv or sis for Ste! Due on January 25, which was nice as it was eminently possible that the conception had happened on Cup Final day! Well done Mr. and Mrs. Evo! Wonder if it was a boy would she let me call him William Shankly Etherington? Nah, no chance! Or Kevin Keegan Etherington ? Even less chance. No, Peter for a boy, Evelyn for a girl. Would I get away with Emlyn? Don't even think about it! Without needing to check the fixture list I knew that January 25th was a Saturday and that furthermore it was FA Cup 4th Round day. There was a 50-50 chance of possibly missing a match. We'd be in the 4th Round of course having strode majestically through the 3rd Round. Anyway, if bruv or sis was like little Ste then there wouldn't be a problem - six days late, Friday child - no prob!

"Oh this year I'm off to sunny Spain. Y Viva Espana!"
No, not us! No chance of us going on holiday - always skint! The constant strains of that classically summer song were heard across Grimwood's shop floor. Mary, let off the leash since her divorce, was off on holiday as a single woman for the first time. She was going to take Benidorm by storm and woe betide any man who got in her way. Mary could break a man's neck with her bare thighs! Mary, whilst being a very attractive woman, also took no shit. She'd taken enough shit while she was wed she told me; now was the time to start enjoying herself. Well bloody good on her I say! I certainly wouldn't have argued with her or fancied a crack off her! I wouldn't have minded a crack *at* her though! Only messin' - I was a very happily (sometimes) married man. The times when I wasn't so happy I could go to Mary, tell her my little problems and be assured that it wouldn't go any further. She sort of looked after me, not in a motherly kind of way but as a more mature friend. Oh how I wished she'd clasp me to those ample bosoms to comfort me!

Apart from Shanks the other big close-season managerial story was that of Don Revie resigning his post at Leeds to take up the reigns as England supremo. The FA, having fired World Cup winning boss Alf Ramsey had been searching for the right man to take over. Joe Mercer had come out of retirement to do a good short-term caretaker job but wasn't interested in the post full-time. Brian Clough was the people's choice. I couldn't really see why. Clough had done a terrific job by leading Derby County to the League title in '71-'72 but hadn't really done enough since (he was at the time languishing at Brighton who had just finished 19th in the Second Division) to justify his own much-vaunted claims for the England job. The FA, quite sensibly, went for and got the best English manager around. Leeds caused something of a sensation by appointing Brian Clough. A strange decision that and not one which was met with universal approval by the Leeds United supporters. The hierarchy among the Leeds players weren't too happy about it either and were not slow to let Clough know it! So it was that the country's two best teams would clash in the FA Charity Shield with new managers. The showpiece game was also to be given a higher profile by being played at Wembley. In recent years the traditional curtain raiser to the new season had lost it's appeal - quite a few League Champions and FA Cup winners declining to take part. Shanks was actually manager in name only. The great man would lead the team out but Uncle Bob was now seen as the man in charge.

I was definitely going to Wembley for the Charity Shield match. Tickets were a lot easier to come by than the gold dust sprinkled FA Cup Final ones. The celebs, hangers-on, wannabe fans etc were only interested in the FA Cup Final. They didn't have time for this pile of shite. Nah, they couldn't go 'cos they'd be walking the dog or mowing the lawn or shopping with their tarts or opening a new supermarket or attending the premier of luvvy's new film or something dead important like that. I'd been going to away matches pretty much on my own mostly since moving to Skem. I hadn't really mated up with anybody sufficiently interested in risking getting their heads kicked in every couple of weeks or so. I'd even lost touch with most of my old mates and saw them only occasionally so home matches too were mostly pretty solitary affairs. One lad whom I had worked with at Walter Holme and still saw from time to time when visiting Ev's sister Linda in her Mum's old house in Hinton Street was Barry Mc.

"Peter, yer goin' to Wembley for the Charity Shield?"

"Yeah."

"'Ow yer gettin' there?"

"Dunno, coach I suppose."

"Well our Kev's goin' down in 'is car. I'm goin' with 'im and another lad Snowy. Wanna jump in with us?"

"Yeah, sound's a bell mate, ta."

"Only one snag though - we're goin' down on the Friday and won't be comin' back 'til the Sunday. We're stayin' at Snowy's sister's flat in London."

"Fuckin' bring it on! Two days in London? Fuckin' right!"

We met up at the Vic in Crosby early in the evening and by the time we left at nine o'clock were well on our way to being completely sauced. I was really looking forward to my first visit to Wembley so the ale was flowing freely in the back of the car as we made our way to the capital. I think the crates of ale were actually taking up more room in the car than people! How the fuck could this be my first trip to Wembley considering we'd played there three times in the ten years I'd been going the match, home and away? Okay, I was too young for the '65 Final and maybe the '71 Final was just a little bit too near my wedding day for me to be able to go even if I could have got hold of a ticket (not that I would have let the little matter of my forthcoming nupts get in the way had I got a ticket) but surely I was **ENTITLED** to a ticket for last season's Final. I think the other lads were getting a bit bored by me banging on about this in my drunken state so to sleep perchance to dream (hopefully a sexy one - I was already missing my darling) for Evo!

"Let me take you by the hand and lead you through the streets of London."
Ralph McTell (real name Ralph May. American, I always thought, but in fact British) was serenading us through the medium of the radio. As we wound our way through the London streets in the early hours on our way to Mary's (Snowy's sister) I did indeed see some incredible sights; much more than on the normal straight there and back coach trips. For instance, it was the first time I'd ever seen two women kissing on the street, well in the flesh that is rather than on a flickering screen. It was the first time really as well I'd seen beggars on our streets. I can't remember seeing them in Liverpool. Yes, I used to see old tramps picking ciggy stumps off the floor and trying to cadge a fag or two but not people actually asking for money; apart that is from the usual "LENDZYERODZ!" outside Anfield (done that myself). I had of course heard about SHELTER and the sterling work they do in trying to house homeless people but I'd never really fully realised how bad the problem was. All this too in our capital city. How sad. I suppose though it goes on in every major city in the world; it was just a shock seeing it at first hand as it were for the first time.

Mary lived in Doughty Street. The name Doughty Street was bugging me. I knew it for some reason but couldn't think why for the life of me. Mary welcomed us even though we'd just knocked her up (I wouldn't have minded) but was still sleep ridden so I decided not to ask her why the name Doughty Street was stuck in my mind 'til later. We placed our four weary, smelly, farty bodies where we could in the hope of snatching some much-needed sleep. A big day lay ahead of us.

Mary fed us a marvellous breakfast before going off to scrub up. She scrubbed up very well too. The boggy, sleepy-eyed Mary of the night before was gone and replaced by a very fit, very pretty lady in her early twenties. There was also the added attraction of Mary not wearing a bra. Very nice! It was all I could do to keep my eyes away from her TSFS when I was talking to her.

"Mary, why does Doughty Street ring such a bell with me?"
"Maybe because Charles Dickens lived in this street."
"That's it! I knew it was something like that! I read a book on Dickens when I was at school. Doughty Street must 'ave stuck 'cos of that."
I felt quite proud to be staying in the street where Britain's greatest ever novelist had lived. Mary lived, I think, in number 30. Certainly it wasn't many doors away from Dickens old house of number 48. Number 48 had now been turned into a Dickens Museum. The museum was closed by the time we set off to catch the tube to Wembley but there was still something awe-inspiring just standing outside the house where Dickens had written some of his greatest works. Apparently, so Mary told me, he had only lived in the house for a couple of years or so but had written prolifically while he had been there. I wonder if people some day will come to visit the Evo Museum at 44 Willow Hey? I somehow doubt it!

"Mary, bloody cover them up will yer!"
I felt sorry for Snowy and his embarrassment at his sister's TSFS being ogled by a load of sex-starved Scousers outside Wembley Park station. That didn't stop me sneaking a few admiring glances myself though!
"Oh shut up will yer Tony. They're only me bloody nipples!"
Snowy's face went as red as his hair. He covered his embarrassment by buying Mary a scarf to cover her TSFS. Not that Mary was in the least bit embarrassed herself. She was proud to show off her nipples. I was quite glad too! Our light-hearted banter sitting on a garage forecourt wall soon stopped though when we suddenly found ourselves surrounded by seven or eight lads. They were okay at first talking to us about how we'd got down etcetera but it was a ruse to get us surrounded. It turned out they were Millwall supporters. I'd had a run-in a few years earlier with the Millwall RHS and ended up, not for the first or last time in my life, with a bloody nose but no other real harm done. The mood, whilst not ugly, definitely had a scent of trouble.

"I can see us gettin' knocked off this wall in a minute."
Barry was clearly shittin' himself as much as I was.
"Well I'm takin' a couple of the fuckers down with me if we do!"
Kev was a big lad and a bit of a hard nut. I could see that he meant
it and felt a bit better. The day was saved by the intervention of a
couple of bizzies who had seen the situation developing. They
moved our potential attackers on and we made our way safely
along Wembley Way to the stadium. Nice one Met lads (for
once)!

I was very impressed by my first real-life view of Wembley
Stadium. I'd been captivated by the place since I was a young lad.
I'd read about the exploits of PC George Arthur Scorey and his
horse Billy - heroes of the first ever Wembley FA Cup Final in
1923 between West Ham and Bolton when George and Billy had
almost single-handedly cleared the pitch of some of the estimated
crowd of 200,000. I know most people thought it was just an
over-sized, ramshackle old shed in urgent need of renovation but
I thought it was the biggest and best ground I'd ever been to.

The match itself was a bad-tempered effort (more of that later)
finishing 1-1 with goals from Boersma and Cherry. A penalty
shootout (or "kicks from the penalty mark to decide a drawn
game" to give it the correct title) would decide whether the
Charity Shield was to go to Elland Road or Anfield. Both teams
had scored all five penalties when the Shield was to be decided
seemingly by goalkeepers Harvey and Clemence taking the
decisive penalties. Up stepped David Harvey - and blasted the
ball over the bar! Come on Clem! Win it for us! What's Cally
doing shuffling forward to take it? Clem's got more chance of
scoring than Cally! Wrong! Cally's penalty, whilst not being the
greatest in the world (well he had slipped as he was taking it)
crept past Harvey to give us the Shield. Shanks in his very last act
as Manager of Liverpool Football Club had kidded the arse off
Mr. Smug - Brian Clough. Nice one Bill! I was glad Phil
Boersma had played as he had previously said he would never

play for Liverpool again after walking out on the squad before the FA Cup Final against Newcastle. Shanks, maybe in a show of loyalty to one of the remaining members of the '60's team, had picked Chris Lawler as substitute. Phil had felt, quite rightly in my opinion, that he should have been at least sub. He had accepted the fact he would not have a place in the starting eleven but had expected the consolation of at least being on the bench and maybe at some point being able to play a part. The main talking point of the match though was not the football but the most famous sending offs in Wembley history. The match had been the usual Liverpool v Leeds affair: Smith kicking Clarke; Clarke moaning to the referee, that sort of thing. Leeds though had one little shit who was to take things to a higher level: Johnny Giles. Now don't get me wrong - Giles was a great player but he was a contemptible little arsehole. Giles butted Keegan, off the ball and out of sight of the referee. Keegan then retaliated and Bremner steamed into him. Keegan threw a punch back and both men were sent off. On their way off Bremner took his shirt off to reveal the whitest body in the memory of man and threw it to the ground in disgust. Keegan quickly followed suit to reveal his marvellously sun-tanned body. Everybody in our end pissed themselves laughing at this.

I went to watch Bremner at a Sportsman's dinner many years later. Billy said that if he had seen Giles butting Keegan then he would have been more than happy to let them sort it out between themselves. As it was, the first thing he saw was Keegan twattin' Giles so he had to back his teammate, which is fair enough I suppose. Both players were banned for eight weeks due to that little twat, Giles. I liked Bremner and always thought he was one of the best midfielders I've ever seen but I hated Giles.

I kept away from the usual pitched battles between our lads and theirs after the match. We were goin' on the piss in London! YIPPEEE!

After touring a few pubs in Old Kent Road, I think - I was only a London learner then, we ended up in some strip pub.

"This is more like it!"

I only said that 'til the stripper actually came on. My God she was ugly! She must have been 70 if she was a day too! What really put me off her though, apart from the bandage on her knee, was the fact she looked like my Granny Martha! Fuckin' 'ell yer can't be watching yer Granny takin' 'er clothes off can yer? Which reminds me of that quaint old Scottish song:
"Och yer canna kick yer nanny off a bus.
Och yer canna kick yer nanny off a bus.
Och yer canna kick yer nanny
'Cos she's yer mammy's mammy
Och yer canna kick yer nanny off a bus!"
Where the fuckin' 'ell did that come from?
Meanwhile back at the Granny Strip Joint:
Things were brightening up! Granny had been paid and was off down to Cricklewood or somewhere to collect her pension. Her place had been taken by a girl, early 20's maybe who could well have been her Granddaughter. This was much more like it! The girl cavorting in front of me on a stage not more than a foot away (of course I was at the fuckin' front!) with her long dark hair, lovely blue eyes, beautiful legs, voluptuous breasts and sticky-out TSFS reminded me of somebody very close to me. It made me yearn even more for my delightful dish at home.
"Get 'em off girl! Come on, show us yer beaver!"
"Come on Peter yer dirty get. We're goin' back to mine now!"
My face turned Snowy's-hair red when I saw Mary fixing me with those dazzling eyes. I wonder what Dickens would have made of all this?

Back at Mary's the whole day was thoroughly dissected. Snowy wouldn't let us talk about anything that rhymed with raspberry ripple.
"We outsang Leeds."
"Yeah, Liverpool Lou was great."
"It was better when we were all singin', "Shankly, Shankly, Shankly, Shankly."
"I thought we were gonna get our fuckin' 'ead's kicked in by those lads at the garage."

"Nah, we'd 'ave twatted them!"

"Fuckin' 'ell, what about that owld bag in the strip boozer?"

"I thought she was all right!"

"Nah, not the young one. The owld one who was on first."

"Yeah, that's who I meant!"

"That young one looked like my missus yer know."

"Fuckin' 'ell Evo, when are we coming back to yours then?"

"Fuck off, she's mine, all mine!"

"I think the lot of youse are pervs!"

"Mary, looking at young ladies takin' their clothes off is not pervin'! Now if I was lookin' at young men takin' their clothes off..."

"See the fuckin' state of Bremner?"

"Yeah, like a fuckin' sterry bottle!"

"Funny when Keegan threw 'is shirt off too."

"Ambre Solaire versus Sterry Milk."

"I think Keegan won!"

"'Ave yer seen Blazing Saddles yet?"

"Yeah, fuckin' brilliant!"

"Funniest film I've ever seen!"

"What about when they're all eatin' beans an' fartin' round the camp fire?"

"Yeah, like this."

"And this!"

"And this!"

"Oh youse are 'orrible yer shower of smelly gets. I'm goin' to bed."

My first Wembley trip had been a great success. There would hopefully be many more to come.

CHAPTER NINE

THE BIRTH OF A BEAUTY

The first League game of the following season was at newly promoted Luton. Kenilworth Road was a really strange ground to go to. We hardly saw a Luton fan outside the ground before or after the match. There wasn't a hint of even one iota of trouble, which of course was just the way I liked it but it was the quietest away game I've ever been to. Luton had a centre-forward called Barry Butlin. Now how could you take someone called Barry Butlin seriously? It sounded like he was gonna run to the crowd any minute and shout "Good morning campers!" Okay I realise that was BILLY Butlin but you know what I mean. Anyway we had to take him seriously when he scored but goals from Smith and Heighway gave us a 2-1 victory and a good start to the season. It was also Kevin Keegan's last match before he started his eight-week suspension for his part in the Battle of the Bodies at Wembley. Tosh's latest "replacement" Ray Kennedy couldn't play because of injury. The signing of Ray from Arsenal for £180,000 was a very strange one on the face of it given as Shanks had signed him when he knew he himself was about to quit. Maybe Shanks was trying to do his best for the club by strengthening the team before he left but to sign a player he knew he was never going to manage seemed strange indeed.

Molineux the Tuesday after was no Kenilworth Road. If the scenes outside had been as quiet as those on the pitch during the 0-0 draw I would have been very happy but it was a good old battle to get back to the station in one piece.

A highly controversial game at home to Leicester saw us win 2-1. Both goals were from penalties scored by Alec Lindsay, the first as early as the first minute. Leicester's Keith "big puff" Weller received a hefty ban for remarks made to the referee after the game. You couldn't really blame him though - both pens were a bit dodgy.

The martial arts boom was at its peak with "Kung Fu Fighting" by Carl Douglas topping the charts. Me and Ev must have seen every martial arts film going. She loved them as much as I did. Bruce Lee was her favourite in films such as: "Big Boss"; "Fist of Fury" and the follow up to "Enter the Dragon" - "Return of the Dragon". I swear to you she actually said this: "It's a pity 'e's dead isn't it. 'E must have made all these films before 'e died." You. couldn't make it up could you? There was one film we saw called, I think, something like, "Hap Ki Do" which involved a story of some bird twatting all her enemies with bobbles attached to her hair. She'd just swing those pigtails of hers and smack the bad guys to fuck! Again, you couldn't make that up. I was quite glad to have Ev with me though in the Badlands outside the Oscar (by now renamed the Focus due to some objection by the real Oscar people). There was no way the TRS or any other RS would tackle Ev, even in her "with child" condition - Ev could kill a man with her bare eyes - a feat she must have learned from my Ma!

The return game against Wolves was an easy enough 2-0 win for us. Highlight of that game was when Kevin Keegan appeared in the Main Stand with his wife Jean and received a rapturous ovation.

My 21st Birthday was spent in the company of Ev's brother John (formerly known as Mad John) and my brother John. "Mad" John didn't join us though when we left the Lithy to spend the rest of the night in town. We were in the Cavern when our John, in scenes reminiscent of a match at Blackpool nine years earlier, kept fuckin' off for ten minute spells. Difference was this time it wasn't pork pies he was surreptitiously throwing down his neck. This time he was expanding his by now already over-expanded mind. He wasn't doing me any harm though so I just let him get on with it. I was quite content to get happily bladdered on the Cavern's shite ale. I didn't want to go to Chelsea (there's a song in there somewhere) the next day so I would be able to have a good lie in and sleep my ale-induced hangover off. Quite how our John dealt with his particular "hangover" I'm not quite sure but that was his business. We won easily, 3-0, at Stamford Bridge but I was rather relieved in a way I didn't go when reports came in of Liverpool fans being booted out of the terraces and on to the pitch after the third goal went in. Keegan's replacement, Phil Boersma, was bang in form netting two of the goals; the other one being scored by debutant Ray Kennedy, now full recovered from his injury.

Phil Boersma's greatest moment in a Liverpool shirt, probably his best ever in football came in the next match at home to Tottenham. Phil scored a scintillating hat-trick. One of the goals came from a run he started in his own-half. That truly was a wonder goal. Talk was of how Keegan could possibly get back into the side after Phil's performance. It was a nice problem for new manager Bob Paisley to have, especially as Ray Kennedy had started his Liverpool career well and had also scored in the 5-2 win against Spurs.

A very fraught 2-1 win against Brentford followed. Brentford Nylons was a huge bedding company in those days with a massive TV advertising campaign. The Kop's chant of, "Yer can stick yer fuckin' nylons up yer arse!" conjured up the most horrible mental images!

Having dropped only one point from our first six games we were obviously top of the League when we made the visit to Maine Road. Quite what made us go in to the Kippax Street for that match I'm really not sure. I'd been safe enough in the Platt Lane stand for the past two seasons. Dave and his Jolly Jalopy weren't going this time though so I threw myself at the tender mercies of Sunniways. I really can't remember whether the coach was late getting to the ground and we made a mad scramble to get in, just going to the first available gate but there were loads of us in the Kippax. Not for very long though. We were sussed well before the kick-off and royally bounced out of there. I actually saw myself on MOTD that night running away from a kicking. I'm not soft yer know! Evo the Trappist Monk watched the match in that funny open corner of the Kippax. Just as well I didn't have much to cheer seeing as we were beaten 0-2.

Quiz question: Who was the only outfield player not to score in Liverpool's record 11-0 victory against Stromsgodset in the European Cup-Winners Cup first round first leg on September 17th 1974?
Answer: Brian Hall.
"He shot, he missed, he must be fuckin' pissed Brian Hall, Brian Hall!"
Poor little Bamber did everything but score. Ray Kennedy almost did the "trick" too. In the end Razor was trying to be fed a goal by the other players. Ray got his goal in the end though but not Brian. Brian must have been really off form that night; I think I would have scored against them!

Keegan's return to League action for the 1-0 win at Carlisle was most welcome as our early season form had dipped. After seemingly getting back on track following the Manchester City debacle with a 3-0 home win against Stoke we then lost the next two games at home to Burnley and away at Sheffield United.

"First goal scored at 37 minutes 49 seconds wins tonight's £100 Golden Goal prize. Consolation prizes of an autographed ball go to ticket holders 37 minutes 48 seconds and 37 minutes 50 seconds."
It was half-time in the League Cup Third Round replay against Bristol City. Steve Heighway it was who scored the goal. Nice one Stevie.
I opened my Golden Goal ticket: 37 minutes 48 seconds.
Yer fuckin' daft twat Heighway! Why didn't yer knock it in a second earlier yer fuckin' knob'ead! Fuckin' one second away from a hundred snots. Christ, what I could have done with that.
Ev was well on the way to having our second child, Christmas

wasn't too far away and money was tight. The autographed ball was a fine consolation prize but that hundred squid would have been nice.

The win at Carlisle had reignited our bid for Leeds' League title. Our now annual home win against them was our fourth successive League victory. Steve Heighway scored the only goal of the game as he had done in the previous season's fixture. Mind you, Leeds were by now on their third manager of the season. Brian Clough had lasted only 44 days before being ousted by "player power". The likes of Bremner and Giles just did not want a man whom had been so vehement in his personal criticism of them and Leeds style of play when in charge of other clubs to be managing them. Clough lasted just 44 days. By a strange quirk of fate so did his successor! Jock Stein had been enticed from Celtic to take charge at Elland Road but the lure of the Scotland job, left open after Willie Ormond relinquished the post, was enough to pull him away from Elland Road. Jimmy Armfield was now the man in charge. He soon found out how tough life could be at the top of the managerial tree when we gave then a mauling. Okay the game only finished 1-0 but we were by far the better team.

Ev was bumping up quite nicely now being six months pregnant.
"Mum why 'ave you got a fat belly?"
"Because you're gonna 'ave a little brother or sister Steven and it's livin' in my belly for now 'til it's ready to come out."
"Is there a little brother or sister livin' in me Dad's belly?"
Cheeky little get!

We went out of Europe on Bonfire Night. The 0-0 draw against Ferencvaros in Budapest was no good to us as they had drawn 1-1 at Anfield so went through on the away goal.

The game at Goodison saw two new signings making their debuts. Phil Neal, a full-back signed at the start of the season from Northampton, only got the message that he was to play on the morning of the match. He then had to go to Anfield to pick his boots up and carried them unnoticed across Stanley Park in a brown paper bag. Terry McDermott on the other hand had signed just a few days earlier, fulfilling his dream to play for Liverpool, and as a big money signing walked straight into the team. The game, unsurprisingly between two teams badly out of form, finished scoreless.

By the time we played Luton at Anfield things were going from bad to worse. We'd forgotten what it was like to win, having not won for six League games and been eliminated from Europe and the League Cup. Cue the return of the fallen hero. Ray Kennedy wasn't really doing the biz for us so Tosh, apparently sent to pasture in the reserves was recalled for the umpteenth time. Tosh's return was greeted ecstatically by the Kop. Big John in return applauded the Kop and gave a defiant salute as if to say, "I'm back again. I've seen off another one!" Tosh didn't disappoint, scoring in the 2-0 win.

The 4-1 Boxing Day win against Manchester City was the best performance of the season so far. Even little Bamber caught the mood, scoring twice. Tosh also netted for the third time in successive games. The FA Cup was coming up, another little Evo would be here soon, everything was looking happy. The only thing spoiling the party was Mud's Christmas Number One, "Lonely This Christmas." Christ, if that song wouldn't make you slit your throat if it was your first Christmas after being dumped then I don't know what would!

So there I was just standing in the Kop minding my own business. Reading the programme just waiting for the teams to come out. That fella doesn't 'alf look like Bill Shankly. Why are there loads of people gatherin' round 'im. Is it 'im? Nah, can't be 'im in the Kop. Doesn't 'alf look like 'im though! Fuckin' 'ell it is 'im. Shankly's in the fuckin' Kop, stood about two feet away from me! That really was a great, great moment. Shanks had always said he'd come in the Kop and stand with his people. I'm not sure but I think he might have done it once before. This time there was no doubt!

"Shankly is a Kopite, Shankly is a Kopite da da da da da da da da!"

"Shankly, Shankly, Shankly, Shankly!"

I don't think anybody even asked for his autograph. I couldn't quite get near enough to touch the great man but I was looking at him close up; that would do me! After everybody realised that this most marvellous man actually was in our midst and those closest to him had swapped stories etc Bill was just allowed to get on with being one of us - **A KOPITE!**

Shanks celebrated Keegan's last minute winner in the 2-1 win against Coventry as much anybody in the Kop that day. Yes, that's right - he stayed right to the very end. Bill practiced what he preached - a game of football lasts ninety minutes and you must go on right 'til the final whistle! It was a great thing for Bill to come in the Kop that day and one of the greatest ever moments in the Kop's history.

SHANKLY, SHANKLY, SHANKLY, SHANKLY.

Having safely negotiated the FA Cup 3rd Round (told yer we would) with a 2-0 home win against Stoke we would be playing at Ipswich in the 4th Round on the day the new Evo was due. I was very, very tempted to go. The Evo babies track record for unpunctuality was on my side but against was the fact Ev had threatened to chop my balls off if I did go. I value my bollocks. I mean, what about that vasectomy lark? It doesn't hurt? It doesn't hurt my arse! Anybody messin' around with your balls and cutting them is gonna fuckin' hurt. I don't care if the surgeon has the touch of Yehudi Menuhin (who does he play for Evo? No one daft arse - he's a violinist) a knife in your plums is fuckin' painful! Anyway, the devastation caused by me listening on the radio to us losing 0-1 was tempered by the fact my bollocks were intact to produce more Evo offspring. Other good news was that should Ev go a week overdue there wasn't a problem as we were away to

Arsenal. There was more chance of getting a knife in my bollocks at Highbury than there was off Ev, even at her vituperative worst, so I decided to give that one a miss. Junior Evo was still showing no sign of making an appearance but would deffo be along well before next Saturday's home match against Ipswich. No problem: even Evo babies weren't a **FORTNIGHT** late!

I didn't get a knife in the bollocks but I did get a knife right along my right wrist. It was a good job I was under general anaesthetic as the surgeon cut away the ugly Ganglion cyst that had grown to golf ball size. Oh this was happy - not only is my hand fuckin' killin' me, I've got a big fuck off itchy plaster and metal thing on my arm and there's no sign of little Evo the day before the Ipswich game.
SALVATION!
"Peter, me water's 'ave broke. Call the ambulance."
HALLE-FUCKIN-LUJAH!
It was 11 o'clock on the Friday night. Nice one. Have her in Ormskirk Hospital. Few hours in labour. Baby born about four o'clock in the morning. Home for a few hours kip. Nice brekky. Back to the ossie to see the baby. Home in time to go the match.
HAPPY DAYS!
NOT!
"Your wife is in slow labour Mr. Etherington. She won't be having the baby for a few hours yet. You might as well go home and get some sleep. Come back at nine o'clock. If she hasn't had the baby by midday we'll induce her!"
Nurse Hammerhead, Ormskirk's hardest midwife had spoken!
What d'yer mean midday? Fuck me, that's cuttin' it a bit fine isn't it? Still, if I get the bus straight from Ormskirk I should be able to get to Anfield on time.
I said ta ra to Ev and set about the hour-long walk home. In the pre-natal panic I'd forgotten to take any money with me to actually get me home from the hospital. Even if I'd had the money for a taxi it wouldn't have made any difference. There was no chance of getting a taxi at four in the morning (that bloody song

again!). I got my head down for about three hours, then went to see little Stevie whom I'd dumped on neighbours John and Mary in the rush to get to hospital. Having assured the little fella that he'd be okay with John and Mary and that very soon he'd be seeing his Mummy with his little bruv or sis it was off back to Ormskirk for the birth of our second child - ETA: 11:00 Hours - hopefully!

NO CHANCE!

Midday arrived. Alarm bells were ringing now but if Ev got a move on it should all be done and dusted in an hour and I'd be celebrating at the match.

"Have you had anything to eat yet?"

Nurse Hammerhead was still on duty (how do they do it?).

"No, I 'aven't. I'm starvin'."

"No, not you Mrs. Etherington. You can't have anything to eat now until the baby arrives. You Mr. Etherington. You couldn't have had anything to eat since last night."

Indeed I hadn't. I'd actually forgotten how hungry I was 'not having had a chance to feed my burgeoning belly since teatime the night before.

"Er, no I 'aven't."

"Very well, I'll sort something out for you."

Half an hour later a marvellous roast dinner arrived for me. Nurse Hammerhead wasn't so bad after all. In fact, I think I was in love with her. Anybody who feeds me is worth loving!

"Bloody good isn't it? I'm the one 'avin' the baby an' you're the one gettin' fed!"

"Yeah, it's dead nice Ev. Lovely roast beef and creamy mashed spuds."

After my wonderful repast I noticed with some concern that the time was now approaching one o'clock. Ev was now under the influence of that gas and air thing which makes imminent mums-to-be do and say very strange things. Now much as I loved my darling she could say and do the strangest things without being under the 'fluence; with gas and air inside her she was a raving bloody loony! Quick - hide the scalpels! Ev's favourite telly programme at the time was The Sweeney so there she was happily singing the theme tune. Ah, leave 'er to it; she's doin' no 'arm.

"I fuckin' 'ate you! Look what yer've got me into!"

"Er…well I think you 'ad somethin' to do with it too yer know Ev."

"Peter, I love you."

"Yer just told me yer 'ate me!"

"Did I?"

"Don't worry Mr. Etherington. It's the gas and air having that effect. Your child will be here very shortly."

Well it better bloody 'ad be! It's half friggin' one! I'll never make the kick off at this rate!

I thought salvation had arrived in the shape of Ev's next mumblings.

"Go the match. Yer gonna miss the match. Nurse; tell 'im to go the match. 'E never misses a match."

"Go to the match? What match?"

"Er, Liverpool are playin' Ipswich. Kick-off's at three o'clock. I'd better go if she wants me to 'adn't I?"

"You certainly will not! You'll stay here with your wife while she has your child! There are plenty of other matches you can go to."

Fuckin' stupid woman! Yer just like all the rest! Yer just don't fuckin' understand!

"Yeah, no problem. I wanna be 'ere."

FUCK!

A bit of good/bad news was that things had moved on since Steven was born and I'd be able to stay with Ev while the baby was born. I was staying firmly at the top end though and just hold her hand. I was goin' nowhere fuckin' near the business end! There I was doing the dutiful husband/father-to-be thing with the kick off just half an hour away. My only chance now was if the baby arrived within the next ten minutes and I got a Fast Black to Anfield; even then I'd miss the first fifteen minutes or so and I didn't really have the money to do that anyway so basically I was fucked.

"You fuckin' bastard. I fuckin' 'ate yer! You do this to me again and I'll fuckin' kill yer!"

The screams could be heard all over Ormskirk. No, not Ev this time - the screams were coming from the next delivery room.

"Christ, that's one unhappy woman in there."

"Yeah, well I'm not too happy either. 'Old me 'and. What 'appened in The Sweeney?"

"I don't know Ev."

At this bloody rate I'd soon need the attention of Regan and Carter to keep my wife from killing me. Mind you, if it came to a straight fight between London's two finest fictional bobbies and the screaming banshee embedding her fingernails into my hand then I knew who my money was on!

"Push Evelyn push!"

Nurse Hammerhead was doing a fine job. She even looked quite attractive in a certain light - the dark.

"Yeah, go on Ev, push."

"Fuck off!"

Where the fuck were Regan and Carter when I needed them?

"Deep breaths Evelyn, deep breaths."

"Go on love yer doin' well. I love yer. Go on. Yer nearly there."

I really did feel sorry for Ev in all that pain. Just after I'd heard a sort of squishy, poppy sound I risked a look at the business end. In amongst all that messy stuff was the head of a beautiful little babbies yed. Sorry, was in Wooly mode then - I mean baby's head. Another scream and a push from Ev, who was by now shredding the palms of my hands to a bloody, pulpy mass with her fingernails (maybe this was how she was trying to kill me), and a helping hand from the midwife formerly known as Nurse Hammerhead and there before me was my beautiful little daughter. Little Ev as she would now forever be known to distinguish her from Big Ev who was actually quite little (I know, it gets bloody confusing for me too) was a tiny bundle of indescribable cuteness. Big Ev was by now sobbing uncontrollably. So was I. To be honest I'd completely forgotten about the time, the match and everything else that was going on

outside of that delivery room until Nurse Niceface announced: "You have a little daughter Evelyn. Six pounds and one ounce. Time of birth: three fifteen p.m. Congratulations."
I was ushered out of the room while the cleaning-up process went on which was just as well as I thought I was about to faint. Big baby aren't I? On a radio somewhere I could hear the strains of the Number One song, "January" by Pilot which was a bit mad seeing as we were well into February. The time was now approaching a quarter- to-four; no chance now of even catching the second-half but I was desperate for news of how the Reds were doing. I walked along a corridor to find out where the radio was when I saw a vaguely familiar face.
"Hiya mate. I know you don't I? Yer work in our place in the filling room don't yer?"
"Yeah, me name's Delvesy. You Evo?"
"Yeah, that's right. Fuckin' missed the match 'aven' I?"
"Yeah, me too. Yer a Red then?"
"Fuckin' right! 'Aven' missed a 'ome game for six years!"
"Me too mate. Twat isn't it? Yer missus 'ad the baby then?"
"Yeah, a little girl. Gonna call 'er Ev after 'er Ma."
"My missus 'ad a lad. Gonna call 'im Alan after the milkman. Nah, after me."
"Any idea 'ow the Reds are getting' on?"
"Yeah, just 'eard we're winnin' three one at half-time. We were two nil up after ten minutes."
"Fuckin' 'ell so we were two nil up when the baby was born!"
"Yeah, mine too. That your missus singin' the fuckin' Sweeney at the top of 'er voice?"
"Yeah, that's 'er."
"She's fuckin' mad 'er!"
"Only as mad as yours wantin' to fuckin' kill yer!"
"Right, I'm fuckin' off now for a pint. Yer comin'?"
"Nah, I'm goin' back in to see 'ow they're doin'."

Big Ev and Little Ev were indeed both doing very well. They were both looking lovely. It was a very contented Evo who picked up my first offspring.

"Yer've got a little sister Ste. She's called Evelyn."
"Me Mum's called Evelyn isn't she Dad?"
"Yeah son. Yer Mum's Big Ev and yer sister's Little Ev."
"Dad, can I be Big Ste?"
"Course yer can son."

Little Ev was a dead ringer for her Mum - the absolute spitting image. I loved them both very much - even if Little Ev had made me miss the match:

MY LITTLE GIRL

8th Feb '75, my head was in a whirl.
I was there to see the birth of my little girl.
Liverpool were playing Ipswich, one of the best teams
    around.
But I was at the 'ossy instead of at the ground!

Your Ma was screaming and shouting and going
    round the bend.
I was there helping out, but not at the business end.
You made me miss the match you know. You're a
    very naughty lass.
Me missing the match was like the Pope missing
    Sunday Mass!

I'd been to every home game for the last six years.
I don't know whether it was you or me who cried
    more tears.
I thought it was all worth it when I saw the sight of
    you.
But I changed my mind when I heard the score; the
    Reds won 5-2!

When you're all grown up and gorgeous, you'll make
me very proud.
Your wonderful looks and personality will make you
stand out in any crowd.
You look so beautiful, my little girl, with your lovely
blonde hair.
Your elegance, charm and grace make you look so
very fair.

When I look at you, my little girl, my heartstrings go
a-flutter.
You cut through my emotions just like a knife
through butter.
When you're hurt, I'm hurt. When you cry, I cry.
When I see tears on your face I want to curl up and
die.

But when you laugh, I laugh. When you grin, I grin.
When I see you smile it makes me as happy as a
Liverpool away win.
To sum up Evelyn how much it is that I really do
love you.
I love you, my little girl, more than I hate Man U!

Out of all Cup competitions we could concentrate on the League.
That would have been great if we could have concentrated! We
were becoming the draw specialists with six on the bounce. One
of these was the goalless Anfield Derby of which I have to admit
I cannot remember one iota: not one single minute; not one single
incident. In a Derby match there's normally one foul, a great
save, a special incident, a chant, something that sticks in the
memory but not in that match. Unsurprisingly the game was
goalless. God, that must have been a bad game! Then we hit a bit
of form winning three on the trot including the performance of
the season in beating Newcastle 4-0 at home. The last goal in that
game was the first in a Liverpool shirt for Terry Mac who was

still finding life hard at Anfield. Also struggling was big money buy Ray Kennedy. With only five League goals all season Big Razor was just not doing the biz but little were we to know Uncle Bob had big plans for him. In what was a crazy season with eight teams including the likes of Carlisle United, who were to be relegated, and Sheffield United topping the League at some point we were still in with a shout going into Easter. The 0-2 defeat at Stoke on Easter Monday whilst not definitely putting us out of the race certainly didn't do us any favours. We did manage to beat the soon-to-be European Cup Finalists Leeds 2-0 at Elland Road though. The 0-1 defeat at Middlesbrough in the penultimate game of the season was the definitive blow to us. Derby County had been handed the League. Not saying they didn't deserve it of course; they certainly did, it was just the League that season was a strange one. Nobody ever really grabbed it by the scruff of the neck and stood out as an outstanding team. Derby's winning tally of 53 points was the lowest in a 42 match League Championship winning season since Chelsea won it with a record low of 52 points in the 1954-55 season. Dave Mackay's Rams were a good side, no doubt, but nothing special.

With nothing to lose now Uncle Bob threw a new centre-forward in for the last match against QPR. We had signed him for a ridiculous fee. Estimates varied from a set of training gear to £500 (yes, five hundred). The highest bid was £10,000 (I think somebody had added a nought or two on to that though). Whatever the amount, Jimmy Case, signed from South Liverpool, turned out to be a bargain. Jimmy had a great game in our 3-1 win though his Liverpool career would blossom not as a striker but in midfield. Uncle Bob the Manager had won nothing that season but had done a very good job in trying to carry on the traditions of Shankly's legacy. Bob Paisley, supreme tactician, was soon to put his magic to good use.

The highlight of the season for me came on Tuesday 29th April. I was a bit disappointed that there wasn't a full house for Bill

Shankly's Testimonial match as there had been at Sir Roger's three years earlier but the crowd of nearly 40,000 there to pay homage to the great man did him proud. Shanks great friend Don Revie managed the opposition and it was a tribute to Don as well as a massive one to Bill that players of the calibre of Gordon Banks, Alan Ball, Alan Hudson, Colin Bell, Billy Bremner and Bobby Charlton should want to play in the match. There were many tears, not least in the Evo eyes, as Bill did a lap of honour at the end of the game to say goodbye to these people who had adopted a Jock as their own. Bill was the closest thing you could get to a Dad without him actually being your Dad. As he waved his final farewells and picked up the dozens of scarves thrown to him by his adoring public I thought how lucky I was to be a Red. How lucky I was to be able to identify so closely to a man of such stature. How lucky I was that I had once met him very briefly and talked to him for but a few short seconds. How lucky I was four months earlier to have been able to share the same square yard of Kop as Bill. **MONEY COULDN'T BUY IT.**

CHAPTER TEN

TONGUES AND TROPHIES

"Evo, geet knob aht!"
This strange noise was emanating from the other side of a double-headed press machine I was working on. Geet knob aht? What the fuck did that mean? I was to soon find out.
"What the fuck are you shoutin' about Lollipop? JESUS CHRIST!"
Lollipop was standing on the other side of the machine with what appeared to be a petrol pump sticking out of his trousers.
"Ee Evo, geet knob aht!"
When I'd recovered from shock and my fit of hysterical laughter I politely declined Lollipop's kind offer to indulge in a bout of donga jousting.
"Yer fuckin' jokin' aren't yer? The fuckin' size of that python! Yer better put that away before somebody sees it and chops the fuckin' 'ead off it."
Lollipop was a loon and a Man United fan which very often go hand in hand.

Bob made only one pre-season signing - a young left-back from Wrexham called Joey Jones. Joey was Liverpool daft - well he was just daft too but to see him playing for the Reds was like seeing your own dreams come true. Joey would have run through two brick walls for Liverpool. He was however very raw. Joey and the team in general were made to pay for this rawness when QPR tore us apart, absolutely annihilated us at Loftus Road on the first day of the season. Gerry Francis ran the show for them but they had several other very good players most notably the mercurial Stan Bowles. Their 2-0 win over us was a statement of intent that they would be mounting a challenge for the title this season.

Yet another crackerjack against Tottenham saw us overhaul a

half-time two-goal deficit to win with goals from Keegan, Case and Heighway. I sometimes felt sorry for Spurs. They always played great football. Always had great games against us. I wasn't sorry for them when we beat them of course. Spurs hadn't won at Anfield since the Titanic sank in 1912 but had come mightily close on many occassions.

A great performance at Elland Road where we totally outplayed Leeds was reflected in the end by a 3-0 scoreline. Ray Kennedy, hitting a bit of form at long last, gave us a half-time lead but it was that man Cally who scored two late goals to give us the winning margin our superiority deserved. He was getting to like this goal scoring lark was Cally!

Now call this a bit big-kiddish if you will but I love it when my birthday falls on a match day, especially if it's a Saturday. There's something about going the match on your birthday. The game at Leicester didn't disappoint as we got a battling 1-1 draw. Ev didn't disappoint either buying me another nice shirt and it didn't even have a flyaway collar!

Jackbit. Baggin'. Ever heard of them? No, neither had I 'til Stan started in Grimwoods. Stan was the broadest of broad Old Skemmers you're ever likely to hear.
"Ee Peter, what's geetin' fer baggin'?
"Yer what?"
"What jackbit's tha geetin'?"
Mary was always very useful in these situations. Her vocation in life had been missed; she should have been a UN interpreter.
"Peter, 'e's askin' yer what're yer 'avin' for yer dinner."
"Oh right yeah. Err…pilchard sarnies but I've actually *got* them, I'm not *getting* them."
"Aye, what's geetin'?"
"No Stan, I've *got* them, not *gettin'* them. If I was gettin' them I wouldn't 'ave them at the moment. I'd be *going* to *get* them at some time in the future; the *very near future* maybe but deffo in the future."

"By the bloody Christ - a fuckin' Scouser tryin' t'educate me! Tha's only fuckin' Irishmen wi' brains kicked aht!" I thought that was quite funny. Didn't agree with it like but funny. I liked Stan. I was to have many verbal Scouse-Wooly jousts with him over the years but they were always entertaining. A big argument was always which was the best team - Liverpool or....wait for it...**SKEM UNITED!** Stan was Skem's biggest fan and wouldn't have it that there was any better team than them in the country. Now that's what I call a fan!

Our attempt to win the UEFA Cup we'd won previously in '72-'73 started off well. We took a one goal lead from the first leg against Hibernian into the return at Anfield but that was overturned by a wonderful Tosh hat-trick in the 3-1 win. The Barmy Anny Road Army was conspicuous by its absence in this match. Oh, there were a few of them there alright but they all had their running shoes on in the face of about 5,000 Edinburgh Hibies taking over their end.

We were up against what was supposed to be a crack Spanish team, Real Sociedad, in the next round. The first leg against the Basque side was won quite easily 3-1. The return at Anfield was even easier as we ran riot to win 6-0. A taste of things to come was provided by a young lad who had made his debut, actually starting the match in the 1-0 win at Middlesbrough, four days earlier. With the tie already won Bob substituted Cally for the red-haired David Fairclough. Davy made an instant impression by scoring within a couple of minutes of coming on. More, much more of that to come!

The League campaign was also going well. After an inconsistent start we were now hitting a patch of form. In the middle of this arrived our old foes: Man United. We couldn't play them the season before because very unfortunately they were in the Second Division having been ignominiously relegated by their neighbours City and more impressively by a goal from former hero Denis Law on the last day of the season. Told you Denis was sound! Tommy Docherty had though built a fine young side to get them quite easily out of the Second Division and they were doing well in their first season back in the top flight. This was to be the first match at Anfield where away fans would be segregated. It took a while for the idea to catch on at other grounds. If only it had been thought of years earlier I would have been saved collapse of the arse and other associated complaints. Even at Anfield the segregation wasn't always used after this but for this match the need for it stuck out like a sore thumb. The exit behind the goal at the Anny Road was split into two by means of two sets of steel barriers running from the exit wall up to the back wall with a corridor in between. It was effective in that it kept the fans apart but there was all kinds of shite being lobbed backwards and forwards between each half. The match itself was a cracker. We naturally won 3-1 but the newly promoted First Division fledglings did themselves proud and would have to be watched in the future.

Cue another VERY bad Evo joke:

Which United player in that game had the same name as a German newspaper?

Answer: Gerry Daly.

Running out of coats!

Our run of form came to a very abrupt end when we were absolutely thrashed 1-3 at home by Norwich. Taking the piss big style was our former reserve team player and ex-Man U thorn-in-our-side Ted MacDougall. Strange player was MacDougall. The nearest he ever got to a first team appearance with us under Shanks was as a non-playing substitute. Tommy Docherty had bombed him out of Old Trafford as soon as he took over as manager with the assertion that MacDougall "couldn't play". Two managers of that calibre couldn't be wrong I suppose; sometimes he did look like he was carrying a sack of Charlie Clarke's goal and Pissy Cissy's moneybag on his back but he was a quite prolific goalscorer. Anyway, this day he had a great game and scored the third goal that sealed the Canaries win. That defeat saw us drop from third place to sixth. As per usual the press went well overboard talking of a crisis at Anfield. The vultures were fed by the following Tuesday's dismal 2-2 draw against Arsenal. Phil Neal's two penalty goals saved us from another embarrassing defeat in front of a very low attendance of just 27,000. It was frustrating that three home games on the bounce against Coventry, Norwich and Arsenal which had we won all three would have put us top of the League had yielded only two points but there was no need for the usual reaction of the hacks. There was even a mini-campaign by those lovely journos to oust Paisley. A scoreless game at Burnley and then a fine 4-0 win at Tottenham put us back up to second place. We went top for the first time in the season by handing out the same kind of beating to QPR as they had inflicted upon us on the opening day. Toshack and Neal scored the two goals but there could have been many more.

We went into 1976 top of the League and in the third round of the UEFA Cup after disposing of Polish side Slask Wroclaw by a 5-1 aggregate. Jimmy Case had scored a hat-trick in the second leg at Anfield already repaying his massive fee! That game was played in thick freezing fog and with a very sparse crowd of 17,000, brass monkeys looking for welders were plentiful.

FA Cup 3rd Round tie at Upton Park. One to stay away from methinks. A lot of other Reds must have thought that too as there weren't many made the trip. One mate of mine who did decided to go in the Chicken Run where he thought perhaps there wouldn't be much trouble for Scousers. After all - who the fuck would think a Scouser would go in there. To complete the disguise he bought a claret and blue scarf outside the ground. Safe thought he. Wrong! He was sussed by two birds, one of whom asked the other: "What's that Scarser doin' with a West 'Am scarf on?" He made his excuses and left. Good job too as Keegan and Toshack gave us a comfortable 2-0 victory.

All the big shithouses (me included) who didn't go to Upton Park were out in force for the trip to the Baseball Ground for Round Four. 10,000 shithouses to be precise, there or thereabouts. There were major problems trying to get into the ground as everybody seemed to be getting pushed into a side street where the entrance to our turnstiles was. There was a massive crush with children screaming all over the place. The police just didn't have a clue what to do. The fact there were only a couple of turnstiles open trying to get thousands of Reds into the ground didn't help their cause. We went out of the Cup courtesy of a Roger Davies goal. Fuckin' nuisance was Roger Davies! He looked shit most of the time but he was a fuckin' awkward, gangly twat who could do the most unexpected. He once missed a chance in front of an open goal at Chelsea from, I kid you not, about two inches. Not in this game though. No, in this game he had to be on target didn't he - twat!

"Ee Peter, look at yon moggy!"
"Where Stan?"
"Theer! Can't tha bloody see?"
"No I fuckin' can't! I can see a little mouse by the door but no fuckin' moggy. What're yer on about?"
"Aye, that's reet. Yon moggy by door."
"It's a fuckin' mouse!"
Mary again:
"Skemmers call mice moggies Peter."
"What? What the fuckin' 'ell d'yers call mice moggies for? A moggy's a fuckin' cat!"
"Nay it's not. A mouse is a moggy!"
"Well what the fuck's a cat then? A fuckin' pigeon?"
"A moggy's a mouse! That's why chayz is moggy meat."
I worked out for myself that "chayz" was cheese. Moggy meat? I fuckin' ask yer!
"Stan, everybody knows a moggy's a cat. Go to Glasgow, Nottingham, London, Birmingham, Liverpool, Belfast, country fuckin' villages, any fuckin' where, even fuckin' Manchester and they'll all tell yer a moggy's a cat!"

"A moggy's a mouse."
Pointless fuckin' arguing with him. Strange people these Skemmers.

Tosh liked playing against West Ham! A superb hat-trick in the 4-0 League win at Upton Park brought his tally against them this season to five. Again though, not many Reds there. My own awaydays had been severely curtailed by the sheer financial constraints of supporting a wife and two children. I'd make the easier away trips but mostly by now the longer trips to London etc were out. It was a pity because they were the awaydays I liked best but that was the way of the world. I had a family and they had to come first. Still wouldn't miss a home match though for anything - expect for the birth of my daughter that is. I was sharply reminded of this on the weekend of Little Ev's first birthday. We were playing Leeds at home on February 7th. Little Ev was ill with a chest infection and it was touch and go at one point whether I would be able to go the match. I wasn't going if she was so ill. Fortunately my beautiful little daughter must have had it on her baby conscience that she'd made me miss the match on the day she was born so thankfully was recovered enough for me to be able to go the match with a clear mind. I really would have hated to miss that one as once again we trounced Leeds with goals from Keegan and Toshack. What a partnership! Helping them was the fact that Bob had produced the greatest masterstroke of his managerial career by switching Ray Kennedy from a struggling out-of-form centre-forward to a left-sided midfielder. Razor didn't have searing pace but he could do absolutely anything he wanted with that left foot of his. Bob obviously saw something in Ray that nobody else had.

A midweek trip to Old Trafford was an awesome, scary proposition. Quite what happened on this occasion I'm not really sure. All I know is I was very grateful that we got in and out without a sign of agro. There was me, BarryMc, Kevin Mc and Snowy in the car. I for one was deffo shittin' meself when we parked very near to the ground. I'd warned the others that because we were going in the Scoreboard End there could well be a repeat of the mad scenes in November '72. I was fuckin' absolutely petrified going up the few stairs from underneath to the terrace itself. To my surprise there wasn't a manc in sight on that terrace; instead it was full of about 6,000 Scousers. It looked like MUFC had got the hang of this segregation thing. We fought out a 0-0 draw without a hint of trouble on the terraces. Okay, this is it I thought - it's gonna go off outside. Not a bit of it though; it was as quiet as the grave. We just got back to the car and drove off. I really couldn't believe how quiet it had been but I was very relieved. It wasn't quite in the same League as a trip to Kenilworth Road but it was very eerie that nothing at all had happened.

Dynamo Dresden were our opposition in Round Four of the UEFA Cup. If we could get past these and into the semi-finals we would have a good chance of going on to win the trophy. There were though some very good teams left in, not least of all Dresden themselves who were establishing for themselves a big reputation, but we were a very good side too and feared nobody. Jimmy Case had earned for himself through his skill and sheer hard work a permanent place in the side. Ray Kennedy had really settled into the left-midfield berth. Young Davy Fairclough was on the fringe of the first team and had an almost permanent berth on the sub's bench. This of course meant that stalwarts such as Peter Cormack and Brian Hall were now out of the team and soon to seeking pastures new at Bristol City and Plymouth respectively. Joey Jones and Terry Mac had been sent back to the reserves to learn their trade in the Anfield way. Tommy Smith had resumed his right-back role he had converted to so well with Phil Neal moving over to left-back. We also had the ideal captain in Emlyn Hughes. The team then was virtually picking itself: Clemence, Smith, Neal, Thompson, Kennedy, Hughes, Keegan, Case, Heighway, Toshack, Callaghan. Dynamo battered us in Dresden but a superb display by Ray Clemence including a stunning penalty save gave us the great result of a scoreless draw to take back to Anfield. Hopes were high obviously that we would win the tie on our own patch. We had been given those hopes literally single-handedly (it really was a great penalty save) by Clem so he was due a fantastic reception three days later before the home match against Middlesbrough. Ray did indeed get a wonderful reception - one of the best I've ever seen for a goalkeeper at Anfield. Disaster though was to befall Ray. Only a few minutes into the game a speculative 30 yard shot from former Leeds player Terry Cooper looked like it was never going to bother a goalkeeper of Ray's stature. Inexplicably Clem let the soft shot squirm out of his normally safe-as-houses hands and into the net. Ray's confidence was shot after that and a further goal from John Hickton sealed the game for Boro before half-time. We were also tormented by ex-Red Phil Boersma. Running the whole show though was a youngster in the centre of midfield. Built like an ox with a great touch and ferocious in the tackle Graeme Souness looked like he could be a real future star of the game. Let's just hope he could be persuaded to ply his marvellously talented trade at Anfield some time in the future

The base that Clem had given us to win the tie against Dresden was built upon with goals from Case and Keegan. It was a very close call though as Dynamo gave us a real scare before we eventually won 2-1. We truly were indebted to Clem. The victory gave us great confidence for the semi-finals. The one team we hoped to avoid was Barcelona. Johann Cruyff, our Ajax tormentor of nine years earlier, was now doing great stuff for the Nou Camp club. We could well do without facing the Flying Dutchman, possibly the best player in the world, again. So who were we drawn against? Yes, you've guessed it...Barca! The only consolation, if any, was that the second leg would be at Anfield. If we could get some kind of decent result, possibly a draw, maybe even nicking an away goal, then we would have a chance in front of a full house at Anfield.

Davy Fairclough was in for the injured Tosh at Carrow Road. Whether Davy was being groomed as the latest in a long line of Tosh "replacements" nobody was really sure. Davy was of a completely different style to Tosh. In fact Davy's style had more in common with the early Stevie Heighway performances than the more robust Tosh. Davy was so exciting as nobody, not even himself, knew what he was going to do next! Davy just got the ball, ran and then let the rest happen as it happened! Simple! Davy's goal it was that beat Norwich. With recovered Tosh back in the side for the next match at home to Burnley Davy was going to have to settle for his now usual place on the bench. Not for long though. Heighway was injured in the first half so on came Davy to terrorise the Burnley defence. Davy had scored by half-time. He added to this with a second half goal to give us the 2-0 win. If Davy wasn't careful people were going to start referring to him as Supersub!

All this set us up, if anything could, for the daunting trip to the Nou Camp. We weren't going to win were we? After all Barca had never lost to foreign opposition at the Nou Camp. Heighway was back in the team. Davy had done the biz against Burnley and was consigned back to the bench. Maybe a little unfair but Bob knew best - and how! I was in the back room of the house listening to the Radio City commentary from Barcelona whilst Ev was in the living room teaching Little Ste to read in preparation for him starting school in September. Ste really was a bright kid who loved reading so it was no drag for me and Ev to teach him to read. The little blighter could even tell the time! The little fella's greatest feat though was that he knew every single name of our squad, even down to the coaching staff. He even knew all the songs seeing as I never stopped singing them around the house. I taught the lad well! I'd barely settled down with my cup of tea and pilchard sarnies (I did like pilchard sarnies - just didn't want them for my baggin', sorry carryin' out, every day) when: "Toshack on the ball. Toshack with a chance! **TOSHACK HAS SCORED!**" Elton Welsby was in paroxysms of orgasmic, commentary frenzy. So was I!

"Fuckin' go 'ead! Yessss!!! Fuckin' go 'ead Tosh! Yer fuckin' beauty!"

"What's the matter? What's the matter?"

"We've just scored! That's what's the matter!"

"Well I 'ope they don't score again, yer gonna wake the baby up!"

Ah shut the fuck up!

Ev was quickly followed in to find out what the racket was by Ste.

"Who scored Dad?"

"Toshack Ste."

Dad and lad singing together:

STEVIE HEIGHWAY'S ALWAYS RUNNIN'.
JOHN TOSHACK IS ALWAYS SCORIN'.
THEN YOU'LL HEAR THE KOPITES ROARIN'
TOSHACK IS OUR KING!

That goal was enough for an unbelievable, stupendous victory. The tie wasn't yet won though; we still had it all to do.

The Anfield Derby clashed with Grand National day. These racing types were very inconsiderate! The game was heading for a goalless draw so up stepped Davy. Tosh went off about twenty-five minutes from time to be replaced by Fairclough. With just two minutes to go Davy took the ball from a throw-in by Tommy Smith on the right touchline at the Kemlyn Road side and then set off towards the Anny Road goal on one of his mad runs. Davy just kept going and going racing past the Everton players like they weren't there. For once Davy knew **EXACTLY** what he was going to do and slotted the ball past Dai Davies at the near post. Cue absolute fuckin' pandemonium! This lad was amazing. Davy hated the Supersub tag but that was exactly what he was.

"DAVY FAIRCLOUGH! DAVY FAIRCLOUGH!"

We even had the time and chance to double our winning margin, which would honestly have been unfair on Everton, when we were awarded a penalty. Phil Neal missed the penalty; hardly surprising in view of the fact he was being bombarded by cans and bottles from the Everton contingent, clearly upset by the

flame-haired wonder's audacity in taking the piss by scoring such a great goal.
AND IT'S LIV-ER-POOL
LIV-ER-POOL FC
WE'RE BY FAR THE GREATEST TEAM
THE WORLD HAS EVER SEEN!
There was a horse running in the National called Davy Lad and Liverpool bookmakers must have taken thousands of pounds from Reds, including my ten bob, staking their odds on a "double". Davy the horse couldn't quite live up to Davy the footballer though and Rag Trade it was that did a Fairclough, leaving the rest of the field for dead. Who gives a fuck about horse shit though? We'd won the Derby and had the rest of the day to celebrate which me, Barry, Kev and Snowy did in the grand manner! That win put us top but only temporarily as QPR were in a rich vein of form. The R's win at Newcastle that afternoon was their tenth out of the last eleven games, the other being drawn. It now looked a straight fight between us and them for the title. Man U were still up there and sniffing round. Their main priority for that season though seemed to lie in the FA Cup which they were now surely going to win seeing as they'd beaten Derby County in the semi-final that day and would be playing Second Division Southampton in the Final. Que sera sera!

April 10th 1976 was a very sad day for me. Not for the fact that I couldn't afford to go to Villa Park to see our 0-0 draw but because I had to take our family pet Dixie to the vet to be put down. Dixie had been run over about a year earlier. He was left with very serious injuries to his left hind leg. We paid the vet's fee, with help from the marvellous people at the RSPCA, to have a pin put in his leg but the poor little thing was never the same again. I suppose the kindest thing to have done would have been to have him put down then but I couldn't bring myself to make that decision. Now was the time though to make the decision to stop our little dog from suffering any longer. Because of the constant pain he was in Dixie had been turning on the kids and had tried to bite Little Ev. It had to be done. It was me of course who took Dixie to the vet to have the deed done. Oh no, it couldn't be Ev! I was the man of the house so it was up to me to handle that sort of thing. Oh yeah Ev - thanks for your fuckin' support! Anyway, I think Ev was busy reading a magazine or something. Can't quite remember what it was but I know it was dead important. People on the bus to Ormskirk must have been wondering why a grown man with a very sad looking dog (I'm sure he knew) was crying. The vet assured me that what I was doing was for the very best so I said a long goodbye to Dixie and left him in the capable hands of the vet. I cried coming away from the vet's and on the bus home like I'd never cried before. I felt like a murderer. I didn't get over that feeling for ages.

"Are you okay?"
"Oh yeah, I'm fuckin' marvellous. I've just sent our dog to 'is death but yeah, I feel fuckin' great!"
"That's the first time I've ever seen you cry."
"I cried when I fuckin' married yer. That's enough to make any fucker cry!"
I shouldn't really have turned on Ev; she was genuinely concerned for me but I was absolutely distraught.
The kids, especially Ste, loved Dixie so I was going to have to concoct a story for them.
"Dad, where's Dixie?"
"We had to give him away Ste 'cos 'is leg was very sore."
"Ah that's not fair. Who did you give 'im to?"
"To a vet son. 'E'll be okay now honest."
"Well why are you crying Dad?"
Ste was a very clued up young kid.
"Oh I'm just a bit sad son. We all loved 'im didn't we?"
"Yeah. 'Is 'e dead Dad?"
"No Ste, honest. 'E's living with a nice vet man in Ormskirk."
"Can we go an' see 'im one day Dad?"
"I don't know son. I don't think so. 'E's better off where 'e is. The vet can look after 'im."

"Oh, okay Dad. Can we 'ave another dog?"
"No son. No more dogs."

Anfield was at its jam-packed solid, atmospheric best for the return against Barca. Johann Cruyff, as expected, was performing wonders for the Catalan side but we were not just holding them we were gradually getting on top and proving to be the better team. We took the lead from the very unexpected source of Phil Thompson. Go 'ead Thommo lad! The Kop was in ferment. I started off standing next to Snowy but ended up about twenty yards from him. This is what we wanted. Two up - we were well in control and looking like we were going to win the tie easily. Cruyff and Carlos Rexach had other ideas. Rexach it was who made us sweat for the win. The final whistle came as a blessed relief but we were in the final of the UEFA Cup and that was all that mattered for tonight. The race for the League title would resume on Saturday but for now it was time for a real Anfield European night celebration.

The Championship race turned our way on Easter Saturday. Stoke's Terry Conroy, a very good and much underrated player, put the Potters 1-0 ahead. By half-time we'd taken the lead through a Phil Neal penalty and a Tosh goal. Ray Kennedy put us 3-1 up with one of his speciality goals- creeping up from nowhere to appear on the edge of the penalty area and then cooly slotting home. Moores then pulled one back before Emlyn produced one of his own specials to restore the two goal advantage and how Crazy Horse celebrated! Stoke were nothing if not doughty fighters though and pulled yet another goal back through Bloor. It was left to Davy, once again coming off the bench, to finish the Potters off. What a game that was and what a result! Better news was to come from Carrow Road. QPR had lost 2-3 at Norwich and had handed top spot to us. With both clubs having two games left to play we had 56 points while QPR had 55. QPR would finish their programme with home games against Arsenal and Leeds, maybe not the trickiest games for them - they should win both. We, on the other hand, were left with trips to Manchester City and Wolves. Wolves were fighting for their First Division lives so neither of them would be easy games. We did have the advantage though of playing Wolves after QPR had finished their programme so a win at Maine Road would leave us knowing exactly what we had to do at Molineux. Against us was the distraction of the two-legged UEFA Cup Final against Belgian club Bruges. Mind you, our players seemed to thrive on the pressure and would probably have willingly played another twenty games that season if asked.

If I was going to Maine Road I would have to minge it. Certainly there was no transport money available. I would have probably just about enough to get into the Platt Lane Stand (bollocks to that Kippax shit after my experience the previous season) and maybe a couple of bob emergency bus fare money but that was about it. So the trusty old thumb was about to make a reappearance.

"I'm goin' to Man City Ev."

"No money."

"I know. I've got a few bob to get me in so I'm gonna thumb it."

"Are you mad? Yer'll get battered if yer on yer own."

"Of course I'm mad. Yer've always known I'm mad. I married yer didn't I?"

"Funny arse. Be careful then. I 'ope they win."

"I 'ope Liverpool win Dad."

"Oh we will son. We will."

A couple of good lifts got me to about a mile or so from the city centre. I was informed by my last lift that if I wanted to avoid trouble it would then be best to get the bus to Piccadilly and get another bus to the ground although he had no idea where that was from. Christ, I was gonna have to develop a manc accent and pretty damn quick or do my deaf mute trick that had served me so well in previous fraught situations. As there were hardly any passengers on the bus into Piccadilly I decided to confide to the driver that I was a Scouser and shittin' meself at the prospect of

118

having to open my mouth on the bus to Maine Road. Manc
Varney was superb.
"You want the Number 14 at Aytoun Street. Don't talk to
anybody; not even the driver or conductor. The fare's seventeen
pence. Just give that to the conductor, say fuck all and get off
where everybody else gets off."
Reg was absolutely spot on! He even made sure I had exactly the
right amount of change so I wouldn't have to open my mouth
faffin' about with twenty pence pieces etc. Having arrived at the
ground very early I bought a ticket for the Platt Lane Stand using
my partially deaf mute trick. I then went in search of a quiet bevy.
I chanced upon a pub, called I think the Parkway, which just
happened to be chocker block full of Reds. Yes, this was more
like it, belting out songs and letting off steam after an enforced
silence. There weren't many in there I knew really well but I did
recognise plenty of old "faces". It seemed everybody was out in
force for this match. We watched the footy previews on the telly
as news was coming through of QPR's win that morning over
Arsenal. It was imperative we won this one. A draw might suffice
but a defeat would almost certainly spell the end for us. We
weren't gonna lose though were we?

By the time the teams ran out I felt we *couldn't* lose. Half the
population of the Platt Lane Stand seemed to be Reds. There
were also thousands of us dotted around the Main Stand and
North Stand too. Completing the contingent were about 5,000
Reds in the Kippax. This segregation thing was catching on! I
was half wishing I was in the Kippax with them as that would
have saved me quite a few much needed bob. Not to worry though
- there were plenty of Reds where I was and we were quite safe.
It was a different story in the Kippax though. The Reds were high
up in the top corner near the Platt Lane Stand and were being
pelted from below and one side by every bit of shite the Moss
Siders could get into the ground. Not that the Scousers kept all
the Mancunians "gifts" to themselves of course! The pre-match
talk was whether Bob would be Uncle Bob and play Jimmy Case

or be Positive Bob, play Davy Fairclough from the start and really go for it. Most Reds opted for the latter. So, thankfully, did Bob. The game was running down to a 0-0 draw with only a quarter-of-an-hour or so to go. We had generally been well on top but just couldn't achieve the breakthrough. Steve Heighway broke the deadlock. I hadn't used the seat I was in anyway as it was right behind a pillar and instead spent most of the match standing in the gangway. I was up and down those bloody steps like a two-year-old on speed. Positive Bob's decision to play Fairclough from the start was vindicated when Davy notched two late goals. It was only after the third goal went in I realised just how many Reds were there. They now seemed to be everywhere. Causing no end of trouble, God love him, was Emlyn who was dancing all over the pitch with Ray Clemence. Emlyn was having kittens, still celebrating the third goal when play had resumed, waving to all sections of the Reds support, especially to those in the Kippax. This was causing untold grief for the Reds on that terrace. We were in for a torrid time outside that was for sure, especially the Kippax based Reds. Plan A was to try get on a coach. The coaches were parked on some footy pitches in Platt Lane. Fuck Plan A - just too many City fans looking for bother to risk that. I was walking along Princess Road asking drivers if they were going to Liverpool - in a Manc accent of course. There were a group of about twelve City lads on the other side of the road all pointing across in my direction. Oh for fuck sake! I'd been well and truly sussed. I don't really know how - perhaps they'd seen me celebrating Emlyn style in the Platt Lane or more likely because I just looked like a Scouse scally. Fuckin' leg it! I *risked* life and limb dodging in between cars and people as I just didn't have a fuckin' clue where I was running to. I just couldn't be caught though as that wouldn't have been risking life and limb it was an absolute certainty! Shit! I hoped one of them wasn't the Gurgling Grotcher aka the Moss Side Spitter - the Gruesome Gollier. Where the fuck was Cainy when I needed him?

"Gerrin! Gerrin'!"

A car door was flung open. The car was still moving but I dived in as the chasing pack was closing in on me.

"Where're yer goin' lad?"

"Where you're goin'! Any fuckin' where! Just get me away from that lot and fuckin' 'urry up! If they catch us they'll fuckin' kill us!"

The driver did a swifty scattering pedestrians on the pavement 'til he could get on a less busy stretch of road. Stirling fuckin' Moss - eat yer heart out! Why does everybody still always refer to any decent driver as Stirling Moss? Stirling Moss retired from Formula One about forty years ago and never won the world title, although he did win lots of Grand Prix (how do you pluralise that? Prix's? Prix? Pricks? Prixes?) especially British ones. Anyway, enough digression. The City lads had been as unfit, as outplayed, as outran and as outthought as their counterparts on the pitch. With us disappearing into the late afternoon yonder they had given up their chase of the uncatchable and were now hauling their fat, horrible, sweaty bodies back to their pits in Moss Side. We were now getting more bother at Maine Road than we ever did at Old Trafford. I vowed never to come here again - 'til next season that is.

"I'm goin' to Skem mate but drop us wherever's convenient for you."

"Crown do yer?"

"Yeah, sound mate."

I had enough bus fare to get to Ma's (I'm the Urban Spaceman) and cadge the bus fare to Skem off my dear old queen. Once I'd got my breath back me and the other four lads in the car discussed my near-death experience.

"Fuckin' 'ell mate they nearly 'ad yer there didn't they?"

"Yeah, thanks a lot mate. If they'd 'ave caught me they'd 'ave fuckin' killed me."

"I know! We saw yer were in trouble, that's why we stopped."

"Yer didn't fuckin' stop! Yer dragged me for abarr a fuckin' mile. Thanks though."

"They 'ad no chance of catchin' yer there mate - you were like the fuckin' roadrunner!"

"I know! Beep beep!"
Sound lads them! Not only saved my life but could belt out a song or ten too!
"And now yer gonna believe us! We're gonna win the League!"
"Oh I am a Liverpudlian an' I come from the Spion Kop!"
"Kopites are gobshites!"
"We all live in a Red and white Kop!"
"Liverpool, Liverpool top of the League!"
"Stevie Heighway!"
"Davy Fairclough!"
"Come on without, come on within. You'll not see nothing (a double negative I know but who gives a fuck?) like the Mighty Emlyn!"
Nice one lads - I'd 'ave been fucked without you.

"Where've yer been Peter?"
"Just been to Manchester City Mam."
"Were yer playing Manchester United?"
"No Mam. Manchester **CITY**."
"'Ow d'yer get on?"
"We won three nil Mam."
"Ow d'yer get there?"
"Thumbed it Mam."
"Don't yer think yer getting a bit old for all that?"
Too old? I'm only twenty fuckin' two!
"I 'ad to Mam. I 'ad no money. Can yer lenz ten bob for the bus fare 'ome?"
"Of course I can son."
That was my Ma all over - wanting me to grow up one minute, then treating me like a kid the next. Dad saw I was in for a mind battering from Ma so interjected.
"I listened to it on the wireless son. That Fairclough's a good 'un isn't 'e?"
"Yeah, 'e's brilliant Dad. Play for England one day 'e will."
Our John was in the house too. That made a change - I hardly ever saw him these days. He was out most of the time when I called to

me Ma's. Maybe he was trying to hide his girlfriend from my pervy eyes. I'd heard all about Janet. He'd been going out with her for quiet a while apparently but this was to be the first time I met her.

"Peter, Janet."

Not big on long introductions was our John.

Oh hello!

"Hiya Janet. Nice to meet you. How long have you been seeing our John?"

I was putting my best posh voice on you see.

"A couple of months I think. How long is it John?"

"Dunno."

I think the answer from our John really meant, "Don't know. Don't care. Now keep yer fuckin' beadies off 'er yer pervy twat!"

Our John must have really loved Janet though because the next thing nearly made me fall off Dad's rocking chair.

"D'yer wanna cuppa Janet?"

Fuckin' 'ell! This *must* be love! I don't think our John had ever made a cup of tea for anybody other than himself in his life!

"D'yer want one Peter?"

Wow! I can't believe this. For me and our John to be civil to each other was, whilst not exactly a first, a very rare occurrence. Then he hit his us all with the coup de grace.

"Ma, Dad, d'yer want one?"

Nah, I must have been hearing things. Dad and John didn't exactly get on like a house on fire. It was unusual for them to be in the same room together even but sure enough it was cups of stewed tea all round from our John. Dad was so taken aback that he actually **GAVE** me a pound for the bus fare home and told me to get sweets for the kids with the change. Now that **WAS** a first!

The first leg of the UEFA Cup Final was going disastrously wrong for us and Phil Neal in particular. Phil had been at fault for both goals by Cools and Lambert that gave Bruges a 2-0 half-time lead. The crowd of just under 50,000 had been stunned by the skill, sharpness and quick-wittedness of the Belgian side.

They were a very good, accomplished team and had totally outplayed us. Maybe the best we could hope for in the second half was to pull a goal back or perhaps snatch a draw - damage limitation in other words because the way we were playing and the way they were playing we were going to lose by about five! Uncle Bob must have rolled his cardy sleeves up and given the team a right bollocking in the dressing room as we came out looking a completely different side. We really tore into the heart of the Bruges defence and were rewarded just before the hour mark by a beauty from Razor. Two minutes late the ball hit the post. The Kop swayed down to see where the rebound was going. Straight to Jimmy Case standing right on the post. Jimmy sort of bundled rather than kicked the ball over the line but who gave a fuck? We were level - that was all that mattered and the place went fuckin' mental! Three minutes later it was bonkers time again as we were awarded a penalty. This was where Kevin Keegan showed his captaincy skills. Kevin wasn't actually captain. That role belonged of course to Emlyn Hughes and what a fine captain of Liverpool Football Club he was. Kevin wasn't Footballer of the Year for nothing though, an award richly deserved as there was no better footballer in the country at the time, and was brave enough to step forward to take the penalty. Phil Neal was the regular penalty taker but his nerves had been shot to fuck in the first half. Kevin had seen that Phil was in no fit state to take the penalty so placed the responsibility on his own shoulders. Good on yer Kevin lad! Come on! YESSSSSSSSSSSSS!!!!!!!!!!!!!

KEVIN KEEGAN! KEVIN KEEGAN!

LIVERPOOL'S GOT KEEGAN IN THE MIDDLE. THAT'S WHY IT'S CALLED SUPREME!

What a game! What a performance! What a comeback! I honestly think that at the time Liverpool were the only team capable of such a fightback. The team spirit was unbelievable. Each player would have ran round the world twice for each other, no question, even those who didn't get on with each other off the pitch. Off the pitch didn't matter. On the pitch was where the biz was done and how! The 3-2 win was a good base for the return but it was going to be one of our toughest ever European games. Bruges had the vital away goals so appeared to maybe slightly have the upper hand. They were playing us though! We had the lead in the bag - they were going to have to beat us to do it. Not only did we have an indomitable spirit we were a bloody good side too so bring it on!

May 4th was historically a good date for us. We'd beaten Inter Milan on that date in 1965 and Newcastle in the FA Cup Final of '74.

May 4 1976: We went to Wolverhampton needing a point to win the League as we had a slightly superior goal average to Queens Park Rangers. QPR, as expected, had won their final game of the season against Leeds. Wolves, for their part, needed to win to have any chance of avoiding relegation as Birmingham City needed to only draw the same night at already relegated Sheffield United. It did seem slightly unfair on QPR that this game was to be played after they finished their League programme leaving us knowing exactly what we had to do to at Molineux. I think the case was though that Burnley and Sheffield United had already been well relegated so the final drop place was to be decided after the final Saturday to avoid any chance of complicity. I'm not sure that was actually the case but it's how I seem to remember it.

We left Bootle at twelve o'clock: Barry Mc, Kevin Mc, Snowy and myself. We took some mad route that took us through the tunnel, North Wales and Shrewsbury: I know, don't ask me, I was only a passenger! We eventually arrived in Wolverhampton at four o'clock. We went straight to the ground where there were already massive queues. At about half-past-five the crush was so intense that a gate buckled and I think part of a wall collapsed, letting thousands of our fans in free. If the authorities had acted after incidents such as this, and believe me it wasn't the only occasion this had happened, then the sad events of nearly thirteen years later could have been avoided.

The official attendance was given as 48,900 but with the people that had got in free there must have been well over 50,000. In any case there were about 30,000 Reds there. Our players came on to the pitch about an hour before kick-off and you could see their amazement at the number of Reds present. Ev was at home listening on the radio; she was actually getting into this being a Red thing now - I think. Apparently Elton Welsby was interviewing Phil Thompson on the pitch. Welsby asked Thommo, who was looking up at all the Reds on the South Bank, "Does this want to make you play for them."

Thommo's reply was, "Play for them, I'd bloody die for them!"

Some Reds had got in to the North Bank and were being escorted to our end by the police. They had this massive flag which read downwards: QPR. Nobody could work out what it was all about until they came nearer and we could see it said:

QUALITY from
PAISLEY'S
REDS.

I wonder if that flag is still around? I'd love to see it again.

The pre-match conversation centred on whether David Fairclough would retain his place or would Jimmy Case return. Most of us wanted David to retain his place after his late-season efforts, especially the two goals at Maine Road. Uncle Bob knew what he was doing though and it was indeed Jimmy Case who was brought in to bolster the midfield.

The players came on to the pitch to be greeted by the loudest version of "You'll Never Walk Alone" I've ever heard at an away ground. Kevin Keegan very nearly didn't play as during the pre-match warm up one of our fans ran on to the pitch and was arrested. Kevin pleaded with the copper to let the lad go and came very close to being nicked himself! Now you won't read that in any book; you had to have been there to know that!

The game started badly for us as Steve Kindon, a big bull of a centre-forward, gave Wolves an early lead. We then proceeded to bombard the Wolves defence, but their goalkeeper, Gary Pierce, was in inspired form. Shots and headers rained in from all angles but there was to be no breakthrough before half-time.

We were attacking the South Bank end in the second half. Attacking was the operative word as there was no abatement of the incessant pressure on the Wolves goal, whilst Ray Clemence was practically redundant. Keegan, Heighway, Toshack and Case all had great efforts saved. Tosh was having a nightmare, so it was he who was expected to be substituted when David Fairclough came on with half-an-hour left to play. However, Mister Paisley got it right again replacing Jimmy Case to give us more attacking options. David got into the action straight away and was causing havoc in the Wolves defence. The breakthrough came after seventy-six minutes when Keegan netted. Loads of lads who had been sitting on the running track, such was the congestion, got on to the pitch before being virtually thrown off by our players. The celebrations in our end had to be seen to be believed. Tosh, who had just been called a " fuckin' big lamp-post" by the bloke standing next to me, turned brilliantly to score the second with five minutes left. Ray Kennedy wrapped things up with a great chip four minutes later. Our ninth Football League Championship had been secured! The triumph had been masterminded by Bob Paisley, his first success as a manager. At the final whistle the pitch was engulfed by our fans. There was potential for bother as some of our lads went towards the North Bank to taunt the Wolves fans but thankfully the police soon dispersed them.

We stopped off for a bevy in a pub called The Three Tuns at a place called Wolstanton, I think. The motorway was absolutely chocker, which brought traffic to a complete standstill. Stuck slap-bang in the middle of the traffic was our team coach! Everybody got out of their cars and were singing and dancing, right there in the middle of the motorway! The players were celebrating too. Ian Callaghan looked pissed and sent us a bottle of champagne out. What a night!

It was a pity Wolves were relegated as I liked going there; it was always a good atmosphere, which I couldn't say about Birmingham who I would have preferred to go down. As it happened Wolves would have been relegated even if they had won as Birmingham drew 1-1 at Bramhall Lane. There were allegations later that the match had been rigged to allow Birmingham to stay up.

We did very well to win the League that season, winning eight and drawing once in our last nine matches. Queens Park Rangers were a fine side who might have won the League in any other season. Their last fifteen matches produced 13 wins 1 draw and 1 defeat; a marvellous record indeed but just not quite good enough. Could our final match of the season see us repeat our League/UEFA Cup double of three years previously?

 Not a cat in fuckin' hell's chance of going to Bruges! We were on lates so snatching bits of the match on the radio and maybe getting off half-an-hour early to watch the BBC highlights was the best I could hope for.
"Ev, if we win go to the Derby Arms phone box abarr 'alf-nine an' phone work. Ted'll answer. Tell 'im the baby's not well an' you want me to come 'ome. That'll give me a chance to get 'ome before the highlights start at ten o'clock."
"Well who's gonna watch the kids?"
"Ask Linda to pop in. Yer'll only be gone five minutes."
"Okay, so it's only if yer win?"
"Yeah, I won't be arsed if we lose. I'll be pig sick."

We'd just got into the canteen for our break as Bruges were awarded a penalty. Raoul Lambert, a great player who had torn our defence apart in the first half at Anfield, had no problem converting the penalty.
"Fuckin' 'ell Peter, that's it. We're fucked! They're ahead now on the away goals."
"Don't be fuckin' stupid Delvesy we're not fucked. We'll be back.

We did it at Anfield - we'll do it there."

Keegan must have heard me.

Elton Welsby's commentary: "Liverpool have a free-kick just outside the penalty area. Hughes touches the ball to Keegan. Keegan shoots! YESSSSS!!!!!!! Keegan has scored!"

Me and Delvesy were jumping all over the canny hugging each other (in a celebratory kind of way you understand). The women were watching impassively as only women can when footy crazy lads are going off their heads.

"Told yer we'd do it Peter. Told yer we'd do it!"

"Did yer fuck! You said we were fucked!"

"Yeah, but I didn't mean that!"

"Oh right yeah, so when yer say we're fucked yer actually mean we're gonna win it?"

"Yeah, yer know what I mean!"

I suppose I did. Alan was every bit as Red as I was really.

That was the end of the scoring so by the time I next had the chance for a quick five minutes in the canny we had indeed secured the UEFA Cup for the second time. All I needed now was Ev's phone call at half-nine and I was laughin'! Half-nine came and went. Twenty to ten - no sign. Quarter-to-ten - nothing. Shit, what's happened? Is Little Ev really not well and Ev can't get out? Is Linda not in so can't watch the kids? Ten to ten it dawned on me: we'd drew! I'd made no contingency plans to Ev if we drew. I'd only mentioned winning and losing. Too much to ask of her to know that even though we'd drew we'd won on aggregate. Fuckin' 'ell, no time now to think of an excuse to Ted for getting off early. I was just gonna have to tell him the truth and hope he let me go. It might be okay though as Ted could be manipulated. He was hard yet pliable, if you know what I mean. Where Eddie was straight down the line, no budging - what he said went, Ted could be talked round in certain situations. I was hoping that was the case this time. In my favour also was that Ted was into footy. He had actually played for Skem United for a while and was apparently a very good player, not far short of League standard.

"Ted, can I get off now please? I wanna get 'ome to watch the match."

"Well Alan Delves has just asked too but okay. I'm going home to watch it too. Want a lift?"

RESULT! How easy was that?

I liked Ted. He was a bit scatty, sometimes got his worms muxed up and very often unintentionally said things that had us in fits of laughter. He wasn't the quickest at getting jokes or retorts to him either. For instance: Ted was once instructing me in the art of putting a blob of glue in an element to hold a bead of ceramic in place. "Take an aerial view of it Peter."

"Bloody 'ell Ted (he didn't like you swearing in front of him), are yer gonna get me a 'elicopter?"

Morocco.

"Ev, why didn't yer ring work?"

"Well they drew. I didn't know what to do. Yer didn't mention anythin' about a draw."

As I thought.

"Yeah Ev but we won on aggregate."

"What d'yer mean?"

"We won 3-2 at Anfield and drew 1-1 in Bruges so that means we won 4-3 on aggregate."

"I still don't get it. Yer drew but yer won?"

"Oh, forget it Ev. Just giz me tea and let me watch the match. It's startin' now."

Congealed egg, sausage and chips had never tasted so bloody good. Life was sweet. As Shanks said, "All ye' need son is the green grass and a ball."

CHAPTER ELEVEN

RED HOT AND DANGEROUS

Summer '76 was the maddest, hottest ever on record. It really was baking hot and seemed to go on for ever. Speaking of records (tenuous link I know) there were some great songs in the charts. Real sort of old style pop records seemed to typify what that summer was all about. Okay, they may sound like a load of old poo now but the likes of "Combine Harvester" by the Wurzels (a real fun song), "Forever and Ever" by Demis Roussos (great kaftan), "Show Me The Way" by Peter Frampton (played the guitar with a tube attached to it and his mouth - made a great sound) and "Dancing Queen" by Abba (still a classic a quarter of a century later) were what everybody was singing that summer. The biggest seller though was "Don't Go Breaking My Heart" by Elton John and Kiki Dee. That was a great song - I loved it. My own personal favourite was, "You To Me Are Everything" by The Real Thing. The words of that just about summed up what I felt for my darling wife. The Real Thing were a boss group who never really went on to be as big as they should have been. I don't know why that was as they seemed to have everything going for them. They were from Liverpool but I likened them to the Four Tops - they honestly were that good. Album of the year for me was "The Eagles Greatest Hits". Every song on that is a classic.

I'm not sure whether it was the heat that had addled my brain or what but I decided to tackle Big Dave. Who's Big Dave Evo? Dave was Mary's husband. Not Mary from work. No, not Delvesy's Mary. No, not Mary with John. No, not Mary with the other John either. If it's confusing for you how do you think I bloody felt? There were Mary's everywhere! Mary was obviously a popular name back then. Not so popular now of course: it's more your Kylie and Britney now isn't it? Mary Whitebits used to make me laugh. Mary Whitebits was other John's missus. Me and Ev christened her that as she used to always wear these blue trousers (never took them off) that were full of white bits, probably from her bedsheets as I'm sure she used to sleep in them. There was a rumour once that she was going to Cammell Lairds to have them removed. Anyway, what made me and Ev laugh was that Mary Whitebits (still following this?) was forever telling Ev that her husband (that's right John. Well done!) was forever tossing himself off in the bathroom. She swore Ev to secrecy. Ev, not being able to hold her own water, of course told me. Ev used to piss her herself laughing at me doing an impression of John pulling himself all over the bathroom. Anyway, back to Big Dave. Big Dave was Big Paul's Dad. Big Paul was called Big Paul to differentiate him from Little Paul who was Linda's son. Big Dave was called Big Dave not only because he was apparently dead big (I hadn't met him yet: that much will become apparent later) but also to differentiate him from Dave with Karen. Our Ste was now Big Ste to differentiate him from Little Ste, Big Paul's brother and obviously Big Dave's son. My two darling Ev's were of course Big Ev and Little Ev. When I was calling one of them I'd just say, "Big" or "Little" - tags which have stuck with them ever since. People look at me strangely when I call them that but Big and Little know what I mean and so do I, which is all that matters. Anyway, back to the plot. Big Paul and our Ste were forever fighting. As our Ste was younger and smaller than Big Paul he usually came off worse. Ste would come in screaming and crying but five minutes later they'd be back playing with each other in the way kids do. As I say, it might have been my heat affected brain that told me I'd had enough of all this and was going round to sort it out with Big Dave.

"I'm fuckin' sick of this. Every fuckin' day it is our Ste comes in cryin' after Big Paul's 'it 'im! I'm goin' round to see 'is Dad."

"Yer can't do that!"

I should have heeded Ev's voice of caution.

"Why the fuck not?"

"'Cos Big Paul's Dad's Big Dave."

"I don't give a fuck who 'e is. I'm sortin' this out once and for all!"

"'Ave yer seen the size of Dave?"

"No I fuckin' 'aven't. I've never seen 'im."

"Well I 'ave, 'e's fuckin' massive! Don't go round on the bounce Peter, 'e'll kill yer! It's not worth it anyway. They're only kids. They'll be playin' with each other again in a minute."

Undeterred by Ev's protestations I bounced round to Big Dave's.

KNOCK, KNOCK, KNOCK, KNOCK, KNOCK!

Mary answered the door.

"Ee arr Mary, this isn't on. Your Paul's always 'ittin' our Ste. 'E's always comin' in cryin'."

"Well what d'yer want me to do Peter? They're only kids. That's the way kids are."

Just then all natural light was blocked as a gargantuan presence filled the doorway. Jesus fuckin' Christ, Big Dave was dead big! Big Dave was like a cross between the Yeti, Saskwatch, BigFoot and Grizzly Adams times ten! Fuckin' 'ell I was dead!

"Eh you, soft arse, fuck off now before I shove yer fuckin' 'ead up yer arse!"

I honestly fuckin' shit myself! I'd come this far though so I couldn't back down without some kind of resistance.

"Yeah, but it's not fair is it? Your Paul's bigger than our Ste."

"GO!"

I went.

I made my jelly-legged, white-faced way home. I actually had to check my skidunkers for poo.

"Christ almighty Ev, 'e's fuckin' huge isn't 'e? Nobody should be allowed to be that big!"

"I told yer. Mary's always sayin' to me, "yer've seen the size of Dave." Did 'e 'it yer?"

"I'm still livin' aren't I?"

"Yer alright?"

"Yeah, I think so. Make us a cuppa please love while I stop shakin'. Where's our Ste?"

"In the garden playin' cricket with Big Paul."

I looked out of the window. Our Ste was batting. My mind flashed back to a red-hot day some twelve years earlier.............

I'd been bullied for the whole of the six weeks school holidays by Tommy H. I was a bit of a weedy kid, not at all street-wise then as I was to become a year or two later, so was quite easy to bully. Tommy was a good couple of years older than I was and obviously a lot bigger. He had hit me every single day. This particular day though he hadn't actually hit me, maybe he was waiting 'til a bit later. Maybe he'd taken pity on me but I doubted it. Maybe he'd just got fed up hitting me; too easy perhaps. Whatever, fact was he hadn't hit me this day. There were about ten of us playing cricket. I was batting. The "bat" was actually a big fuck off four by two. It was that big I could hardly hold it never mind hit a cricket (in this case, tennis) ball with it. Tommy was fielding in Mrs. Lynch's garden. Pilch was running in to bowl. Tommy was watching for the moment of Pilch's delivery. I don't know what came over me. Maybe something had just flashed through my brain and I'd spotted my chance. I vaulted Mrs. Lynch's low garden wall. **FUCK OFF!** Before I'd actually realised what I'd done I'd summoned up all my strength to smash the four by two right across Tommy's face. It made a terrible crack. Well I was off like a fuckin' rabbit with it's arse on fire! Half-an-hour later Tommy's Ma came to our house with Toothless Tommy in tow.

"Lily, look at this! Your Peter's 'it our Tommy with a lump of wood an' knocked all 'is teeth out!"

LILY EYES!

"Fuck off! Your Tommy's always 'ittin' our Peter! 'E comes in every day cryin'. Serves your Tommy right."

Fuckin' go 'ead Ma!

Tommy's Ma went home with her tail between her legs and Tommy without his teeth. Tommy never hit me again.

I was stirred from my childhood reverie by the sight of our Ste lifting the bat. No Ste, don't do it! **FUCK OFF!** The sight of the sponge ball spinning high into the air and into a garden many yards away was a joy to behold! A six for Ste! Nice one son!

Kids eh? Who'd fuckin 'ave 'em? Enjoy them while they're young though 'cos they're a pain in the arse when they grow up!

This coming season, I'd decided, I was going to have a season ticket. I set about saving the fourteen squid it was gonna cost me. That was, literally, hard work believe me! It was no fun working twelve-hour shifts in that searing heat. That was just the way it was gonna have to be though unfortunately. There was no way I was gonna afford it on my normal wages. I was just about to start my four hours overtime one blazing June day. Maybe I'd get a nice cushy little number sitting down by the door gluing elements I thought. Shit, hoped I wasn't gonna be taking elements out of the furnace. I'd fuckin' melt! You'd be able to fry chips off my fat for a year!

"I've got a job for you outside Peter."

RESULT! Fuckin' nice one Eddie!

"Go with Phil and paint the roof."

Fuck off! Yer 'avin' a fuckin' grin aren't yer?

"Paint the roof Ed? What d'yer mean?"

"Go up and paint out the skylights; stop the sun comin' in."

"It's fuckin' nearly 100 degrees outside Eddie. Fuck knows what it is on the roof; I'll fry!"

"Phil 'asn't complained."

Well fuckin' work a fuckin' 'olic Phil wouldn't would he? 'E'd probably do it for fuck all!

"Ah, come on Ed; 'aven' yer got anythin' else for me?"

"No, that's it. Make sure youse do it properly or yer'll be back up there tomorrow."

"Come on Evo, let's go to it."

Fuck off Lovelace Watkins.

Phil was the spitting image of Lovelace Watkins - a cabaret singer of the time.

Now, while I'm not exactly scared of heights I don't fuckin' love them either. A metal splinter in my little finger could almost reduce me to tears so the thought of falling off the zillion foot high roof had me a quivering fuckin' wreck. I mean, the very least I was gonna get away with was a gang of broken bones but for me death was a near certainty. The old women, not all of them females, were laughing at me as I collected the brushes and paint while Phil went for the ladders. It was alright for them just sitting there by the door, taking the sun and the fresh air in. They were okay in the comparative shade of the factory.

Fuck off yer shower of fuckin' witches. Fuckin' sittin' there coolin' yer fuckin fat fannies! Close yer fuckin' legs - yer breath stinks!

It was no laughing matter up on the roof.

"Phil, I'm gonna fall!"

I wasn't taking the piss. I was seriously shitting myself.

"Yer won't. Yer'll be okay. Just 'old me 'and."

"I can't Phil. I can't!"

I was absolutely rigid and unable to move from the edge of the roof.

"Okay, well just sit there then but make sure Eddie doesn't see yer. 'E's 'ere 'til 'alf-six too. If 'e sees yer doin' fuck all 'e'll sack yer."

Getting sacked was the least of my worries at the moment. Preserving my life was uppermost in my thoughts. That and the fact Sue Barker and Chris Evert would be on the telly when I got home. Sue and Chris were fit as! Possibly the two fittest players ever to play at Wimbledon. Phil was fuckin' made up. He was a skippin' an' a jumpin' along the roof like Dick Van fuckin' Dyke in Mary Poppins.

"Yer alright there Peter?"

Yeah, I'm fuckin' sound! Frightened to fuckin' death. Sweatin' me fuckin' bollocks off and yer could fry a fuckin' egg on me 'ead! Oh yeah, I'm fuckin' superb!

"Yeah, fine thanks Phil. Thanks a lot mate. Yer doin' me a big favour."

"Okay, yer owe me a pint."

Fuck off!

I did at least have Phil's radio up there though to entertain me while my head boiled. It was getting on for five o'clock when the radio got lashed from a great height. I kid you not, "Up On The Roof" by the Drifters came on. Diddy fuckin' David Hamilton was taking the piss!

"What the fuck was that Peter?"

"The radio fell off the roof Phil."

"Fell off? 'Ow the fuck did it fall off?"

"Don't know Phil. Maybe a gust of wind caught it."

"Wind? There 'asn't been any fuckin' wind for abarr a month!"

"Well I don't fuckin' know. It just toppled off."

"Fuck me; my missus'll kill me!"

Not if I fuckin' throw yer off the roof first.

The best fourteen pounds I've ever spent were handed over to the girl in the ticket office. Go 'ead. Passport to freedom! No longer would I have to miss Cup Finals 'cos I couldn't get a ticket. While having a Kop season ticket didn't actually guarantee a ticket for a Cup Final there was a bloody sight better chance than if you didn't have one. No more queuing for hours to get in for big home games. No more having to leave the Fountains Abbey at half-one to make sure I got in.

The '74 Charity Shield crew of me Barry, Kev and Snowy reunited for this season's encounter against Second Division Southampton who had beaten the mighty Manchester United in the previous season's FA Cup Final. We were going on a coach from some club in Crosby; I really do forget which one, a social club or the Legion, something like that. We were leaving the club at some unearthly hour of the morning - something like 6 o'clock. Two 6 o'clocks in one day? Anyway, the club was open at 5 o'clock serving breakfast and best of all....ale! I'd never been in any establishment serving ale at that hour. Happy days! What a deal that was: a flim got us breakfast, coach ticket, match ticket and carrying out for the coach including a big fat ham shank (a proper one I mean, meat on a bone, not the rhyming slang version silly! I think that was available for an extra quid though!) - couldn't argue with that. The match tickets were for seats - I would have preferred to be standing behind the goal but couldn't really complain, even if sitting at the match was an alien concept to me (except for my safety first tactics at Maine Road). We were dropped off at about midday somewhere in London. It was very convenient that it just happened to be near where Snowy's sister Mary (her of the extra-long TSFS) lived. It was also very handy that we'd pick up from there at midnight giving us plenty of time to go sightseeing after the match. MY ARSE! Well, sightseeing of a sort I suppose as a few days previously I'd seen a pub called The Apple Tree on The Sweeney. Snowy assured me Mary lived near there so that was where I would be having a post-match pint or four. Ev would be dead jealous, as The Sweeney was her second fave TV prog after Corry. It was good seeing Charlie's old gaff again. I was deffo gonna have to visit there sometime. We had our dinner at Mary's. Mary actually liked to call it lunch but then she was getting Southernised. Midday meal to me and any other self-respecting Scouser is dinner NOT lunch and always will be.

The match itself wasn't great. Because of the intense heat players on both sides just seemed to be going through the motions. Tosh scored the only goal of the game and that was just about that. All I could think of was how quickly we could get out of there. I've never known heat like it. After our lap of honour the Southampton fans, normally a pretty well behaved bunch, got hot and bothered the police. Saints turned into sinners; pelting our players as they were about to go into the tunnel. Tosh actually headed an orange back into the crowd. Joey lashed most of the shite thrown at him back at them! Imagine that happening now?

The Apple Tree was a fine pub. A little bit posh for my liking and bloody expensive too but then we *were* in London. Scenes from the Sweeney had indeed been filmed in there. I was assured that I was standing in the very spot where Regan had twatted a villain. Ordering ale in London could be a bit of a nightmare sometimes though.
"Brown mixed please mate."
"What's a brown mixed guv?"
"Brown ale mixed with mild ale."
"We don't sell mild ale down 'ere."

"Okay, a brown bitter please mate."
Billy the barman opened a bottle of brown. That's fine. I couldn't understand though why he kept pouring bitter into the pint glass above the half-pint mark.
"Err....that's not quite what I meant."
"That's what you asked for - a brown and a bitter."
"Yeah, but yer've give me a bottle of brown and a *pint* of bitter. I didn't ask for that. I asked for a brown bitter. A brown bitter is 'alf a pint of bitter poured into a pint glass and then a bottle of brown poured into it."
"Strange fuckers you Northern monkeys."
"Doesn't matter mate; I'll 'ave it as it is."
I thought that was the best policy, as any minute now I was either gonna die of thirst or a severe beating from Billy. Snowy fared no better.
"Pint of golden."
Nice start Billy - 'alf a lager in the pint glass. Shit, e's toppin' it up with cider!
"Ee arr mate, that's not a fuckin' golden!"
Snowy wasn't quite as diplomatic as I was.
"Yes it fackin' is! 'Alf a fackin' lager and 'alf a fackin' cider!"
"Nah mate, that's a fuckin' snakebite. They won't even serve yer with that up our end. It sends everyone loopy; as if they're not loopy as it is!"
"Never fackin' 'eard of it guv. What's this fackin' golden supposed to be *up your end* then?"
"'Alf a lager in a pint glass topped up with 'alf a bitter. Fuckin' simple mate!"
Couldn't be arsed with this mixing drinks any more. Imagine if we'd have asked for a black and tan or a pint of fifty? Everybody seemed to be drinking lager now anyway. Nice cold drink in this roaring hot weather. Think I'll try a pint of that.
"Pint of lager please Billy."
"Which one?"
"I dunno. Err… that one there. Yeah, that one. That looks okay. That Stella Artois thingy."

"You sure?"

"Yeah, why?"

"Well if that fackin' snakebite stuff sends you fackin' Northerners round the twist this does the fackin' same to the punters round 'ere."

Terrible language these Cockneys haven't they?

"Well ee arr, giz a pint of it anyway."

"That'll be fifty pence guv."

"Fifty fuckin' pence? I could get pissed for a fortnight with that at 'ome!"

"Well you're not fackin' at 'ome are you! You won't need many more of them anyway."

Billy was only right. First sip - **FUCKING HELL!** Oh, that's good - strong but good. A very unusual taste but I think I could get to like this gear. Half a dozen Stellas later and I was being poured on to the coach, talking about me Granny and telling everybody I loved them. Billy by then was my best mate too. That was the start of a very long love affair with Stella. She's always been good to me and never let me down. She's given me a sore head on more than one occasion but we always get together again. Here's to Stella - the real Lady of Lager!

CHAPTER TWELVE

GIVE A LITTLE WHISTLE

Having won his first managerial trophies Bob was determined to bring the European Cup to Liverpool for the first time this season. To this end he had strengthened our squad by bringing in the latest of Tosh's "replacements", the ex-Everton player David Johnson from Ipswich. The bad news though was that Footballer of the Year Kevin Keegan had announced he was leaving Anfield at the end of the season when his current contract ran out. A lot of Liverpool supporters felt this was a kick in the teeth to a club that had made him what he was - by far and away the best player in the country. Kevin had said that he wanted a "new challenge". I said: "MY ARSE!" As far as I was concerned the word "challenge" didn't come into it; money was the deciding factor. Keegan was after a big payday. He knew he could get far more ackers playing abroad than he ever could in this country. It wasn't just me who felt that way either. Liverpool were the best team in the country and one of the best in Europe. We were out for an all out assault on the European Cup this season and we could well have done without this. The fans felt betrayed by Keegan. Why didn't he want to play for us any more? Surely any player would want to play for the Football League Champions. Kevin assured everybody that he would still be giving one hundred per cent for the club in every game. I for one believed him on this, as there was no other way he could play. It was very disappointing though that my biggest hero since Sir Roger wanted to go and play his football elsewhere.

So it was that Keegan's name was no longer the first one chanted by the Kop in the pre-match warm up. Keegan later said that the crowd stopped chanting his name at all. That's just not true. His name did get chanted - just not first. Replacing Kevin as the hero of the Kop was Joey Jones. Joey wasn't the best player in the world - in fact he wasn't even the best player in his house! Keegan had more skill in his little toenail than Joey had in the whole of his body. What Joey did have though was that he was a Liverpudlian and a Liverpudlian through and through! Joey had as an undying, unquenchable spirit and passion for the club as me or any other Kopite standing there watching him play. First game of the season at home to Norwich Joey came thundering out of the tunnel in the way he did; fist clenched to the Kop, running towards us like a madman and showing off his Liver bird tattoo. A REAL KOPITE!

OH JOEY JOEY!
JOEY JOEY JOEY JOEY JOEY JONES!

The players looked good in their new shirts. The old round-necked shirts had been phased out by most clubs, preferring a gaudy looking v-neck with a collar attached. Liverpool and Arsenal were probably the last two clubs to change from the traditional look. We were now wearing shirts with a shallow white v-neck. David Johnson had a solid if unspectacular debut actually playing alongside Tosh. Steve Heighway scored the goal that got us off to a winning start.

"Evo, I'm startin' a footy team off in 'ere. Just gonna call it Grimwoods like and we'll join the Skem League. Fancy playin'?"
"Yer fuckin' kiddin' aren't yer Tony? I'm shit. I play footy in the park with our Ste. 'E's better than me and 'e's not five yet!"
"Well just come trainin' an' play five-a-side an' that. I've got loads of players so if yer don't fancy it yer can go sub but yer can play if we need yer."
"Okay then. Yeah, I don't mind bein' involved but I'll only play if yer stuck. I'll do the fund-raisin' an' that. I like watching the Sunday footy sometimes anyway. I was thinkin' of takin' up the reffin' a few years ago in the Crosby League when I lived in Litherland."
"Yer don't wanna do that Evo. Everybody 'ates the refs!"

I made my debut for Grimwoods coming on as sub against Ormskirk Hospital. I'd like to say I did a "Davy Fairclough" and turned the game with my supersub antics giving us a draw after being three goals down. I'd be telling you lies though - I came on twenty seconds from the end after Tony Jones had been injured scoring our equalising goal. I didn't even get a kick of the ball. I did kick their winger though. I might be shit but I'm hard to get past! I had enjoyed doing the linesman's duties though for referee Ronnie Ford.

"You did a good job there son. Ever thought of taking up the whistle?"

"I did a few years ago ref but I'm not sure now. I've just 'eard all that shit you've put up with. I think I'll stick to playin'. Everybody knows I'm shit at that so they don't moan at me."

I made a couple more fleeting sub appearances before I was really thrown into the fray for my first full appearance as we only had the bare eleven players. We were playing BOC who were known as a very good team with the likes of Jimmy Mahon and Jimmy Flanagan in their team. They also had a shit hot left-winger called Ray Gauntlet. Ray was the fastest thing on two legs in Skem whilst I was possibly the fattest. So what position was I picked to play? Yes, you've guessed it - right-back. We actually did quite well to hold them to a four goal defeat but I had a torrid time. They had seen I was shit so kept playing the ball out to Ray. Ray must have thought all his birthdays had come at once as he glided effortlessly past me time and time again to lay on the goals for Mahon and Flanagan. I did manage to kick him a couple of times though but I think that was when he was beginning to feel sorry for me and had become fed up of taking the piss out of me. I decided there and then while unravelling my body after being turned inside out and back to front by Ray that my playing days were over. I dragged my ravaged body to Skem United footy club bar - The Blue Rooms to the locals - to enjoy a much need pint or four of Stella: a lady I was now becoming quite fond of. The ref who had been in charge of our match, Chris Abbot, was in there with another ref: Tom Hughes. I went over to Chris to shake his hand.

"Alright ref. Yer 'ad a good game there. Thanks."

"Okay lad. I'd like to say the same about you but you got roasted there didn't you?"

"Yeah, ref. I'm bloody shit I am. I'm packin' it in now. I was thinkin' of takin' up the reffin'. What do I need?"

"A broad pair of shoulders."

"A pair of ears that don't work." Tom interjected

"A blind eye that you can turn now and again."

"And loads of money!"

"But yer get paid three squid a game don't yer ref?"

"Yes, but that all gets taken up with your kit, washing it etcetera."

"Come on Chris, most of it gets spent in here after the game. Then there's all the meetings we attend. Loads of ale there too. So yes, you do need a few bob."

"Okay lad, there's a referees course coming up soon at the Liverpool County FA's office in Bold Street so give us your details and I'll get you on that."

"Yes, you should pass that and get your Class Three. You can start reffing games then."

"I'll give you some of my old kit 'til you can get some yourself."

"Yes, and I'll give you a whistle, notebook, pencils and a stop watch."

"Ah thanks a lot refs. I appreciate that. Eee arr, what are youse 'avin'?"

I really did appreciate it too as money was very tight at home so there was no way I was going to be able to afford all that gear 'til I could get a few games under my belt and save a few match fees to pay for my own kit. They didn't spend ALL of their match fees on ale did they?

The Reds were going great guns in the League. We'd won five of the first six games; the only points dropped being the 1-2 defeat at Birmingham where Johnno opened his account for us. Included in this run was a very good 3-2 win at Derby after being 1-2 down at half-time. Keegan had kept to his promise of 100% commitment and was really doing the biz for us. Tosh was still weighing in with goals so things were looking decidedly good.

We'd gone out of the League Cup at the first hurdle to West Brom but that was seen as a blessing rather than any great loss. I didn't like Liverpool losing any game. If we were playing a Norwegian Fifth Division team in a friendly I wanted us to win 20-0. If we had to bow out of any competition early though then the League Cup would be the one any Red would choose. If defeat in the League Cup meant that fixtures would be less cluttered and we had a better chance of achieving our real goal of winning the European Cup then that was fine by me. We'd been drawn against Crusaders from Northern Ireland in the first round; the first leg to be played at Anfield. We made terribly hard work of a 2-0 win. Crusaders refused to come out of their defensive shell even when they were two goals down. Damage limitation was obviously their sole objective. That was fair enough I suppose. They had no chance of winning the tie and didn't want to play the home leg seven or eight goals down with the subsequent drop in attendance. Bob was almost Shanklyesque with his post-match comment: "They finished the game with ten men. Nobody was sent off. One of their players crossed the halfway line in the second half and was shot for desertion."

Our League run was ended by an awful 0-1 defeat at Newcastle. I knew it was terrible as Phil Neal told me so. I was in town on the Monday after the Newcastle defeat for the first evening of the two-night Class Three refereeing course. I'd taken the day off work so I could go to the Odeon in the afternoon and see the film everybody was raving about, "One Flew Over The Cuckoo's Nest." They were quite right to rave too. What a film that was. I cried at the end. I know I'm a big softy but the ending of that film combined with the superb acting of Jack Nicholson was enough to reduce anybody to tears. Do I sound like Barry Norman? And why not! Anyway, back to Phil Neal. I was in Lime Street station when I saw Phil standing by a pillar. Just standing there all on his own he was. Nobody was bothering him for autographs or anything but he was about to be accosted by me.
"Hiya Phil. Bad defeat yesterday."

"Yeah, we were shit. It's always hard up there. Shit weather and everything. We just couldn't get going."

"Ah, never mind Phil, we'll still win the League and the European Cup. 'Ow come yer not in Belfast? I thought visitin' teams 'ad to be in the country the day before the match."

"We can't fly in 'til tomorrow 'cos of the troubles."

"Oh aye yeah I forgot about that. What are yer doin' ere Phil?"

"I'm meeting a friend off the train. What about you?"

"I've just been to see "One Flew Over The Cuckoo's Nest." Great film it is Phil, yer wanna go an' watch it."

"Yeah, I've seen it. It's brilliant."

"I'm doing a referees course later. I'm gonna ref in the local Sunday League."

"You must be fuckin' mad lad. It's bad enough for the refs on a Saturday with us. You'll have to ref all the lads pissed up after a few beers on a Sunday. Good luck anyway."

"Thanks Phil. Can I have yer autograph please?"

"Yeah, sure."

That was sound! Phil didn't have to talk to a scally like me. Mind you, I did have my best clobber on to impress at the FA: dark blue velvet jacket, light brown Oxford bags and brown wedge shoes. Evo knew how to dress to impress! The following night was great for me as the Reds won 5-0 in Belfast and I passed my Class Three with flying colours. I was ready to start my refereeing career. YIPPPEEEEEEEE!

I spent most of the 0-0 home draw against Middlesbrough watching the ref to see if I could pick up tips for my whistling debut the following day - not that I did of course. I was suitably kitted out for my big day and at least looked the part if nothing else. The big test was going to come on the pitch though. Dealing with twenty-odd hairy arsed Sunday League players wasn't going to be easy, especially as most of them were older than I was - 22 was no great age to be starting a refereeing career. Most refs only started in about their mid-thirties, usually after their playing career had been ended by injury. My playing career had been stopped through my being a bag of shite. The other refs were a big help to me. They could see that I was very nervous entering the changing rooms. I of course knew Tom Hughes and Chris Abbot. I had also earlier been introduced to the Skelmersdale Sunday League referee's representative Terry O'Brien. Terry in turn introduced me to the League Secretary, the legendary Tommy Rogers. Tommy was known as a strict disciplinarian and a stickler for the rules. I'd obviously seen him around the playing fields of Skem, especially Blaguegate Lane, as he went about his task of making sure players not only stayed in line but also that they got their game of football on a Sunday as trouble-free as possible. Tommy was about five foot four, looked like Hiram Holiday, stuck his head out and shoulders back like a strutting cock and gave it to you straight but was sound as a pound. I'd been told, not to say, warned of his straight-talking manner but was slightly unprepared for just how straight.

"Tommy, this is Peter. He's reffin' Ormskirk Hospital versus Ashfield this afternoon. Peter, this is Tommy Rogers, secretary of the League."

"Alright son. Yer okay?"

"Err… yes thanks Mr. Rogers."

"Don't call me Mr Rogers son. Call me Tommy."

"Oh, okay Tommy."

"Eh, yer in for a treat when yer ref the Commies son. They're a great team. My lad Tommy plays for them and me son-in-law, Jimmy Wilson. Smashin' team they are! Anyway, yer a bit young to be a referee aren't yer son?"

"Err… yeah Tommy. I was playin' for Grimwoods but I wasn't very good so I decided to pack it in and start reffin'."

"I know! I saw yer playin' the other week against BOC an' yer were bloody awful! Yer'll 'ave to be a better bloody referee than yer are a player though or yer won't last five minutes up 'ere with this bloody lot!"

HE WASN'T BLOODY MESSIN' EITHER!

"Okay Tommy I'll try."

Tommy then put his iron fist of discipline inside the kid glove of compassion.

"I tell you what though son, if any of these lot give yer any shit you come an' see me. I'll stop them playin' football. They might think they're all roughy toughies out there but if yer take their football away from them they're like big babies! It's like cuttin' their bloody 'eads off!"

He was right too. It was something that stuck with me as I could identify with it - if you took *my* football away it would be like cutting *my* head off.

As it happened I didn't have to go and seek Tommy's reassuring cutting off of heads - not after my first game anyway. I did okay in Ormskirk Hospital's 6-2 win over Ashfield. I was a bit shaky on offsides, didn't quite know how to run diagonals or figures of eight but overall was okay. Most of all though I enjoyed it - something I had never really done when playing. I did love playing but because I was no good just didn't enjoy it. If I could have played even at the lowest of the low Sunday League standard I'd have been happy but no, my on-field football career was to be refereeing. My off-field football career was to continue to be following the greatest football club in the world.

The Anfield Derby was virtually won after 12 minutes when we raced into a two goal lead through Heighway and my mate Phil's penalty. A further goal four minutes before half-time from Tosh more or less wrapped everything up bar the shouting. Even the Evertonians couldn't find any post-match excuses although they did have the consolation of reducing the deficit with the best goal of the game - a real thirty-yard cracker from Martin Dobson. It had to be good to be beat Clem from that range.

A long, arduous journey followed four days later to the shores of the Bosphorous. Trabzonspor of Turkey were known to be a pretty good team. Ali Kamel scored the only goal of the game. The second leg at Anfield was going to be very difficult indeed for us. Of course, if we wanted to win the European Cup nobody was going to hand it to us on a plate.

The usual great following of Reds were present at Elland Road the following Saturday. I'd heard there was a minibus going from the Mucky Duck so I made the arrangements to go on that. I was going to be safe with them - there were some right fuckin' nutters aboard. I actually felt quite privileged that the hardcases of Digmoor were allowing a soft Church Farmer to travel with them. If we got any trouble at Elland Road I was just gonna have to get stuck in or look a right fuckin' divvy. Thankfully there was none outside the ground pre-match. Leeds had converted the old Cowshed into a smart new terrace with a stand above it. The posh new surroundings hadn't appeased the Leeds hoolies however. There was a large presence of them in the paddock next to us looking to give us as much shite as they possibly could. Ray Kennedy gave us the lead after 72 minutes but hardly looked arsed about it. Razor, normally quite animated when celebrating a goal, could hardly raise his arm. It looked as if the long journey to and from Turkey had really taken it out of Ray much more than it had from any of the other players who themselves were looking absolutely knackered. Sadly, it later transpired that this was the start of Ray's debilitating illness: Parkinson's Disease. The minibus was parked quite close to the motorway so we were set for a quick getaway. We were on our way as gangs of Liverpool and Leeds lads were knocking shite out of each other in a subway. I was glad to have missed that one. The other lads on the minibus hadn't been involved either so no face lost - that was good.

Johnno's early season form had evaporated. He was now in and out of the side sharing striking duties with Tosh. Tosh himself was now struggling through games. He was finding it hard to see off his latest "replacement" - something he'd had no trouble doing for years. Tosh's persistent thigh injury that had dogged him for years was now finally beginning to catch up with him. The development of Davy Fairclough was also going fairly slowly. A big plus though was the emergence of Terry Mac. With the aid of Bob and the coaching staff Terry had honed his game to such an extent that with his powerful runs he could very often be relied upon to get on the end of Razor's long range bombs. This was most in evidence during Terry's outstanding performance in the 3-0 home win against Aston Villa. Terry's Man of the Match performance was rounded off by a marvellous goal.

I'd been pestering Terry O'Brien to give me a game in the Premier Division of the Skem League. I'd reffed three games in the First Division so felt I was ready to tackle the hard lads in the Prem. After the torrid ninety minutes of the Polaris versus Plough game I was wishing I hadn't. I'd heard all about the Polo centre-forward Eric Sealey but was totally unprepared for him. Within about ten minutes Eric had me held up by the scruff of the neck, my feet dangling about two feet from the ground. I was too shit scared to be able to do anything about that so Eric did virtually as he liked for the rest of the game. Maybe this refereeing lark wasn't such a good idea after all.

The expected difficult return leg against Trabzonspor didn't turn out that way as we won very easily 3-0 with goals from Heighway, Johnson and Keegan. We'd started our quest to at last win the European Cup very well and could now look forward to the quarter-finals in March, four months hence. Happy days!

Bubbles was one of the loons from Grimwoods. He was a bit of a weird loon too. He was okay in an okay kind of way but there was just something strange about him. He was also a professional photographer and apparently a very good one at that. He had done stuff for people in work at very reasonable rates: weddings; christenings; family photos, that sort for thing. Bubbles came highly recommended so I asked him if he could take a few family photos for me. The photo shoot was arranged for the Saturday of the game at Sunderland; a.m. obviously - I didn't want Bubbles interrupting me listening to the match. So what time did he turn up? Yeah, fuckin' three o'clock! Why did people insist on blighting my life by interrupting my footy? I didn't ask for a great deal from life, just not to interfere with my footy.
"Bubbles, where the fuck 'ave yer been?"

"I was doin' a weddin' this mornin' an' got a late bookin' to do one this afternoon."

Not once did Bubbles look at me while he was telling me this. His eyes for not one second diverted themselves from Ev. His gaze was focussed mainly on Ev's very prominent bust. My darling's marvellous, pendulous breasts were a sight to behold no doubt but I didn't want every Tom, Dick and Bubbles feasting their pervy eyes on them! I suppose I couldn't blame him though - she was fuckin' beautiful. Her figure, after the battering it had taken from her second pregnancy, was now fully restored to its usual amazing beauty.

"Ee arr Bubbles, are yer gonna get on with this? The match is about to kick off. I wouldn't mind listenin' to it if yer don't mind."

"Err..yeah, okay."

Bubbles Bailey was about to start the great Evo mug shot incident.

"Let your wife sit on a stiff, hard chair."

Phew, thought he was gonna say somethin' else there!

"What for?"

"So you can stand behind her and have the kids standin' either side of you."

"Fuck off Bubbles! We'll look like a fuckin' Victorian family on a day out to New Brighton!"

I was no professional but I just knew that would look shit. It took Bubbles nearly an hour to set all his lighting equipment up. Once the "studio" was up and running he spent another hour or so snapping merrily away. I was very concerned about the amount of photos he was taking and especially how many he wanted to take of Ev sitting on her own. Most of the group photos were of me, Big Ev, Ste and Little Ev on the couch. If they all came out okay I'm sure they would look very good. One of the photos was spoiled though as by now I had the radio on while Bubbles did the biz. Davy scored what was to be the only goal of the game about fifteen minutes from time. What should have been a nice family photo turned out to be a mass of arms and legs with me in mid air and the word "FUCK" as in the first word of "fuckin' go 'ead" framed on my lips. The rest of the photos though were absolutely superb. Bubbles gave them to me in work a couple of days later. He gave me a stack of photos and at a very reasonable rate too. I asked him what he'd done with the load of photos he took of Ev.

"Your wife is very beautiful you know. I'll show the photos to modelling agencies. She can earn two quid an hour you know modelling."

"Yeah, I know what kind of fuckin' modellin' you've got in mind! No thanks Bubbles."

I did take some of the photos of Ev off him though. We were on lates so the kids were in bed when I got home. I gave Ev the stack of family photos and deliberately left the solo ones of her 'til last.

"Oh these are great aren't they Peter? Ah, look at our Ste there. Ah, look at the smile on our Ev."

"I know Ev, they're sound. Ee arr, 'ave a look at these."

"They're brilliant!"

"I know. Bubbles reckons yer can earn two squid an hour modellin'. I told 'im to fuck off though."

"Yeah, I don't wanna be doin' that!"

"Yeah, I said yer wouldn't wanna do it. D'yer know what Ev, I know we 'ave our battles an' our ups and down an' that but I 'ave to say this - you are fuckin' gorgeous and I love yer very much."

"Come on, get upstairs while we're both in a good mood."

Thanks Bubbles. Money well spent that lad!

Best performance and funniest, maddest moment of the season so far came in the home match against Leicester. Heighway and Tosh scored to help us to a 2-1 half-time lead. The fun and games were only just starting however. A Phil Neal penalty twenty minutes from time put us further ahead. Two minutes later Anfield went mad. Honestly, the Kop went absolutely fuckin' ballistic. Why? Because......**JOEY SCORED!** Now I've told you earlier how much I loved Joey so I'm not being unkind to him, in fact he would admit it himself, when I say that if you saw Joey with the ball just outside the opposition penalty area then you would also expect to see a dead pigeon on the roof a couple of seconds later. Not this time though. Joey's 25-yard thunderbolt fairly rifled into the Anny Road net to give him his first ever goal for us. Even Emlyn couldn't catch Joey as he legged it towards the Kop. As Joey came nearer and nearer the Kop you could see the biggest, broadest smile ever in the memory of man spread right across that mad grid of his! His Liverbird tattoo festooned arms were pumping like mad as he as skipped and jumped like a two-year-old kid towards us. I honestly thought he was going to jump in the Kop. By this time Phil Thompson had caught up with the loon; Joey must have been getting knackered for Thommo to catch him. I wish they had have jumped in the Kop. There, standing side by side, going mental and nearly within touching distance of us were the two biggest Liverpudlians ever to take the field wearing the red shirt. Joey and Thommo epitomise what Liverpool Football Club and being a Liverpudlian is all about. Keegan wrapped up the scoring, capping his own great performance, by slotting home a penalty eight minutes from time. Kevin showed his own sense of humour and gave us all a laugh by trying to imitate Joey's celebration. Nice try Kevin but.....**THERE'S ONLY ONE JOEY!**

Mad arse repeated the trick in the next home game! Cue same berserk celebration. Even better this time though as it turned out to be the winner in the 2-1 win over Bristol City. Again the goal was scored at the Anny Road end. I wish he could have scored at our end - he *deffo* would have ended up in the Kop with us! I really was made up for Joey. He'd only really got his chance in the team at the start of the season as Tommy Smith was still fulfilling a contract by playing in the United States at the start of the season. Phil Neal moved over to right-back allowing Joey to take up the left-back berth. Joey grabbed his chance with both hands, feet and whatever else he could! The big thing in Joey's favour for a chance of actually staying in the team was that he **WANTED** to play for Liverpool. That desire coupled with his own good performances ensured Joey did indeed keep his place upon the Anfield Iron's return. Good on yer Joey lad!

CHAPTER THIRTEEN

OLD ENEMIES - NEW FRIENDS

We went into the top-of-the-table clash at Ipswich three points clear of them. By the end of the day that lead had been reduced to one after Ipswich's 1-0 victory. Ipswich had a game in hand, at Birmingham the following Tuesday, which they duly won 4-2 to go a point clear of us. Ipswich's game the following Saturday was postponed giving us the chance to go back to the top if we could beat QPR at Anfield. Rangers had failed to build on their marvellous last season when they ran us so close for the title and were now languishing in 16th place only three points off the relegation zone. Whether or not the game would go ahead was in doubt right up 'til kick off time as thick fog enveloped Anfield. When QPR took the lead we were beginning to wish it hadn't. We equalised ten minutes before half-time when a great run by Phil Neal ended with him hitting a shot across goal. The ball hit the far post but Tosh was on hand to net the rebound. There is a marvellous photo by the great photographer, Harry Ormesher, taken from right behind the Kop net that shows QPR 'keeper Phil Parkes standing in his own goalmouth with not another player in sight as the rest of the pitch was enshrouded in fog. The game was heading for the draw, which really wouldn't have done us, but we won the match with two late goals from Keegan and Kennedy.

Sweeneyspeak was sweeping the country. The antics of Regan and Carter in the top TV programme were spawning a strange new tongue. Local colloquialisms would be mixed with the Cockney rhyming slang used by the fictional bobbies. Local rhyming slang, in this case Scouse slang, was added to make a sometimes unfathomable mix.
"Peter, lenz a Plymouth."
"If I knew what a Plymouth was Ronnie I might lend yer one."
"Yer know, a Plymouth - a grey'ound."
"No I don't fuckin' know Ronnie. I 'aven' gorra fuckin' clue what yer on about."

"A Plymouth. A Plymouth Sound. A pound."
"Oh a squid. Well why the fuck didn't yer say that then? Not like you that though Ronnie is it to be skint an' on the cadge."
I handed the two ten bob pieces over (they'll always be ten bob pieces to me) with little optimism of ever seeing them again.
"Ta Peter. Yer sound's a pound."
"Yeah, just make sure I get it back Ronnie."
I never did get that Plymouth, I mean grey'ound, I mean pound back.

Another great exponent of Sweeneyspeak was Terry O'Halloran.
"Peter, bring some dosh in tomorrow and we'll go for a gargle after work."
"Dosh?"
"Yeah, yer know, money."
"Oh right. What's a gargle?"
"A Don Revie."
I knew that meant a bevy. I used that one myself. I duly brought the dosh in and went for a gargle with Terry. Terry was my bevying partner and a good one at that for quite a while. Terry would regale me with tales of gangsters in Liverpool. It seemed he had mixed with that crowd for a while and knew a lot of them. I don't know whether most of the tales were true, although he had no reason to tell me lies, but they were entertaining anyway. Terry was still suffering from a broken toe sustained during the previous red hot summer. There was a woman worked in Grimwoods who was desperate for Terry to shag her. She had pestered him for ages to take her for a drink. Terry being a man of the married persuasion had steadfastly refused her advances. She had mithered Terry something rotten all week when we were on late shift to take her for a drink after work on the Friday night to the Plough and Harrow and then shaft her senseless up at the Beacon. To get her off his case Terry agreed on the Thursday to take her for said drink and shaft the following night. Terry of course had no intention of doing so. She came into work on the Friday dolled up to the nines wearing a pair of the highest high

heels you've ever seen. Terry told her he wasn't taking her and indeed never had any intention of taking her to the Plough nor anywhere else, as he was a married man. Of course this was not taken too well. An hour or so later Terry was standing up working on a machine wearing just shorts and a pair of sandals (Grimwoods never were very big on safety). She walked up to Terry and without hardly breaking stride stamped on his foot, ground her stiletto right in, twisting and turning her foot as she did so and then just carried calmly on her way up the factory. Terry didn't give her the satisfaction of screaming out loud but the state of his middle toe some three months later was testimony to the terrible injury she had inflicted on him. It was funny though.

Our most embarrassing defeat in years came at Villa Park. Not that Villa weren't a good side of course. They were on the fringe of the title race and had a crop of good players such as the young Andy Gray, Brian Little, Frank Carrodus, Dennis Mortimer and Allan Evans. It was the manner and size of the defeat that came as such a shock. Villa were 5-0 (yes five nil) up inside half-an-hour. Razor pulled one back five minutes before half-time but that was little more than a consolation goal. Thank God Villa took their foot off the pedal in the second half or we could have been looking at a ten goal defeat. Villa were brilliant that night, especially Andy Gray. The young Scot tore us to pieces and looked to have a very big future in the game ahead of him.

We fared little better three days later against West Ham. West Ham were bottom of the First Division whilst we were top despite our mauling at Villa Park. We went down 0-2. That was the famous occasion when supposedly only seven people booked on the Special, which then had to be cancelled. I wasn't there myself but apparently there were a good few Reds who'd got the ordinary. It's something I hit my old Anny Road mates with when they start singing about how us Kopites were gobshites:
"Where were you at Upton Park?" I sing at them. Where were the dead hard Road Enders against the West Ham lads? Not that I was there of course but it does wind them up, which is nice.

The defeat at Upton Park had dropped us to second place. Crisis at Anfield again! Disarray in the ranks! The cracks are starting to show! Of course we'd heard it all before. So what did we go out and do in the next match? Go out and twat Stoke 4-0 that's fuckin' what! In front of a Christmas crowd of 50,000 too. Fuck the press!

Next stop: Maine Road. Oh, that's all I fuckin' need, a night match at what had become the scariest away ground in the country on a freezing cold day in between Christmas and New Year. I had the fuckin' flu too wouldn't yer just know it! What d'yer mean I didn't 'ave to go? Of course I 'ad to go! I had the money so why shouldn't I go? Ev hadn't spoken to me since Boxing Day - I think I'd only put one sugar in her tea instead of two or something dead wrong like that - so it was a great relief to get out of the house. I can't really think why I didn't get the train from Upholland or Wigan to Manchester. Anyway, I ended up in Wigan and got a bus from there. That was the bus ride from hell. It took about three hours on our tour of places I'd never heard of - I'm sure we actually got into Yorkshire at one point. I'd been hoping to get to Maine Road early to buy a Platt Lane Stand ticket. I really didn't fancy paying to get in the Kippax and risk getting my head kicked in on a night like this. There were hundreds of City lads waiting for buses to Maine Road at Aytoun Street. If I was sussed I was fucked. I had my seventeen pence bus fare at the ready. Just hoped it hadn't gone up in the last eight months. It hadn't: nice one! Luckily, or so I thought, there was a pay gate for the Platt Lane Stand so I dived in there. The Platt Lane Stand was normally a safe place to be for a Scouser. I'd been in there three times previously and had no trouble. There were normally plenty of Reds in there. This time though it seemed I was the only Red in that stand. There were none dotted around the other two stands as there usually were either. It seemed every Red who'd made the trip were on the Kippax doing battle. I was feeling absolute shit! Deffo the worst I'd felt since I'd had pleurisy nine years earlier. Hope I wasn't getting that again. I deffo didn't need sussing as soon as I got sat down.

"Fuckin' Scouse bastard."

Oh shit! I could only hear him from behind me. I was gonna have to front this. He couldn't be that hard anyway or he'd be in the Kippax with the other loons. A bit like myself actually! I turned round expecting to see a young lad who looked at least a bit hard. Sitting before me was a 40-something whale.

"Yeah, dot's yer duckin' broblem?

Sorry, "What's yer fuckin' problem?" Remember, I did have the 'flu.

"You shouldn't be in 'ere."

"Well, I fuckin' am so fuck off."

Shit, I'm gonna get me fuckin' 'ead kicked in 'ere. Not by the hump-backed whale of course but by the other owld arses if they kicked off.

"Keep your fuckin' mouth shut durin' the match."

"Fuck off!"

Fair enough on the other City fans around him they told him to leave me alone as I wasn't causing any bother. Nice one lads. I might do the same for one of your young fans when I'm forty-odd. City, kicking towards us, took the lead in the first half. It had to be Joe fuckin' Royle who scored too didn't it? Fuckin' ex-Everton. Bollocks! Whalebone behind me was going fuckin' mental and slapping everybody on the back he could lay his hands on, including me. I actually think he got a few sly digs in too but I couldn't be arsed to have a go back as I was too sick, in more ways than one. We were playing like a bag of shite so Johnno was brought off to be replaced by Supersub. City really were shit scared of Davy after he'd tormented them the previous season. With just a minute to go Davy panicked Dave Watson to such an extent that with Davy snapping at his heels soft arse put the ball into his own net past the bemused Joe Corrigan.

FUCKIN' GERRIN YER FUCKIN' BEAUT!

I was jumpin' all over the place. I turned round to give it loads to Willie the whale but he'd fucked off. Probably thought the game was won and gone to the nearest watering hole for his celebratory pint of plankton. That made it all the better. Fuckin' wanker!

The bus to Piccadilly was negotiated safely enough but fuck me there were hundreds of City lads waiting at the entrance to Victoria station. There was no fuckin' chance of getting away walking through that lot. Luckily I wasn't sussed. I walked around the side of the station looking for some kind of safe entrance. I found one purely by chance. There were a set of stairs leading to a platform but they were guarded by a set of railings. Luck was definitely on my side tonight as there was a gap I was able to squeeze through.

"Oi 'ave you got a platform ticket?"

Shit! There was a guard on the platform but I was in mood for him either.

"Does it look like I've got a fuckin' platform ticket? I've 'ad to come up those stairs to get way from the City fans."

"Platform 4 to Liverpool"

I couldn't be arsed telling him I wasn't going to Liverpool so found my own way to Platform 6 for the Wigan train.

"And make sure you buy a ticket!"

Fuck off Ivor the Engine!

"Okay mate, thanks."

I had to make sure I caught the last bus from Wigan to Skem or I was fucked for getting home. There were a few lads getting on it as I legged it out of Wigan station. Sound, clearly said on the front 395 - Skelmersdale Town Hall. Laughin'! Wrong!

"Town Hall please mate."

"What Town Hall?"

"Skem Town Hall."

"Well, yer only said Town Hall. Yer might 'ave meant Southport Town Hall."

"It's only goin' as far as fuckin' Skem isn't it so I obviously meant Skem Town Hall."

"I won't fuckin' let yer on in a minute!"

"Ah for fuck sake mate, look I'm fucked, I can do without this."

"Get off the fuckin' bus."

"No, I will fuck. 'Ere's me fuckin' fare just fuckin' take it will yer!"

Why were bus drivers/conductors the bane of my fuckin' life? I was rescued by the lads I'd seen getting on the bus. They turned out to be lads who played in the Skem League - Larry Trencher, Eddie Pinno, Alan Southern and best of all Dave Tisdall. Dave was a bus driver. He knew the twatty driver of this bus so intervened on my behalf. They were all Road Enders too so Twatty Bollocks wasn't gonna mess with them.

"Yer coulda got battered there Peter, 'e's a 'ard fucker."

"I don't care 'ow fuckin' 'ard 'e's supposed to be Dave. Who the fuck does 'e think 'e's talkin' to? Fuckin' blurt. I've 'ad one twat of a day; I don't need arse'oles like 'im givin' me any more grief than I've already 'ad."

Fuckin' Man City again! I was getting so much grief when I went there that I wasn't gonna go again - ever! Well, 'til next season that is. My grief wasn't yet over though.

"Wher've *you* been?"

"Ah no please Ev, no. I've 'ad a fuckin' awful day and I just don't need any more grief."

"Yer've been to Man City 'aven' yer?"

"Yeah, I fuckin' 'ave so why ask?"

"Why didn't yer tell me where yer were goin?"

"'Cos yer weren't fuckin' talkin' to me. Yer 'aven' said a fuckin' word to me for three fuckin' days. What was I supposed to do, fuckin' tell yer in sign language?"

"Yer coulda just told me."

"Fuck off will yer Ev. Leave me alone. I've got the 'flu."

"I didn't know yer 'ad the flu!"

"Well yer wouldn't would yer? Yer 'aven' been any fuckin' where near me for three bastard days!"

I really was getting fed up of all this. I'd done fuck all wrong and was getting constant grief. Was there any fuckin' point to it? If I hadn't been a big lad I would have cried. Nothing bugged me more than her not talking to me. I'd rather have had a fuckin' chisel in the head or something but this silent treatment was shit.

"'Ave yer 'ad anythin to eat?"

"No. Please Ev, just leave me alone. I feel like shit. I've got a poundin' headache. I just wanna get me 'ead down and go asleep. I'll let yer moan at me tomorrow but for now, please, please, please leave me alone."

"Come downstairs then and I'll cook yer somethin'. Then I'll sweat that 'flu outta yer. I'm sorry."

STRANGE WOMAN!

The sadist disguised as a computer programmer at the Football League had given us the tasty, mouth-watering fixture of Sunderland at home on New Year's Day. Oh fuckin' marvellous! I'd just got over the 'flu, been at a party 'til five in the morning, was goosed and just wanted to stay in bed all day. Why did the Football League hate me? What was the point of playing matches on New Year's Day? Everybody was fucked! I just about got through our 2-0 win without throwing up.

"Errrrrr......Peter, errrr......yer goin' the match Satdee like der la?"

Baz had started in Grimwoods the previous summer, having just moved to Skem from Bootle. He had been quite hard to get to know at first, keeping himself pretty much to himself. Once he got himself settled though EVERYBODY knew he was there. Baz was a year or two older than me and, as I say, originally from Bootle so I suppose I should have already known him. He knew all the Bootle lads I did and knew our John very well. I'd never met him before in my life though so I suppose we'd just moved in different circles. Baz was wasting his time in Grimwoods. He'd missed his vocation in life. Baz should have been a professional Scouser. Baz was the archetypal, stereotypical, whatever you want to call it, Scouser. I'm sure Harry Enfield must have met Baz at some point and based his "SCOUSERS" characters on him. Baz would say the maddest things that neither I nor anybody else could quite understand. I used to sort of get what he meant so in the end I had an ear for Bazspeak so to speak.

"Yeah Baz. Are you goin'?"

"Errr....yeah like er der la. I'll errr....get the sponds and errr...see

what the crack is on de errr…'urdy gurdy like errr la."
Quick translation: "Yeah, no problem. That is if me missus let's
me 'ave the money. I'll ave to see what the score is on that."
Baz was a sound guy. He really made me laugh. He was also, I
sort of guessed, a bit of a hard case. There was only one person
in the world he was frightened of - his wife. He was totally,
absolutely, shit scared of her. I suppose though, in a way, we're all
frightened of our wives aren't we? I know I was of mine but then
I'd had an array of dangerous objects launched at my head for the
past five-and-a-half years. I had a right to be scared!
"Okay, get to ours for twelve o'clock then. Delvey's comin' too."
Crystal Palace brought a good following to Anfield for the FA
Cup 3rd Round game. Most of their fans were in the Anny doing
battle with the Road Enders but there were also a fair few of then
in the paddock causing fuckin' mayhem. They were picking on
old men and kids just wading in to anybody before them. A load
of lads had got themselves together at the bottom corner of the
Kop and were ready to vault the wall and sort out the gobshites
in the Paddock. Keen to join them were Baz and Delvesy.
"Ee arr…errrr…let's get over there and fuckin'…errr…do them
in. Fuckin' Cockney twats!"
"Yeah, come on, let's crack some 'eads."
That was a favourite of Delvesy's, "let's crack some 'eads." I
suspected that Delvesy would have had trouble cracking an egg
never mind a head; a massive scar where somebody had
Krookloked his nose bearing massive testimony to his lack of
hardness.
"Fuckin' behave will youse. The bizzies are there now anyway."
It was a good job the bizzies had sussed the situation as that could
have VERY ugly. On the pitch Third Division Palace were giving
us a right pounding. Clem was having to be at his world-class
best to deny Palace the win they deserved with a string of
outstanding saves. Baz and Delvesy missed the last five minutes
of the match as they'd gone to see if they could "crack some
Palace 'eads".
"Errr….yer shoulda seen the ag after the game there Peter.

Errrr....loadsa Road End round the paddock. I was sittin' on top
of the gate an' jumped down on the Palace."
"Did yer Baz? Marvellous."
Another of Baz's favourite sayings, that he used mostly in work
was: "Err.....de balloon's gonna go up an' errrrrr..........when it
does go up it'll stay up!"
I think that meant: "Somethin' big's gonna happen in this factory
soon that might well affect the well being of us all and when it
does happen it will be somethin' VERY big." Don't take that as
gospel though.

I was getting right into the refereeing now and would travel
virtually anywhere to get a game. I couldn't afford to go to
Norwich so accepted the appointment to ref a schoolboys match
in Crosby: Crosby and Litherland Boys v Kirkby Boys. Bloody
difficult place to get to by public transport from Skem is Crosby
but I managed it. When I saw an old face from the past just before
kick-off I was half wishing I hadn't bothered. It was the old gym
teacher from St. Wilfred's - Arthur Stevens - Stevo to his enemies
of which he had many amongst us Willies lads. During my four
years at the Willies I never saw him in anything else other than a
baggy black tracksuit. He was still wearing it now. I truly hated
him at school. He was forever skitting me for having no kit and
made me cry in front of the other lads on more than one occasion.
I was hoping he wouldn't recognise me. No such luck.
"Hello Peter, how are you? Nice to see you again. I never thought
you would take up refereeing."
*Yeah, well yer were wrong weren't yer! Yer never thought I'd ever
amount to anything 'cos I was shit at every sport goin' an' told me
as much. Nice to prove yer wrong!*
"Oh hello Mr. Stevens. Nice to see you too. What are you doing
here Sir?"
I just couldn't get out of the habit of calling him Sir. I suppose it's
something that is ingrained at school - you respect teachers, no
matter how much you didn't like them.
"I'm scouting for Everton. There are a couple of lads I'm looking
at in this match. How long have you been refereeing?"

"About three months Sir."

"Are you enjoying it?"

"Yes Sir, very much."

"Well, I hope you have a good game. Good luck and I'll come and have a chat to you after the match."

"Okay, thanks a lot Sir."

Christ, I couldn't believe how nice he was to me. He seemed really genuine too. Maybe the monster he was (perhaps had to be) in school was replaced by a caring, good person outside of school. What a game that was! The final score was 6-6. I'd had a great game and Stevo did indeed come to see me after the game.

"Well done Peter, you were brilliant. You really surprised me. Excellent refereeing. How high are you hoping to go?"

"I don't know really Sir. I'm just quite happy with what I'm doing now. I've been told if I really want to go to the top I'll have to start reffing in Saturday Leagues but I'd only be able to do that every other Saturday and I don't think most Saturday Leagues would accept that."

"Why only every other Saturday Peter?"

"I've got a season ticket for Anfield Sir and there's no way I'd be able to concentrate on any game or whatever I was doing if I was doing it while Liverpool are at home."

"Oh yes, I remember, you were always a big Liverpool supporter when you were at school. Missed a few days school too I seem to remember queuing for tickets. How are you getting home?"

"Well I live in Skelmersdale now Sir but I'm going to my Mam's in Bootle so I'm getting the bus from Crosby terminus."

"No, don't be wasting your money doing that. I'll give you a lift."

I was getting to like new Stevo!

"Thanks a lot Sir."

Once we were in Stevo's car I nearly fell through the floor when he called me Evo!

"Are you married now Evo?"

It really was a shock. It was disconcerting enough him calling me Peter rather than the Etherington I'd always had at school. For him to call me Evo really threw me.

"Yes Sir. I've got two kids too - Steven's five and Evelyn's nearly two."

"Oh that's nice."

Right, now for the real test! I'm gonna make a big confession 'ere. Let's see if yer still nice to me after this!

"Sir, remember when I was off sick for about six weeks when the World Cup was on?"

"Yes Peter I remember that."

"Well, I wasn't sick sir. I bunked off school so I could see all the players training at Goodison."

Come on then Stevo - kick me out of the car and report me to the Board of Retrospective Punishments For Truants or whatever you call it.

"I know. I saw you watching Russia and Germany there."

"You saw me Sir?"

"Yes."

"Why didn't you report me then?"

"Because I was bunking off too. I'm a football fan the same as yourself Peter."

I couldn't help it. I just fell into a heap in the car laughing. Stevo soon cracked up too. I decided to hit him with another one.

"Sir, do you remember the end of season match against the leavers when you were juggling the ball on your head showing off and it bounced off your head past Mr. Breen?"

Stevo laughed uproariously.

"Yes Evo, I do remember that. Old Breeny wouldn't speak to me for a week after that."

"Well did you see the poem on the boy's toilet wall about it?"

"Yes. I suppose you wrote that didn't you?"

"Yes sir, I did."

"I thought that might have been you. Dennis Costigan saw it. He said it was probably you as it looked like your handwriting. He said you were quite good at English and a bit of a poet."

"Yes sir; English was about the only thing I was ever any good at."

I was almost sorry when our journey ended and we'd reached my Mam's. I was half-tempted to invite the old goat in for a cup of tea but that would have been just a step too far. Stevo was a good age then so I suppose he will have passed away by now. If he has I hope he's looking down at me from the great gym in the sky, probably still wearing his baggy black tracksuit, and having a little chuckle at this.

Having safely disposed of Palace in the replay far more comfortably than the 3-2 scoreline suggests we would face another lower division club - Second Division Carlisle United in Round 4. Mark Blackburn was coming to this game with me. Mark worked with me in Grimwoods and we were big mates. He was a fairly quiet type of guy with a dry sense of humour.
"Evo are yer goin' the match on Saturday?"
"Yeah Mark. Why, d'yer wanna come with us?"
"Yeah, I wouldn't mind. What time shall we leave?"
"Whatever time you want mate. What bus d'yer wanna get?"
"The big red one."
It made me chuckle anyway.
I was reffing a match Mark was playing in one day. He was quite a good player and was on an amazing run from his own half. I was keeping pace with him (honest) and was running alongside him. It wasn't fair me putting him off but he was a mate so it was allowed.
"I bet yer miss."
"Fuck off Evo!"
"Go on, I bet yer miss."
"Fuck off!"
Mark was now just outside the opposition penalty area.
"Go on, miss."
Mark pulled his shot horribly wide. Once he got his breath back he slaughtered me.
"You're the fuckin' referee! Yer can't say things like that to me! Yer fuckin' fat bastard!"
I ran back down the field, backwards as all good refs should, pissing myself laughing. Mark's team won the match so no harm done but he has never let me forget that! Anyway, back to the

match: Carlisle didn't trouble us anywhere near as much as Palace had. We won easily 3-0 with two goals from Keegan and another from Tosh. Such a pity that Kevin was going at the end of the season. He was in great form but European clubs weren't exactly knocking his door down to sign him up. The only sniff of interest came from Real Madrid. Such was the lack of interest that Kevin "supposedly" said he would consider joining another English club. This really outraged us, especially as Manchester United had been mentioned. Whether he actually said it is a matter for conjecture - it might have just been the press causing trouble, I wouldn't put that past them, but whatever it didn't go down well at all.

CHAPTER FOURTEEN

NIL-NIL BY MOUTH

I was really looking forward to the trip to Old Trafford. Yes, you heard right and I wasn't being sarcastic. We were top of the League, a point ahead of Ipswich and Manchester City who both had games in hand on us - three and two respectively. We'd got no bother there at all last season and I was going with the same lads in the car so there should be no problem. Only I never got there did I?

I was on the short, ten minute walk (seven minutes if I ran but I was early for once) to work. It was very cold with ice, black ice at that, on the roads but was thinking happily of the match tonight, quite confident we'd get at least a draw to consolidate our position. Jack Wallbank's car pulled up.
"Come on Peter, get in."
"Thanks Jack. Bloody freezin' isn't it?"
"Aye lad. Black ice on road too. I'll 'ave to be careful."
Jack's car skidded, must have hit said black ice and crashed into George Caldwell's car who was approaching work from the opposite direction. My head hit the roof of the car. Jack and George got out of their cars unharmed, inspected the damage and agreed that it was a total accident, nobody to blame, black ice had caused it. They were hanging around doing whatever it is drivers do in these situations. I was still in the front passenger seat of the car nursing a sore head - a VERY sore head.
"You okay Peter?"
"Yeah, I think so Jack. 'Ead 'urts a bit like but I think I'll live."
Actually it was hurting more than a bit - it was friggin' killing me by now.
"Well we've got to sort this out so you get to work to make sure you don't clock on late. Tell Ted we'll be in soon."
As soon as I started walking I knew something was wrong. I didn't quite know where I was although I could see the factory

about a hundred yards ahead of me. I headed for that but just didn't seem to be making headway as my legs weren't working properly. By the time I clocked on I was wobbling all over the place. I was sitting in the canteen trying my best to drink a cup of coffee but actually spilling most of it. I had my head in my hands and was deffo feeling sick. The coggy on my head was rising at a rate of knots and would soon be the size of Mount Snowdon.

"Bloody 'ell Peter, you look like death warmed up."

I knew what Tommy Goodwin meant but why did people say such things? I mean, has anybody ever conducted an experiment where they have actually put a corpse in an oven at Gas Mark 4 - 180c say for twenty minutes, taken it out, left it to cool slightly on a rack, then checked what colour it is and what it looks like? No, I doubt it. In much the same way I doubted whether anybody had actually boiled shite to see what colour it goes, as in my Ma's favourite saying, "You look the colour of boiled shite."

Another one of those old wives sayings, 'cos surely it is only old wives who say them, I'm sure you'd never get an old husband or any man for that matter saying them is, "Don't put your coat on indoors or you won't feel the benefit."

What fuckin' benefit? Can anybody at all tell me what kind of benefit I'm supposed to feel by *not* putting my coat on before I step outside? What if it's blowing a gale outside or freezing cold, lashing it down or worse - snowing? What am I supposed to do, freeze my bollocks off for five minutes outside before I put my coat on? What fuckin' benefit is there in that?

"I know Tommy. I don't feel well. I think I'm gonna be sick."

"Go an' see Ted an' tell 'im yer goin' the 'ospital. Ask 'im to get somebody to take yer."

I stumbled to Ted's office, ready to pass out at any minute.

"Hiya Ted. Jack and George 'ave crashed their cars. I was in Jack's car and banged me 'ead. I don't feel well. I'm goin' to Ormskirk ozzy. Can yer get somebody to take me please."

"Can't yer get a bus?"

Well, I could get a bus yer fuckin' cretin but I'd probably die on the way. Besides, 'avin' enough money to get me a bus to

Ormskirk was not the first thing I thought of when I left 'ome 'alf-an-hour ago. Just fuckin' sort somethin' out for me will yer before yer 'ave two deaths in yer office 'cos if I'm gonna pop 'em I'll make sure I take you out first!

"I can't Ted. I feel that bad I probably wouldn't even make the bus stop."

"Okay, I'll get Arthur to take you."

Let the saints be fuckin' praised! 'Ow 'ard was that?

"Thanks Ted."

Arthur had just about managed to get me to the Casualty entrance when I collapsed in a heap as I stepped out of his car. I came round what was probably only a minute or so later to find two nurses undressing me. Now as you can understand, in different circs I would have been quite pleased with this - bloody ecstatic even. Even in my concussed state I recognised one of the nurses as Mally Clarke, centre-half for Ormskirk Hospital. The other nurse, although quite pretty, was not going to arouse any carnal thoughts in my jumbled, coggied head as all I could think of was that I was in serious trouble here as I'd booked Mally the previous Sunday for calling me, and I quote, "Egg on legs." Mally was now surely gonna extract revenge by cutting my knob off or something. Mally and she nurse then exploded into fits of laughter as they got my kecks off. No, not at the size of my shrivelled up acorn; that was to come. I looked down: horror of horrors. I always knew I should have taken more notice of me Ma. Lily was forever telling me, "Always make sure yer've got clean underwear on. Yer might get run over."

Now this was one I never could work out. I mean, you probably start putting your own underwear on when you're about five, right? Okay, so say you live to the average life expectancy of about seventy. Take it also that you're probably gonna go out on average once a day for the rest of those 65 years. A quick reckoning (I've been on Countdown you know) tells me that you have to check for clean underwear over 23,000 times. At a conservative estimate of 10 seconds a check that works out at over 64 hours. 64 hours of your life wasted checking your Bill

Grundy's to make sure they're clean in the highly unlikely event you're gonna get steamrollered. Now come on, that's not on is it? I mean, if you do get snotted by a big fuck off truck or something you're gonna shit yer Bill's anyway aren't you? 64 hours? Christ, that doesn't bear thinking about does it? I mean, that's like having eight days off work sick. Imagine going to your doctor and saying, "Doctor, I need eight days off work to check my skidunkers." I mean, what would the learned one write on your sick note under that bit, "I have examined (INSERT NAME) today and certify he/she is suffering from.......... He/she should refrain from work for eight days"? It would probably have to be something like, "Checking his/her thundercrackers" wouldn't it. Can you see your boss going for that? No, me neither - mine certainly wouldn't! Hmmmm…but hey - I'd put clean skids on this morning - brand new ones in fact. Yeah, even my befuddled brain could work out that as Ev had done no washing this week I'd had to put on a pair she'd bought me for Christmas that I'd vowed I'd wear only in the direst emergency.

OH SHIT!

My eyes fell upon the posing pouch Ev had bought me, singularly failing to keep my meat and two veg in their rightful place, with a picture of a rose thorn and the legend emblazoned upon them,

"JUST A LITTLE PRICK."

I fuckin' hate you sometimes Ev!

Once Nursies had undressed me and squeezed me into the shittiest pair of jimjams ever - two sizes too small for me at that - I was deposited into a bed on Phillip Ward - Men's General to join the assorted geriatric loons currently serving their time there. A doctor came along in due course to examine me.

"You are suffering from concussion Mr. Etherington. We'll be keeping you in for obs."

I knew obs was observation from the three days I'd spent in Wythenshawe Hospital seven-and-a-half years earlier after suffering a severe beating at Old Trafford. Shit, the match! I was gonna have to get outta here soon. It was nearly midday now. I've

gotta phone Kev to confirm pick up time in Bootle at five o'clock.
"'Ow long will I be in for Doctor? I'll be out for teatime won't I?"
"I'm afraid not (*yes, I know the joke*) Mr. Etherington. You'll be
under observation for at least twenty-four hours, maybe longer."
Oh fuckin' deep everlastin' eternal joy! I've gotta get out. I'm goin'
the match!
"Okay Doctor. Does my wife know I'm in here?"
"Yes, the gentleman who brought you in has informed her."
*Arthur's not a gentleman. Nice enough fella like but yer deffo
wouldn't call 'im a gentleman.*
"Thanks a lot Doctor."
Well that's okay anyway. Ev knows so she'll be in soon to see me.
That'll give 'er time to phone Kevin Mc, tell 'im what's 'appened
and maybe arrange for 'im to come to Skem and pick my ticket
up. 'E can sell it on to somebody so I won't lose any money. I
know a mate of 'is was after one.
"Hello Peter. How are you mate? Been in the wars eh?"
Shit, Mally! Wouldn't yer fuckin' know it? Fuckin' 'ell he saw my
horrendous skids.
"Eh Mally, listen, about that bookin' on Sunday. I know yer didn't
mean anythin' nasty by it. Just frustration an' that wasn't it? I tell
yer what, I won't put it in. I don't want yer payin' a fine just for
callin' me "Egg on legs." We'll just forget about it eh, okay?"
"Fair enough Peter, that's no problem. The other lads were saying
you were the shittest ref we've had this season but I told them you
weren't that good."
Yer takin' the fuckin' piss now! Don't fuckin' milk it!
"Okay Mally. Nice one."
"They were telling me to mark you 1 out of 10 but I stuck up for
you. I said at least your kit was clean so that's worth two marks
alone. So that's what I marked you - 2 out of 10."
Yer not just milkin' it now - yer fuckin' creamin' it.
"Okay. Do me a favour though; don't mention those 'orrible
fuckin' bills to anybody will yer?"
"Peter, referees shouldn't swear! Richie doesn't swear!"
Yeah, but Richie doesn't drink, doesn't smoke, doesn't go with

loose women and makes all 'is own dresses. Now fuck off yer 'airy piss takin' twat!

"Yeah, sorry Mal. Yer won't say anythin' about me skids though will yer?"

"Okay Pete. You owe me though."

I'm lettin' yer off with the fuckin' bookin' aren't I? What fuckin' more d'yer want Dracula - fuckin' blood? Yeah, I suppose yer do don't yer?

"That's fair enough Mal."

I'll owe yer for the next match I ref yer. After that I'll book yer just for walkin' on the pitch.

"Mally, any chance of somethin' to eat mate? I've 'ad nothin' all day."

"No, sorry, you're nil by mouth."

No I'm not; I'm Peter Evo.

"What d'yer mean Mal?"

"Because you're concussed and under observation we can't allow you anything to eat or drink in case you bring it back up. You can have small sips of water to take your medication."

You are fuckin' jokin' aren't yer?

"I was in 'ospital with concussion a few years ago Mally and it wasn't like that then."

"Things have changed now Peter."

Oh I'll just fuckin' starve to death then shall I? Never mind, Ev'll be 'ere soon she'll bring me somethin' in.

"Okay Mal, fair enough."

"Right, I'm finishing my shift soon. I'll try to make your stay here as comfortable as possible."

Fuck off!

It was fuckin' hard work watching all the owld fellas eating at teatime. Even the ones in to have their Farmer Giles sorted were having at least *something* to eat. Hang on! Maybe this was a plot by Mally to exact his revenge. Maybe cutting my cock off was against medical ethics. THIS was his revenge - starving me to death! I'd thwart his dastardly plan! I'd just seen Nurse

Hardknock passing. She looked a right battleaxe but she wasn't going to deny a man in need was she?

"Nurse, can I 'ave somethin' to eat please? I'm starvin'."

"Of course Peter. I'll just go and fetch you a chicken curry from the kitchen. I'll bring some apple pie and ice cream too for your pudding."

LIKE FUCK SHE SAID THAT!

She answered me with just three words. Yes, you've guessed: "NIL BY MOUTH."

Twat!

Anyway, where's Ev. It's five o'clock now and no sign of her. She shoulda been well 'ere by now. What's 'appened to me Man U ticket?

Ev, being Ev, turned up at seven o'clock. It was instant hard on material for me when she walked in. She had a pair of black boots on (ah, what memories I have of those), the miniest of white leather mini-skirts with a red leather coat over it, the top couple of buttons open to reveal her skimpy low cut top, her puppies straining at the leash to be free of it and their constraining half-cup bra.

"What are yer dressed like that for?"

"I thought I'd cheer yer up."

"Yer've cheered me up and the rest of this fuckin' ward too! D'yer realise I've brought the average age of this ward down to about seventy-six? The poor owld gets'll be 'avin' 'eart attacks!"

Ev bent over to kiss me. I looked around and all the geriatrics (is he a German striker?) were feasting their eyes on Ev's skimpy black knicks - making the same tents in their beds as I was. Dirty owld gets! I don't suppose I could blame them though.

"Wher've yer been anyway?"

"I phoned the ozzy and they told me to come in at visiting time so I did."

"Yeah, there was visitin' this afternoon too so yer coulda come then."

"I phoned this mornin' an' they told me yer were comfortable so I thought I'd leave it 'til tonight."

"Well of course they'd tell yer I was fuckin' comfortable! They say that about every fucker! Yer could 'ave a cut finger or be at death's fuckin' door 'avin' the last rites and they tell everybody that asks yer comfortable. Comfortable could mean fuckin' anythin'! Comfortable anyway? What's fuckin' comfortable? I'm not comfortable! I've 'ad fuck all to eat all day an' I'm trussed up in a pair of fuckin' pyjamas I'll need a bastard shoehorn to get out of. Yer didn't go out an' buy me a pair of pyjamas did yer?"
"No."
"Now why doesn't that fuckin' surprise me?"
"Well yer don't wear pyjamas at 'ome."
"Think abarr it Ev - I can't fuckin' sleep in me knack in ozzy can I?"
"Well they told me on the phone they'd supply them."
"Yeah, but look at what they've fuckin' give me!"
"It would 'ave been a waste of money anyway. Yer'll be out soon."
Yeah, like that fuckin' skirt was a waste of money. Paying thirty bob in Ethel Austin's for that when yer could've bought a fuckin' belt the same size for twenty-five pence!
"Right, okay. Yer 'aven' brought me anythin' to eat either 'ave yer?"
"No."
I fuckin' hate you!
"Why the fuck not?"
"I asked them should I bring anythin' in and they said nil by mouth or somethin' like that!"
"Well yer shoulda took no fuckin' notice! Ev, I'm Hank Marvin' 'ere!"
"Who's Hank Marvin?"
"Fuckin' forget it!"
Then she hit me with the coup de grace (that's not a sharp instrument by the way).
"I gave Mr. Appleton yer ticket for the match."
"What?"
"'E called abarr five o'clock for 'is insurance money. 'E said 'e wanted to go the match but didn't 'ave a ticket. I told 'im you were

supposed to be goin' but yer were in ozzy so yer wouldn't be able to make it. 'E asked could 'e ave the ticket so I gave it to 'im."

"Mr. Appleton's a Man United supporter!"

"I know but you can't go so I thought 'e might as well 'ave it, save it goin' to waste."

"I don't fuckin' believe this! *You* sold *my* ticket to a *Man United supporter*?"

"No."

"Yer just said yer did."

"I didn't. I didn't sell it to 'im - I *gave* it to 'im."

"Nah, yer takin' the piss now. Yer only messin' aren't yer Ev? Yer phoned Kevin an' told 'im I couldn't go. 'E came up to Skem, bought the ticket off yer and then passed it on to 'is mate who was after one. That's what 'appened wasn't it?"

"No, honest, I gave it to Mr. Appleton."

Further argument was pointless. I was banging my head against a very large brick wall. Besides my head now hurt and I mean PROPERLY hurt! As well as the raging horn I had a raging headache. There was also the very important fact that we were in a hospital. There are lots of nice, sharp objects in hospitals. I didn't fancy a scalpel or something in my eye so I shut up. I was just drifting off to sleep when Jack came in. I felt sorry for Jack. He was so apologetic. I had to keep reassuring the old fella that it wasn't his fault - anybody could skid on that black ice. He insisted on giving Ev a lift home and gave her a few bob to make sure she could come in and visit me or take me home whatever the next day. He didn't bring me any scran or pyjamas though. It was hallelujah time when my next visitor arrived. Pat Asp was another Grimwood loon and I do mean LOON. He was a great laugh, never stopped telling jokes, had an answer for everything but was well and truly loony toons! He had though in his wondrous, splendiferous marvellousment brought me a big gang of sarnies.

"Ee arr Evo. I know what's it's like in 'ere; they never feed yer and it's not as if yer tart ever remembers to bring anythin' in for yer."

Pat got Ev eyes for that. Sound Pat. He didn't bring me any

pyjamas though. Ev stayed behind for a couple of minutes to say ta ra to me in her own inimitable fashion. Tonsil tickling when you're ill is not very good for your constitution. It is good for making tents in your bed though. As her hand slipped ever so gently "accidentally" over my donga I reminded her to dress down a bit the following day. *I* couldn't take much more of this, *never mind* the poor old buggers sharing my incarceration.

As soon as everybody got off I settled down to listen to the match on the radio. We drew nil-nil (quite an appropriate scoreline I suppose in view of the fact I was nil by mouth, but not for much longer - he he he!) in what sounded like quite a decent game. That was a good result at Old Trafford. I was gutted to have missed it. I hadn't missed a trip to Old Trafford (apart from when they were in the Second Division - he he he!) for seven seasons. My only consolation was the thought Mr. Appleton was having as torrid a time in amongst the Liverpool supporters in the Scoreboard End as I'd had in amongst the United supporters in the same end four-and-a-half years previously. I soon put that unkind thought out of my head. Mr. Appleton was a nice old man who didn't deserve anything like that and I hoped he'd be okay. As soon as the match finished it was lights out in Stalag Phillip. I slid under the covers to enjoy my clandestine feast. What was on the sarnies? Ah Pat, you're a fuckin' star! Roast beef and mustard!

HAPPY DAYS!

With my belly full and my headache settling down I gave it a little think about getting away with a five-finger shuffle. Ev had looked as fit as tonight and had turned me on. I'd have to do it in the bed though, as I wasn't allowed out of my temporary prison. Nah, can't risk those telltale stains. That didn't bother the gerries though as there was more shuffling going on in that ward than in Caesar's Palace! Dirty owld gets!

"Nurse, nurse! Bring me a bowl quick! I'm gonna be sick!"
It was three o'clock in the morning and I was yacking like a good 'un.

"What have you been eating? You're supposed to be nil by mouth!"

"Nothin' nurse, honest!"

"You have! Look at that!"

There was indeed the unedifying evidence of bits of beef and bread in the bowl. There were also the obligatory diced carrots although I hadn't had carrots, diced or otherwise, since Christmas.

"Oh me mate just give me a butty nurse. I was starvin'."

"You stupid young man!"

Oh that's very nice of yer to call me young. What am I like - a naughty fuckin' schoolboy?

"I know. I'm sorry nurse."

My own fault I know. I should have stuck to nil by mouth. The medical people know what they're doing and do it for all the right reasons. For me to ignore that was stupid in the extreme. I was bloody starvin' though. I now properly felt like a bag of shite. Hmmm... I'd have to try that one time - get a bag (would it be a paper bag or a plastic carrier bag?) fill it full of shite and then grope round the outside of it to see what it feels like. The Doctor's round later that morning confirmed my worst fears - I was indeed a bag of shite.

"You ignored nil by mouth Mr. Etherington. A very silly thing to do."

"I know Doctor; I have been told."

"We'll have to keep you in for more obs."

Yer just punishin' me for my terrible crime.

"I realise that Doctor."

"You might have been on your way home now if you hadn't ignored nil by mouth."

See, I told yer!

"Yes, I realise that too Doctor."

"Your blood pressure is very high. We can't allow you home until that is normal."

Alright, alright, give us a fuckin' break will yer. I did wrong. Fuck me - the crime of the century or what? No wonder me fuckin' blood pressure's high! Just let me 'ome - there's more chance of it gettin' back to normal there than in this fuckin' hellhole with you lot givin' me all kinds of grief. But then again, I'm only gonna get grief when I go 'ome, so yeah - yer might as well keep me 'ere for the rest of me natural. I'm not checkin' me fuckin' skids every day though!

"Okay Doctor. It won't happen again I promise you."

The Doctor looked as if he was of Middle Eastern origin but I thought it not a good time to tell him about the Arab with amnesia - Mustafa Got.

My ravaged (not ravished - I wish!) body must have been getting back to something approaching normality - if there ever was anything normal where my body's concerned - as I was allowed a little something to eat at teatime. Nothing much like - a little bit of dinner, a couple of slices of bread and an apple but it tasted like a Jacobean banquet to me - not that I've ever been to a Jacobean banquet! The same visitors as the previous night dutifully arrived. Jack was still apologising, Ev had dressed down just a little but was still getting gerry eyes and Pat brought another big bag of sarnies in.

"Ah Pat, I can't eat them mate. Thanks like but I spewed them all back last night and I got a terrible telling off. They fed me a bit at teatime but said that was all I was allowed now 'til tomorrow. I wanna escape from 'ere as soon as poss so I'd better do as I'm told."

"Okay Pete. We'll eat them then."

They did too! The fat bastards sat round my bed munching away on turkey sarnies while I was fuckin' starvin'!

BOLLOCKS!

I loved my Ma but she was the very last person I wanted to see right now.

"I believe yer've been in a car accident son."

No Ma, I'm lyin' 'ere for the good of me fuckin' 'ealth!

"Yeah Mam. I'm okay now though. I'll be out tomorrow."

I knew what was coming next:

"Did yer 'ave clean underwear on?"
No Ma, I'd 'ad me skidunkers on for a week and there were fuckin'
big skid marks all over them!
"Yeah I did Mam."
"Well that's alright then."
Oh yeah, of course it's fuckin' alright! It doesn't matter 'ow 'urt I
was like. It doesn't matter that me 'ead feels like it's got a fuckin'
rock in it. It doesn't matter that I coulda been killed. In fact it
might 'ave been better if I'd been killed: I did 'ave clean sweats
on after all. No, deffo, all that matters is that I 'ad clean grunds
on.
"I know Mam. I always listened to you Mam. I always check me
underwear's clean before I go out."
"Ah, yer a good lad Peter. Isn't 'e a good lad Ev?"
Piss off Mam! I'm TWENTY-three not three!

It was getting on for midnight that night when I realised I hadn't
had a poo for nearly two days. Now that wasn't normal! I'd had
hardly anything to eat like but still and all the owld innards
shoulda been working better than that. I was a bit too
embarrassed and didn't want to feel like a gerry to ask a nurse for
help with a commode (still wasn't allowed out of bed) so I
decided I could hold on 'til morning. WRONG! I woke about
three o'clock absolutely bursting for a number two.
"Nurse, I need the toilet."
She brought me one of those funny piss bottles that really look
like they should be musical instruments rather than a urine
receptacle.
"Err…no nurse, it's err…a number two I need."
"Oh right. I'll help you on to the commode."
I'd never felt so embarrassed in all my life. Even through the
curtained screens my red face must have lit up the darkened ward
as I farted, splurted and cacked my way through the next five
minutes. Have you ever tried using one of those commodes? I tell
you what; it takes great feats of ingenuity, balance, bravery and
nerve to master it. Respect to you gerries for that! I'll tell you this

too; if those nurses were on a million pound a week it wouldn't be enough. They really must see some terrible sights. For this particular nurse the sight and smell of my poo, which had been building up for over two days remember, was almost too much. The poor nurse visibly flinched as she took the bedpan from the commode to empty it. Seriously, and no pun intended, that really is a shitty job. Seriously too, I do really feel for NHS medical staff. Overworked, understaffed and underpaid. Maybe one day this country will find a government willing to pay these people what they're worth but I doubt it.

I made good my escape the following day with the medical warning that I should take it easy for a few days, put my feet up and maybe only return to work on Monday. Against wifely advice I passed myself fit, having taken the Evo medical and fitness test, to attend the following day's match against Derby at Anfield. Bring it on!

CHAPTER FIFTEEN

HORSES FOR COURSES

A goal down at half-time to Derby so who did we send for? Joey! Well, Tosh equalised but Joey it was who put us ahead with one of his specials. Only trouble about Joey's three goals for us so far was that they'd all been scored at the Anny Road end. The Kop were dying for him to score one at our end. For all he went bonkers when he scored at the Road end and ran down towards us anyway we wanted him to score one in front of us. I'm sure Joey felt that way too. Keegan wrapped the win up for us with the third goal five minutes from time.

FA Cup draws were being kind to us. We faced Second Division Oldham Athletic in Round 5 at Anfield. We won quite comfortably with goals from Case, Keegan and a Phil Neal penalty. We were now ready for our biggest test of the season - the European Cup Quarter-Final against St. Etienne of France. "Les Verts" (The Greens) as their fans called them were a fine side. They had lost, very unluckily, 0-1 to Bayern Munich in the previous season's European Cup Final at Hampden Park and were strongly tipped to win this season's competition. We lost the game 0-1 through a goal by Bathenay. That was not at all a bad result in the circs. With the crowd behind us in the second leg we were all hopeful of turning the game round. It would, however, be a very stiff task. Lads who went to St. Etienne spoke of the very intimidating atmosphere. Bread was in very short supply in the UK at the time due to a strike, I think, by bakers. Apparently the French hoolies were throwing bread at our lads. They deffo weren't getting thrown back though! A lad I know who went, Derek Keir, told me that the Reds there were singing, "You're not gettin' yer bread back. You're not gettin' yer bread back da da da da da da da da!" Our crowd wouldn't be throwing anything at anybody other than a wall of noise at the St. Etienne players. If the St. Etienne fans thought they'd created an intimidating atmosphere in France then they ain't seen nothing yet!

The game against Newcastle was notable for two things; one of them the shape of the future, the other a very sad moment for one of our players. This match was the first one to be sponsored at Anfield. Bell's Scotch Whisky were the benefactors on this occasion. Bell's had for years been involved in football sponsorship through their Managerial awards. Steve Heighway scored as early as the 11th minute to secure victory. All this however was overshadowed by a very serious knee injury to Phil Thompson that was to keep him out for the rest of the season. That was tough on Thommo as he had become a real stalwart of our defence. Thommo's physique belied his strength. His greatest ability though was reading the game. He hardly ever put a foot wrong, knowing just when to tackle and when to jockey. His partnership in central defence with Emlyn was rock solid (apart from the nightmare at Villa Park) and he would be sadly missed in the quest for the Treble - that was for sure.

The Treble bid went slightly off the rails however the following midweek when we lost 0-1 at Tottenham. Ipswich drew 1-1 the same night at home to Newcastle. We were top on 40 points but Ipswich were right behind us trailing by only a point, with two games in hand and a superior goal difference that was worth another point in itself. Ipswich kept the pressure up with a 1-0 home win against Bristol City. For our part, we put ourselves in great heart for the return against St. Etienne with a great 1-0 victory at Middlesbrough. The game against the crack French team really was going to be our biggest for years. Most people saw St. Etienne as possibly the best team left in the competition. Everybody connected with us; players, management team and most of all the fans felt that if we could win this tie then we would go on to win the European Cup. It was going to be bloody tough though!

I left for the match straight from work at five o'clock with my boss Alan Bowen, his young son Alan and Alan junior's mate. They were going in the paddock. I took my place in the queue for the Kop, the end of which was outside the King Harry. You could tell it was going to be a special night as the air was crackling with tension and excitement. The queue seemed to be moving very slowly. I was beginning to worry whether or not I would get in. At six o'clock all hell broke loose, as there were rumours that the gates at the Anfield Road end were shut. I was near the arches by now and was making a determined push to get in. The dreaded bell rang to signal that the gates were shutting and with one last huge effort I just about managed to get through the turnstile before the gate slammed shut behind me. Strange, when I think back, that matches of this magnitude were not made all-ticket. Snowy didn't get in even though he had a ticket for the Kemlyn Road such was the confusion and pandemonium. Once inside the Kop I pushed and shoved my way towards my usual spec in the middle. There were over 55,000 people in the ground creating an electric atmosphere. St. Etienne had brought 6,000 supporters with them, but I'm sure a lot of them didn't get in, as there were many Reds in the half of the Anny Road allocated to the Frenchmen. Some lads had risked their lives by climbing on to the Anny Road end roof; it was that sort of night. The pre-match conversation centred on the need to score at least two goals to be sure of winning the tie, whilst also having to be very careful not to concede a dreaded away goal. St. Etienne had shown enough in the first leg to suggest they were quite capable of scoring at Anfield. Players such as Janvion, Bathenay and Rochetau were among the best in Europe at the time. Also up for discussion was whether John Tosh would play or possibly be replaced by Davy. Tosh had been kicked to bits by, and had made little impression against, the Argentinian centre-half Oscar Piazza in the first leg; not for nothing was Piazza known as "The Wild Bull of the Pampas". The fact that Piazza had been booked in that game for kicking Tosh and was therefore suspended from the second leg probably got John the vote.

The St. Etienne fans were singing, "Allez Les Verts" prompting the Kopites to reply, "Allez Les Rouges." A huge banner in the

Kop read, "Joey Eats Frog's Legs." The players came out to a tumultuous, ear-splitting reception from all around the ground. Kevin Keegan was back after missing the game in France through injury. We were all hoping Kevin was the man to win the tie for us. Emlyn Hughes won the toss and elected, obviously, to kick towards the Anny Road in the first half. We won a corner in the second minute, which was played short by Steve Heighway to Kevin Keegan. Kevin floated a cross in to the penalty area, which deceived goalkeeper Curkovic and nestled nicely in the far top corner of the net. Mayhem ensued as we celebrated wildly; a breakthrough so early on was much more than we could have hoped for. St. Etienne gradually clawed their way back in to the game, spurred on by the magnificent Bathenay. Clem had to make two fine saves; one of them, from a blistering shot by Rocheteau, was probably his best ever - even topping the penalty save in Dresden the previous season. For our part we were worryingly missing good chances and half time arrived with no further breakthrough.

Five minutes into the second half Bathenay scored with a superb, dipping twenty-five yard shot. We were now going to have to score another two goals to win the tie and with their defence being brilliantly organised it seemed we were heading out of the European Cup. Liverpool, however, were made of stern stuff and roared on by every Red in the crowd, and I do mean everyone, not just the Kop, we continued to hammer away at the French defence. Reward was gained in the fifty-ninth minute when Tosh flicked on Cally's cross for Ray Kennedy to score with a low shot. Game on!

With fifteen minutes left to play the tired, battered and injured Tosh was withdrawn to be replaced by Davy. Davy immediately caused problems with his lightning speed. The crowd were roaring on every Liverpool attack but with time slipping away it seemed all our efforts would be in vain.

With six minutes to go Razor played a long ball down the left. Davy used his searing pace to get on to it, rounded three defenders and shot low past Curkovic. The place went absolutely mental! I swear I have never seen anything like it. I was celebrating like a mad man. The Kop was a mass of heaving, jumping, wriggling, barmy bodies. Davy had ran towards the Paddock and was besieged by the rest of our players, Emlyn being particularly animated as only he could when celebrating one of our goals. Going just as mental in a bed at Park House Nursing Home in Waterloo was Phil Thompson who was recovering from his knee injury. Phil later said his screams were that loud two nurses came rushing into his room thinking he had done himself a further injury. Once everybody in the crowd got their breath back, "You'll Never Walk Alone" bellowed all around the ground. Nobody in the ground was sitting down. People in the Kemlyn were standing on their seats singing and dancing.
The most almighty roar I have ever heard in my life followed the final whistle.
"Liverpool are magic", sang the Kop, and indeed we were; players and supporters. To overcome a team as good as St. Etienne was really a great feat. In any other season they would have won the trophy I'm sure.
WE'RE GONNA WIN THE EUROPEAN CUP!

We met First Division opposition for the first time in the Cup run in the shape of Middlesbrough. We had again been drawn at home. A crowd of nearly 56,000 - even bigger than the attendance for the St. Etienne match was in attendance. Boro', roared on by a large, vociferous support gave us plenty of problems in the first half. Second half goals from Fairclough and Keegan put us into the semi-final. Outshining everybody though was Tommy Smith. The old war-horse had been brought out of almost semi-retirement to plug the massive gap left by Thommo's injury-enforced absence. I don't suppose renewing centre-back acquaintances with Emlyn was high on Tommy's list of most wanted but I'm sure he was more than grateful to be playing a part in the exciting climax to his last season. Tommy had stated quite clearly that he intended to retire at the end of the season. To that end Tommy's Testimonial match had been arranged: to be played two days after the European Cup Final. All Reds were hoping that was just one of three trophies we'd be parading that night.

Everton were also doing well in Cup competitions. They were in the middle of three games against Aston Villa to decide the Football League Cup Final. The second of these games had been played at Hillsborough on the same night as we'd played St. Etienne. They had also played on the same day as we'd beaten Boro' - disposing of Derby County in their Quarter-Final tie. Hopes were that both clubs could be kept apart to possibly produce the first ever all-Merseyside Cup Final. Those hopes were firmly dashed on Monday lunchtime. Yes, that's when they used to do the FA Cup draws, and at Lancaster Gate, FA Headquarters, too, not in a TV studio! The FA Cup Semi-Final dress rehearsal at Goodison Park was a dull affair finishing goalless. As an exercise in sussing out opponents strengths and weaknesses nothing much was gained by either side to take into the match at Maine Road. One player who hadn't played in the Goodison match we would have to watch though was Duncan McKenzie. Duncan was a slippery eel of a player whose tricks, turns, undoubted skill and match-winning ability could well trouble our defence. He was a bit flash for manager Gordon Lee's liking but the Evertonians loved him. Speaking of which there were some marvellous Evertonianisms doing the rounds. One of them was that McKenzie was a better player than Keegan. Hmmm...think not! Neither did Don Revie who had Kevin as a regular in the England side whilst Duncan wasn't even thought of. Duncan was a fine player, no doubt, but he was no Keegan. The funniest one I thought however was their assertion that the League Cup was harder to win than the European Cup because you had to play more rounds in it. Now, come on! I'm not even giving that one a think!

The 3-1 home win against Leeds on Grand National morning was a piece of piss. Our old foes were nothing like the force they had been in the Revie era. It was quite sad to see them languishing in mid-table really considering some of the epic battles, on and off the pitch, we'd had against them. The day was about to get better. I went to Ma's after the match. Mam was busy picking out her 28 each-way selections for the National. There was only one horse Dad was backing. Dad was convinced Red Rum was gonna win his third National.

"Yer 'avin' a bet son?"

"Nah Dad, I'm boracic lint."

"Ee arr, 'ere's ten bob. Put it on Red Rum; it's gonna piss it."

"Okay, ta Dad. 'Ow much are yer 'avin' on it?"

"Just the same ten bob Peter."

I thought that was strange. Dad had backed Rummy with a good deal more money than that on its two previous National wins.

"Come on son. Let's go an' put these on. I'll buy yer a bevy in the Corry."

"Ee arr John, put these on for me."

Ma handed Dad a sheaf of betting slips you could have reprinted War and Peace on.

Dad put my half a quid on for me, put War and Peace on for me Ma and then put his on - two pound win on Red Rum.

"Thought yer were only puttin' ten bob on Dad."

"That was for yer Ma's benefit. She woulda gone mad if she knew I was puttin' two quid on. Never tell them 'ow much yer puttin' on. Never tell them 'ow much yer win either. Sometimes don't tell them you've won or even 'ad a bet at all. In fact, best to tell them fuck all about anything, ever!"

Dad was by now in early retirement from work through ill health. I thought back to the days when I was a kid and he was working. It was nothing for him to put a week's wages on one horse. Of course more often than not the horse would lose. That would mean untold hardship for us all at home for the next week. Dad wasn't the only man to do it though; that happened in plenty of households. It was just the way it was back then. Dad had obviously toned his betting down a lot now but I could see his point in not telling Ma how much he'd put on. I liked a little bet myself now and again but only on a very small scale. I'd bet on the National and maybe a couple of other times a year but that was about it. Andy Pandy was the big pre-race favourite and had in fact been backed down to 11-2. Rummy was twelve-years-old and carrying a bit of weight so started the race at 9-1, a price he'd been when winning his first National - a good omen. We watched the race in the Corry. Four fences from home it was clear the winner was either gonna be Rummy or Churchtown Boy. Rummy took advantage of his rival's stumble at the third last to romp home a winner by twenty-five lengths. Dad and me went mental. Dad then rushed over to the bookies to collect our winnings. He returned half-an-hour later with the dosh.

"Shoulda seen the queues in there Peter. Everybody musta been on it! They've stopped payin' out now. They're tellin' people to come back at five o'clock or on Monday mornin'."

"Good job yer got ours now then eh Dad. 'Ow much did me Mam win?"

"Fuck all!"

"What, she didn't 'ave Red Rum in all those bets?"

"She didn't even 'ave a place!" I'll give 'er a few bob though."

"Worra yer 'avin Dad?"

"What d'yer think I'm 'avin' lad? A TREBLE RUM!"

"Two treble rums please luv."

"Evelyn'll kill you when yer get 'ome."

"Ah, I'm not bothered Dad. I'll be well drunk by then."

The day just kept getting better. Ipswich had lost 1-2 at Manchester City. That all meant we were now top with 45 points. Ipswich, their games in hand now played, were second with 43 points and their goal difference was now only one better than ours. Manchester City were third on 42 points and with a game in hand on both us and Ipswich.

Dad and me staggered along the entry between the back gardens of Fernhill Road and Grogan Square. We then both promptly fell over Dad's back garden wall. Dad was twenty squid better off. I was quite happy with my flim.

"Come on Lil, get ready girl. I'll take yer the ODVA."

"In a minute. Won a fiver eh big licks? Smashin'!"

"In a minute" was one of me Ma's favourite sayings. Ask her to do anything and Lily would say, "In a minute" whether she was gonna to do it in five seconds time or five hours time!

"I won a fiver too Mam!"

Why didn't I listen to my Dad? Telling Mam was my biggest mistake.

"You make sure you tell Evelyn 'ow much you won too Peter."

"I will Mam, honest."

"Well make sure yer do 'cos I'll be tellin' 'er next time I see 'er."

Snitch!

"Okay Mam."

My rum riddled brain was desperately trying to work out just how much I should tell Ev I'd won. She would probably guess I'd won something due to the advancement of my inebriation; trick would be telling her what she would believe. Mind you, there shouldn't be a problem - she never believed anything I ever told her anyway! I couldn't tell her I'd won a flim. I'd spent nearly half of it by now anyway and she would surely have the other half off me. Ah, bollocks to it! Let the truth be told - for once! What am I - a man or a mouse?

SQUEAK, SQUEAK!

I could hardly believe my eyes when Ev opened the door to me. She had a lovely red dress on. All the war paint was in place. Her hair was beautifully done. In fact she looked ready for a night out.

"Why're yer all dressed up Ev?"

"I've been waitin' for yer to come 'ome. I 'ad a bet on Red Rum an' got two pound back. Come on; let's go over the Derby Arms. Lena's mindin' the kids."

"Oh, okay Ev, Ta. Yer a jammy get. One bloody bet a year yer 'ave an' yer come up. Nice one though."

"Did you 'ave a bet?"

"Nah Ev, I was Bernie Flint. Me Dad won a few bob though. 'E took me to the Corry for a bevy."

Alright, call me a bad man. There was no point telling her now I'd won a few bob seeing as she'd already won was there? Besides, I didn't wanna steal her thunder. It made a change for her to pay for the ale. We were having a great time in the Derby. Ev was quite happy to pay for the ale and best of all I'd be able to stash the dosh and use it to go to Stoke on Easter Monday. A few little white lies, nobody was hurt - happy days! We were both well bladdered by the time we fell into bed. I was Tommy Stack and Ev was Red Rum as we re-enacted the big race. Mind you, it took us a bit longer than ten minutes to pass the finishing post!

The warm glow of post-coital harmony was about to make me tell all. I didn't get the chance.

"Peter, I've got a confession to make."

"What's that Ev?"

"I won four pound, not two."

"No problem Ev. Why didn't yer tell me yer won four squid then?"

"I thought yer'd get a cob on 'cos I'd put forty pence on a 'orse."

"Nah. Yer took us out anyway didn't yer an' yer've got a few bob left for yerself so that's okay. Yer shouldn't really tell me lies like but I still love yer."

"I love you too. Come on let's go to sleep."

I'm a bastard aren't I?

We won the first leg of the European Cup semi-final in Switzerland against FC Zurich very easily even after conceding an early goal from a Risi penalty. Phil Neal equalised that goal. Steve Heighway put us ahead and Phil completed the victory from the penalty spot.

The game against Manchester City was a brutal affair. Keegan gave us the lead just before half-time. Brian Kidd equalised this goal and promptly caused a near riot, giving the ups to the Kop after he'd scored. We had the last laugh; Steve Heighway scoring the goal that gave us a vital victory.

I was in buoyant mood when I got back to Ma's. Ev was there with the kids. I was hoping we could get off quite early, get home, sort a babysitter and go for a drink or three. Lily was about to scupper all plans and drop me in the deepest of deep shit.

"What did yer do with that fiver yer won on Red Rum Peter? Did yer give it to Ev for some new clothes for the kids?"

Oh, fuckin' bollocks! How the fuck was I gonna lie my way out of this one. I looked to Dad for inspiration. No chance. He just scuttled off after throwing me a quick glance muttering something about being caught short.

"You said yer didn't 'ave a bet!"

"Well, yer know, err Ev, I err didn't really. It was err like me Dad's money."

"Yeah but you kept the money didn't yer Peter? Yer went for a bevy with yer Dad and kept the rest."

Fuck off will yer Ma, yer've got me in enough shit already. Giz a fuckin' break will yer. What's the matter - don't yer love me anymore?

"Well err, yeah, sort of."

It was no good. Ma had dropped me in the shite but I was digging myself so much further into it I'd be in Australia soon. Stop digging Evo.

"Yeah okay. Me Dad gave me 'alf a quid for a bet. I put it on Red Rum. I won a flim. I spent 'alf of it in the Corry with me Dad an' I kept the other 'alf. What's wrong with that?"

Everything.

Ev wasn't gonna 'ave a go at me in front of Ma but I'd get it in fuckin' spades when I got home. The journey home was conducted in complete silence save for the kids playing up running up and down the bus. I was banished to the back of the bus whilst Ev and the kids were at the front. I had a plan. It would only delay the grief I was certain to get and would probably lead

to a whole lot more but it was the only plan I had. I walked down
the bus just before it stopped at the Alex. Our stop, the Derby
Arms, was the next one down.

"Ev, look, I'm sorry. Don't give me the silent treatment."

"Fuck off."

That was just the response I'd expected, hoped for even.

"Bollocks to this I'm goin' for a pint."

I'd timed it just right and was able to dive straight off the bus and
into the Alex before Ev had the chance to give me a volley. I
watched Match of the Day in there knowing I'd have no chance
whatsoever at home. I went home when I thought it would be safe
and everybody would be in bed. I crept silently up the stairs and
into bed being careful not to wake Ev up. The plan was working
so far. I crept out the following morning to go refereeing. I hoped
I wouldn't get any shit today: I just wasn't in the mood for it. I was
refereeing a Premier Division game, The Tanner versus The
Highwayman, so there was every chance I would. It was the first
offside decision I gave when I heard it:

"Eh yer pancake!"

"Excuse me, what did you say?"

"I called yer a pancake. That was never offside!"

"Yes it was."

"I waited before I played the pass to make sure he was onside."

"Well you waited too long. He was offside."

"Pancake."

"If you call me a pancake again I'll have to book you"

"Pancake."

"Can I have your full name please?"

"Joey Laycock."

"This is an official caution. If you commit a further cautionable
offence you will be dismissed from the field of play for persisting
in misconduct after having received a caution."

"'As your missus been givin' you a 'ard time?"

"Yeah, she 'as actually."

"Well don't fuckin' take it out on me!"

"Yer did call me a pancake Joey."

"Okay, I'm fuckin' sorry. Can I get on with the game now and start playin' football?"

"Please do."

And what a player! Joey could hit a ball from midfield forty or fifty yards and drop it right at the feet of a forward or winger. He was a joy to watch but a fucker to referee. He never left you alone from minute one. He was fair though and backed me on occassions if he thought I was right, telling his teammates to get off my back and let me get on with the game. I had a good rapport with Joey - even if he did call me a pancake! The Tanner won 4-0. Joey scored two of the goals and laid on the other two.

"Good game Peter. Yer 'andled that well."

"You said I was a pancake!"

"Ah take no fuckin' notice of me. Yer comin' for a bevy with us? We're all goin' to Richmond 'Ouse."

"Yeah, might as well Joey. Fuck all to go 'ome for only a load of grief."

This was the part of refereeing I was really getting to love - having a bevy with the players after the game. They could be calling me all the names under the sun but it was all forgotten after the game. Sure, they'd be pointing out my mistakes but for the most part I'd be congratulated on handling the game well. Having a drink with the players was a good way of getting to know how they operated, how their minds worked, their little idiosyncrasies etcetera. This was all good information to have for future reference. Mostly, if the players knew you were a decent bloke off the pitch they were less likely to give you a hard time on it. That's my theory anyway. My excuse if you like. Not that I've ever needed an excuse for a bevy! I stayed out for as long as I could, that is 'til I'd spent the last of my £3 match fee before heading for the mother of all grief. By this time I was well and truly pancaked. If I could just get home and get to bed - no dinner, I'd been a naughty boy - then sleep 'til morning I might be able to delay grief for a while longer. I'd creep out early and get to town for the Crown's coach to Stoke. I had my little stash from the Rummy winnings so I'd be okay. Yeah, good plan that. I might even be able to delay the grief 'til Tuesday afternoon seeing as I was on earlies. Walking up Willow Hey I thought somebody's dinner smells good. Ain't fuckin' mine though. I'd 'ave to put up with making myself a bit of toast before I scampered off to bed to avoid the Great Goddess of Grief. That's strange, it's coming from our house! Deffo, yeah, opened the door and there was a lovely smell of roast dinner. Not mine though; she must have done it for herself and the kids but I'd be getting fuck all, I'd been a bad lad remember.

"Sit down and eat yer dinner."

"What?"

"You 'eard."

Laid before me was a feast fit for a king: Bernard Matthews Turkey Roast - that was gorgeous - I loved it; gangs and gangs of roasties - loved them too; veg all over the place. I didn't know whether to eat it or climb it! All topped off by Ev's special cockroach gravy. Ev was fuckin' shit at making gravy. There would always be big black lumps in it that the kids used to call cockroaches. It didn't spoil this dinner. Ev would never have made a Cordon Bleu chef but she could do a decent roast dinner when she had a mind too. She'd pulled out all the stops on this one. What was it all in aid of though? I just couldn't work it out. She wasn't speaking to me after all and I was due a shedful of grief.

"Thanks Ev. It looks lovely that."

I moved towards Ev to give her a little kiss. She shied away from me.

"Ee arr, what's that all about? Yer make me a lovely dinner and then push me away."

"I'm leavin' yer."

"Yer what?"

"You 'eard. I'm leavin' yer. I'm takin' the kids and stayin' at our John's or our Linda's 'til I can get somewhere to live off the Council down there."

"Oh don't be fuckin' stupid Ev! Yer can't fuckin' leave me just 'cos I didn't tell yer I'd won on the 'orses!"

"I can and I am. That was bad yer keepin' that money from me. Yer just like yer Dad you."

Well that's 'ardly fuckin' surprisin' is it seein' as I'm 'is fuckin' son yer stupid fuckin' mare! Of course I'm like 'im in certain ways but 'ave yer ever 'ad no money for a week 'cos I'd lost all me fuckin' wages on a 'orse? The answer to that one's fuckin' no! 'Ave yer ever 'ad to go fuckin' grovellin' an' snivellin' to bastard fuckin' rip off moneylenders to feed the kids for a week? The answer to that one's fuckin' no too! So if yer gonna go just fuck off and get out me fuckin' sight!

"Ah, come on Ev, I'm sorry. Please don't go." (Donald Peers 1969)

"I'm goin'."

"Well 'ow come yer done me a lovely dinner. What's that all about?"

"I wanted to make sure yer 'ad yer dinner before I left."

"Yer a strange fuckin' woman you Ev. I love yer to death but yer fuckin' strange."

"Well yer don't love me enough."

"I can't fuckin' love yer any more than I do."

"It doesn't matter. I'm goin'. Yer needn't think yer goin' to Stoke tomorrow either. I found yer little fuckin' stash so I'm takin' that with me. Yer shoulda give me it last week an' this wouldn't 'ave 'appened, but no, yer had to think yer were bein' clever didn't yer. I took yer out an' yer let me spend me money knowin' you 'ad loads yerself."

Pointless arguing any more with her. I'd rather have had a chisel in my head than this. I kissed the kids ta ra. The dinner was there before me. Little point it going to waste so I walloped it before going to bed to hopefully sleep it all off. Perhaps it had all been a bad dream, I'd wake up and Ev would be at my side.

I woke up early having set the alarm for the trip to Stoke. I went to retrieve my little Stoke stash. Shit, she had taken it after all! Back to bed for a few hours. The house was as silent as the grave. It would normally be filled with the sounds of the kids playing and laughing. Ev would be screaming at and laughing with them in equal measure. I was missing them already. Maybe she'd come to her senses, realise I hadn't knocked an old lady over the head and robbed her handbag, then come back to me, where she belonged. Ev had done this in our early days in Skem, that was for sure and was probably understandable as she had terrible trouble settling. She had come back then but this was different. There was a different feel to this that told me she probably wouldn't be back. This feeling made me sick to my stomach. Here I was all alone in this empty house, nursing a big, fat hangover, head the size of Birkenhead, listening to a match I should have been at and missing the wife and kids I loved so much. The question is - why? What had I done that was so terribly wrong? Was that fair? Was life fair? We drew 0-0 at Stoke. That wasn't fair either - we were all over them.

I hauled myself to work for the rest of the week - earlies isn't the best shift to be on when your head's as chocker as mine was - and just about got through it. Ev hadn't been in touch at all. I'd given up all hope of her actually coming back to me but she would surely have to show her face soon to arrange payments for the kids and to collect clothes etc. I couldn't wait for the week to end and get to the match against Arsenal to get my mind off all this.

The 2-0 win over Arsenal certainly did take my mind off things for a couple of hours or so. We were absolutely superb: real Championship material. Neal and Keegan scored but the margin of victory should have been far greater. I went straight home after the match preferring not to face the inevitable barrage of questions from Mam who would by now have heard the jungle drums about my latest split from Ev. Besides, Ma wasn't exactly my favourite person at the moment. Of course I loved her to death and she hadn't dropped me in the shit for malicious purposes I was sure but nevertheless she had done and it hurt. Guy Fawkes had nothing on Lily Evo! Okay, it was my fault in the first place for being a dickhead but I didn't deserve what I was getting now.

I didn't have enough money to go for a bevy so it would be a lonely night in front of the telly with the likes of Larry Grayson, Bruce Forsyth, Cilla Black, Jimmy Tarbuck and Mike Yarwood to keep me company. Oh fuckin' marvellous! As I was about to open the front door I could hear muffled noises from within. Shit, that was all I needed for Bobby the Burglar to be paying me a visit right now.

"Hiya Dad!"

"Hiya Dad!"

I was so glad to see the kids again I didn't realise Ev was sitting on a corner of the couch.

"Hiya Big."

"Hiya."

"'Ave yer come for some clothes an' that?"

"No, I've come back."

"'Ave yer, really, for good?"

"Well, 'til you pull a bloody stunt like that again."

"Look, I'm sorry, but I don't really think I did that much bad."

"'Ave yer learned any lessons while I've been away?"

"Yeah, 'ow to make decent chips. Want me to teach yer?"

"Yer a bloody cheeky get!"

"Ev, look, if we fall out again please feel free to just twat me dead 'ard over the 'ead with somethin' dead 'eavy."

"I might just keep yer to that."

"Honestly, it's better than the Tremeloes treatment."

"What's that?"

"Silence is golden."

"Piss off!"

"No seriously, getting a bonce full of metal hurts for a day or two maybe but when yer leave it's like yer rippin' me 'eart out. I'm nothin' without you an' the kids Ev an' yer know it. What made yer come back?"

"Because I love yer. Yer might be a bastard but yer my bastard."

"Fair enough."

CHAPTER SIXTEEN

A TREBLE CHANCE

The second leg against FC Zurich was little more than a formality anyway after the brilliant result in Switzerland but in the way we did things we made absolutely sure with two goals by Jimmy Case and another from Keegan. By now Joey had become definitely the most popular player ever to play for us. Banners about him were appearing all over the place. Following on from **JOEY EATS FROGS LEGS** was **JOEY MAKES THE SWISS ROLL**. Joey's popularity really was incredible. Incredible too was the time, effort and commitment that went into making these banners. I think there were quite a few bedsheets went missing in Merseyside homes around that time.

Maine Road was split down the middle, as you would expect, for the FA Cup semi-final. I saw Evertonians at that game I hadn't seen for years - some I didn't even know were footy fans never mind Evertonians. The Evertonians in their half of the Kippax very kindly donated their empty beer cans to us. We didn't really want the effort of taking them to a recycling plant so returned them to our friendly foes. Apart from that the usual Derby banter abounded. Davy Fairclough got one of his rare starts but within just a minute must have been wishing he hadn't. Davy galloped down the right-wing and into the penalty area. Roared on by us we fully expected Davy to squeeze the ball inside the near post as he had done against our rivals last season. Davy took a swing at the ball that had by now become lodged in the mud-heap masquerading as a football pitch. Davy completely missed the ball with his right foot. His left foot went from under him and Davy was on his arse slithering around in the mud like an overgrown eel to the chagrin of us and the great delight of the Evertonians. Talking of arses: Tommy Smith was looking for a new one after his was worn out through being put on it twice in the first ten minutes by Duncan McKenzie. This type of forward gave Tommy more trouble than most. Tommy would have been better dealing with the missing Bob Latchford whose rawer brute force was ideal for Tommy's game. Indeed Latchford had barely ever had a sniff of a chance when playing against the Anfield Iron. Terry Mac, by now well entrenched as a regular in the team, spotted David Lawson off his line. Terry took aim and delicately, carefully chipped the ball over the Everton 'keeper's head. That goal was later voted as the BBC Goal of the Season and quite rightly too. The goalkeeper was badly positioned, of that there is no doubt, but it took a special shot of stunning precision to get the ball up, over Lawson's head and down in time to nestle neatly into the top corner of the net. Everton and McKenzie in particular continued to play very well. It was an Everton I for one didn't know could play this well. Allied to no little skill was a burning determination, matching our usual level of commitment that I thought we had the patent on. The Blues finally got what they deserved when Jim Pearson, surely playing his best ever game in an Everton shirt, dispossessed Emlyn near the touchline. Pearson crossed for McKenzie to slot firmly home. Everton continued to be the better team in the second half so it was against the run of play when we took the lead in the 73rd minute. Ray Kennedy hit a free-kick that Lawson elected to punch rather than risk dropping the ball in an attempted catch. This proved a big mistake. The ball went only as far as the edge of the penalty area. One of Ray Clemence's goalkeeping theories was that if you were going to punch the ball make sure it would land somewhere near the halfway line: I wouldn't have liked a dig off him! Jimmy Case, not best known for his heading ability, strained every muscle and sinew in that sizeable neck of his to guide the ball over Lawson with a looping header. Everton teams of the past would have folded but this Gordon Lee outfit was made of sterner stuff. The impressive Martin Dobson, a very elegant player with a touch of grit to his game, was replaced eight minutes from time by the less obviously talented but big-hearted Bryan Hamilton. A minute later Everton were level again. Man of the Match McKenzie, on this occasion totally overshadowing Keegan, once again mesmerised our defence. His cross cut out our entire back four and Clem leaving Bruce Rioch with a simple tap-in at the far post. Just one minute later came possibly the biggest ever talking point in British domestic football; certainly the biggest ever in the long, illustrious history of Merseyside Derbies. A left-wing cross by Ronnie Goodlass was flicked on by McKenzie's head. The inrushing Hamilton got the faintest of touches to divert the ball past Clem. There was no protest from our players. Clem looked aghast at the concession of a goal that had probably blown our treble chance. Everton players and supporters alike looked as if they had won the pools. The first thing I do or try to, because of my refereeing training, when a goal has been scored is to look immediately to the linesman to see if the goal stands. If he is not running back towards the centre-circle then - no goal. I swear to you, and it's a point that as far as I'm aware has never been picked up on the television replays, the linesman on our side of the field, Colin Seel, running the half at the end the goal was scored had his flag raised. I then looked immediately to the penalty area. Referee Clive Thomas, whom I never really liked, too affectatious for me, was stood in the goal area clearly indicating a free-kick to us. When it was realised the goal was disallowed Red relief was unbounded whilst Blue blood boiled, and quite rightly so on this occasion as it turned out, at the injustice of it all. All that Clive Thomas has ever said about the incident is, "there was an infringement." Evertonians have ever since put the blame totally on Mr. Thomas. Mr. Thomas, probably in an attempt to protect his linesman, has never mentioned the fact that Mr. Seel had his flag raised. I believe that but for the raised flag Mr. Thomas would have allowed the goal to stand. There was after all nothing clearly evident to raise doubts about the goal's validity. Had Mr. Seel and then in turn Mr. Thomas thought that Hamilton was offside? There may just have been a case for that looking at the replays but if so it was VERY marginal - certainly our last defender, Joey Jones, *looked* to be playing everybody onside. This though remember was in the days when the benefit of any doubt on these decisions went to the defending side; a clause that since, thankfully, has been amended to favour the attacking side. Had that been the case in 1977 the goal would have stood. Had the two officials thought that Hamilton handled the ball into the net? If that is the case then they were clearly wrong as the ball DEFINITELY came off Hamilton's hip. Whatever the case I honestly don't believe Mr. Thomas cheated. I can understand Evertonians *feeling* cheated as they clearly deserved to win the game and the goal should have stood but to accuse Mr. Thomas of DELIBERATELY cheating them is out of order. Well, there's my take on it. You can agree or disagree with me at will but the whole incident was to be consigned to the history books four days later.

The greatest goal I've ever seen at any level of football came the following day in the Skem Sunday League Cup semi-final between UpHolland Labour Club and Courtaulds. Ray Gardner of UHLC started it after winning possession on the edge of his own area from a Courtaulds corner. Ray passed it to centre-half Joe McCann. Joe played a great ball out to Tony Givnan on the left-wing. Tony was greased lighting and shit off a shovel combined times ten. He skinned the full-back and crossed deep to the edge of the penalty area. Ray Gardner had continued his box-to-box run and met it full on the volley. If the net hadn't stopped it the ball would have ended up in Wigan. Good job it didn't as the Wiganers would probably have made a pie out of it. It truly was a great goal. I was linesman and had to halt my run (okay brisk jog) back to the halfway line to applaud the goal. On the pitch and dancing like John Travolta on roasties was UHLC manager John McFarlane. John, along with John Brough and John Twist ran the Skelmersdale Everton Supporters Travel Club (see, they're not all from County Road!). The club took a set amount of money each week from members and guaranteed travel to every Everton game, home and away. There was a tale of a lad who insisted on going to a mid-week game at Norwich even though he was the only one who wanted to go. The club paid his taxi fare there and back. I was stuck for transport for the replay. I was having a drink with John and his players in the Labour Club after the match and asked him if me and Baz could travel with them on the coach if there was room.

"Absolutely no problem Peter. Just clear it with Twisty and Broughy and stick to our rules. There's women and kids on the coach so we try to keep the language to a minimum."

That was fair enough. Me and Baz got a bit of stick on the coach but nothing more than good-natured banter. I don't know why but there seemed a hell of a lot more Reds at this game than Blues.

"You don't get a second chance against Liverpool" was by now becoming a well-worn cliché. It certainly proved the case in this tie. We took the lead after half-an-hour courtesy of a Phil Neal penalty. Tommy Smith had learned from his gruelling experience against McKenzie in the first game so put the shackles well and truly on the mercurial Duncan this time. Late goals from Jimmy Case and Ray Kennedy gave the scoreline a somewhat flattering appearance but we certainly did deserve to win it. Many bevvies were sunk in the Denmark before we boarded the coach for home. It amazed me how the Evertonians had taken defeat even though they were obviously gutted. I know if we'd been beaten I would have gone into mourning for a week! We were still well on course for the treble with Borussia Moenchengladbach and Manchester United awaiting us in the two finals.

If the game against Manchester City was brutal then the clash with Ipswich was purely vicious. The 2-1 win was marred by the most inept display of refereeing I've ever seen. Peter Willis was the culprit who allowed a head butt by Mick Mills on Steve Heighway to go unpunished. Steve had to go off with a massive cut over his eye. Davy Fairclough came on to replace him and was promptly booked by the hapless Mr. Willis because he hadn't received a signal to come on to the field of play. Amazing! Mr. Willis caused a near riot with that piece of ineptitude. It was no excuse I know for the lad who ran on to the pitch and offered Mr. Willis his glasses but it was understandable. No excuse either for the idiot who threw a bottle from the Kop that smashed against the crossbar. We won the game 2-1 but I dread to think what would have happened if we hadn't. That win put us three points ahead of Ipswich with two games in hand. Our biggest threat now was coming from Manchester City. They had beaten Derby 4-0 and were now level with us on points. Our goal difference was one better than theirs. We did have a game in hand on them though.

Kevin Keegan gave us a 1-0 win in the FA Cup Final dress rehearsal against Man U. Kopites were no opera singers but this song wouldn't have sounded out of place at La Scala:

WE'RE ON OUR WAY TO ROMA ON THE 25TH OF MAY
ALL THE KOPITES WILL BE SINGIN'
VATICAN BELLS THEY WILL BE RINGIN'
LIVERPOOL FC WE'LL BE SINGIN'
WHEN WE WIN THE EUROPEAN CUP.

With four League games left to play we were now within touching distance of the title. I desperately wanted to go to' the away games at QPR and Coventry that would probably give us the base to win the title at home against West Ham on the last Saturday of the season. I really wasn't too keen at the possibility of going to Bristol City on the Monday before the FA Cup Final. I'd heard from the Evertonians who'd been there this season that it was a very scary place to go. As for the Cup Finals: if I qualified for a Wembley ticket that was a definite - I had enough money for that but would probably have to sacrifice the away League games. Rome was a definite non-starter though. I'd thought of every way I could to raise the money but it just wasn't feasible. I was reading, seeing and hearing of Reds getting up to all kinds of dodges to raise the money themselves. Apparently they were selling family heirlooms, cars and anything else they could lay their hands on to get the money together. I had nothing to sell - simple as that. I wasn't going to Rome and that was that. It was galling though to see people who hadn't been to a match for years boasting how they were going to Rome and what great Reds they were because of it. I knew it was a load of old arse but what could I do about it? Good luck to the lads going who, like me, never missed a home match and followed the Reds to as many aways as possible but the part-timers did my head in. My sour mood was somewhat lifted by the fact I'd qualified on my season ticket for an FA Cup Final ticket. I felt I'd finally got what I deserved. I had to miss the QPR game due to chronic lack of finances. Going to Wembley wasn't going to be cheap and that was going to be first and foremost. Our 1-1 draw at Loftus Road meant that with the right combination of results we could win the League at Highfield Road so I was desperate to go. Help came from a very unexpected source.

"Yer goin' to Coventry tonight?"

It was nine o'clock on the morning of the game so I had no chance. No money and besides I was due in work at half-two. Best I could hope for was snatches of the match on the radio.

"Nah Ev. We've got no money 'ave we?"

"They could win the League tonight couldn't they?"

"Yeah, but 'ow do *you* know?"

"Read it in the paper."

"Bloody 'ell! You're gettin' good aren't yer? Still got no dosh though."

"'Ere, go an' cash the Family Allowance book and get to Coventry."

"What? Yer sure?"

"Yeah, go on. Yer missed Stoke didn't yer. I'll phone in work for yer and say yer sick. Just work a bit of overtime later in the week to make the money up for yer day off."

Christ, this woman never ceased to amaze me!

"Right, ta Ev."

I was off to the Post Office and on the bus to town within the hour before Ev had a chance to change her mind. I made sure I'd showed her how grateful I was in the time-honoured way before I left.

It was a good job I'd left for town early as I only just about managed to book myself on to one of the many specials that were going. The Crown was chocker with Reds who'd had the same idea as myself. By the time we boarded the specials we were all well oiled. Upon arrival at Coventry station we were herded towards the ground where the bizzies wanted us to go straight in. There were too many Reds, literally everywhere, for them to impose their will on us though so we headed for the Mercers Arms. It became clear very early that this was a night when our support would probably outnumber the Coventry faithful. After a good sesh we made our way on to the West End Terrace which was split 50-50 between Liverpool and Coventry. The open terrace at the other end was also full of Reds with others dotted around the stands on the other two sides. It really was some sight. When the crowd was announced as over 38,00 we started singing, "30,000 Scousers." That was a bit of an exaggeration but there weren't far off that many. The game itself was a bit of a non-event. Coventry desperately needed something out of the game in their battle against relegation whilst we were happy with a draw and maybe get the points we needed from the final two games. News came through that Everton had drawn 1-1 at Manchester City so if we won here we'd win the League for definite. The 0-0 draw in the end though kept everybody happy so we needed just a point from our final home game against West Ham to make certain of the title. We duly clinched the title with another scoreless draw. West Ham were more than happy with their point that virtually secured First Division status. A lot of West Ham supporters had made the trip but didn't get in because the gates were closed so early with nearly 56,000 people inside Anfield. Quite a few Hammers fans forced entry in to the ground by running into the main entrance and into the Paddock and Main Stand causing havoc as they went. Others had forced their way into the Anny Road where they were engaging in battle with our lads. Our tenth League title was certainly well celebrated after the game but not by the Road Enders. They were ignoring the on-pitch celebrations to get stuck into the West Ham hardcases who had legged it out of the Anny Road as soon as the final whistle sounded. Quite why the West Ham lads were wearing sheepies on such a red hot day I've no idea but they were very kindly relieved of them by the Road Enders before they made their journey home.

Our joy at winning the League was tempered by the thought that this was only the first leg of the treble and we would have to work mighty hard to secure the other two trophies. A worry also was an alarming lack of goals in the last few matches. Our League season ended with a 1-2 defeat at Bristol City five days before the Wembley meeting against Man U. This of course didn't really bother us as we had already won the League but it was a vital result indeed for Bristol City. They preserved their place in the top flight three days after this game with a 2-2 draw at Coventry amidst many allegations of shennanigans from Sunderland who lost 0-2 at Everton the same night. The allegations centred round the fact that Coventry Managing Director Jimmy Hill had deliberately delayed the game at Highfield Road. Hill was a great friend of the Bristol City manager Alan Dicks. Everybody at Highfield Road therefore knew well before the end of their game that Sunderland had lost at Goodison meaning that a draw would keep both Coventry and Bristol up. Whether these allegations were true or not is a matter for conjecture but I for one wouldn't have put it past the chin-faced wonder. Hill and Bruce Forsyth were once both on Merseyside and decided to have a face to face meeting: Jimmy was on the Pier Head - Brucie was in Birkenhead. Anyway, enough of that, we had bigger and better things to occupy our minds.

Fletcher's, Sandy Lane, Skem were running a coach to Wembley. That's nice and handy thought I so booked Delvesy and me on it. Delvesy for some strange reason had got it into his head that as this was my first Cup Final and he'd been before that he was taking me to the Cup Final in a way that a man would take his ten-year-old son. It kept him happy though so I went along with it. The Lawrenson's, Crown, Sunniways, Home James rust buckets I'd got so used to were the lap of coach luxury compared to the virtually horse drawn effort we boarded at Sandy Lane. It might have been okay if used to take a load of old Skem pensioners to Blackpool but it certainly wasn't suitable for a long journey taking footy fans to Wembley. The driver too must have been used only to Morris Dancing troupes. He stopped at a service station clearly marked "Man United only." We just about managed to get off the coach, have a piss and get back on in one piece before the coach was bombarded with everything from bottles to ice creams. I gave it half a thought to get off the coach and wallop the ice cream stuck to a window (it was very hot) but decided discretion was the better part of valour. Not so Delvesy who was screaming at the bombarding Mancs about "crackin' skulls" in his usual manner. He also muttered darkly the same sentiments at the three Man U supporters on our coach. The three lads were doing no harm so Delvesy was spoken to by the more sensible people on the coach. No skulls were cracked.

Approaching Wembley it became clear that Man U fans heavily outnumbered Scousers. There was hardly a Liverpool supporter to be seen whilst Man U fans were running rampage everywhere. Dopey Dan the driver man did his best to get us killed by parking smack bang in the middle of the Man U coach park. We got off the coach and ran the gauntlet of hate 'til we could get on to free ground. There were running battles everywhere. I just wanted to get in the ground and out of the way of trouble. Inside the ground my estimate of a 60-40% split for Man U was proven to be about right. I've no idea where they got all the tickets but there were plenty of Mancs in our end. They got royally booted around for their cheek and were being taken out of our end in their droves. It was hard to concentrate on what passed for pre-match entertainment: police dogs displays; model aeroplanes; gymnastic displays; marching bands etcetera. "Abide With Me" and the National Anthem were replaced in our end by "You'll Never Walk Alone". Maybe a lot of Reds had stayed away preferring to save their money for Rome. Whatever it was we were hopelessly outnumbered but were still giving a good account of ourselves. It was weird singing "Come on you Whites"; United having won the toss for the right to play in first choice strip. What chances there were in the first half seemed to fall mostly to us although we weren't playing particularly well. Kevin Keegan was having probably his most ineffectual game ever in a Liverpool shirt. People were accusing Keegan of not trying. I'm not sure if that was the case but Kevin's cause wasn't helped by the fact it was widely known he was off straight after the match for talks with the West German club Hamburg. Valencia of Spain were also rumoured to be waiting in the wings should there be any breakdown in the transfer negotiations. Steve Heighway had the shackles well and truly put on him by young Jimmy Nicholl while Arthur Albiston in the other full-back position was having the game of his life. Pearson scored the opening goal. I really hated him. He seemed to typify the arrogance and "we're better than you" attitude United had - an attitude that showed a total lack of respect for anybody else. Our equaliser came with one of the great FA Cup Final goals. Joey played a hopeful ball up to Jimmy Case on the edge of the penalty area. Jimmy swivelled and hit the ball on the volley as it dropped in one smooth, graceful movement. Stepney in the United goal was still grabbing at thin air long after the ball had rippled the back of the net. Game on! We were surely going to win it now. Pity was, nobody had told our players. We just didn't seem to take heart and build on that. When Jimmy Greenhoff scored United 's winner I was very nearly physically sick. Ian Callaghan had replaced the sadly out of touch David Johnson to bolster our overrun midfield. With hindsight it might have been better to play Davy Fairclough. Davy was itching to play and was mightily upset at being left out of the squad altogether. The game was well and truly up when a tremendous shot from Razor crashed against the United crossbar. It wasn't to be our day. I'm not sure that United deserved to win but I know we were definitely not firing on all cylinders so I suppose we didn't either. A big factor maybe in Bob's team planning was that any replay wouldn't have taken place until June. Madness I know but that's the FA for you. Bob wanted the game done, dusted and won at the first time of asking but it wasn't to be. Too many of our players had an off day all at once. Whatever it was, United had won the Cup and we'd lost our treble dream. It was bad enough watching the United players and management cavorting round Wembley with the Cup but to see our weary, bedraggled players so distraught was a sorry sight indeed. Ray Clemence was in tears, blaming himself for at least United's first goal. Clem was the ultimate professional and any perceived mistake was magnified to him two hundred fold. Emlyn was also badly affected. As Captain of our club and the deserved winner of the Footballer of the Year award Emlyn probably felt it worse than most. Emlyn wore his heart very much on his sleeve; he knew no other way. The gauntlet of hate we'd experienced getting off the coach was as nothing compared to the gauntlet of scorn we had to run getting back on it. The dead hard Mancs were skitting us to high fuckin' heaven. Their particular targets were a couple of women who were dressed in all kinds of Liverpool regalia. The Mancs were ripping rosettes off their dresses and then worse still lifting their skirts up. The women were clearly very frightened. I wanted to rip the Mancs fuckin' 'eads off but there were just too many of them. The ladies plight was ended when the more sensible United supporters came over and rescued them. One of them even gave the ladies' tormentors a right hook. I was very pleased about that to say the least.

Bob had a massive task on his hands to lift the spirits of the team for the biggest match in Liverpool FC's history just four days later. How on earth could the players get over this to ensure we all enjoyed a glorious summer as winners of the European Cup? Joey had the answer. The team coach was on it's way to Watford station to catch the train back to Liverpool; no post-match banquet for our players - they had far more important things to occupy their minds.

"What are you going to do when you get home Joey?"

The question by the interviewer, I think Brian Moore, on the coach was an innocent enough one.

"I'm gonna kick the cat! And the bloody dog!"
The coach rocked with laughter. Joey had managed in one fell swoop to lift the spirits. Clem helped things along even more as the party were waiting on the platform. He broke into an impromptu chorus of our Cup Final song, "Yeah, we can do it!" Okay, our players were no Rubettes, more Lillettes, but that unquenchable spirit was back and was to count for a lot in the Eternal City.

For some reason, again I'm not sure, I think I might have walked up and down the stairs too many times or something, Ev wasn't speaking to me. For once this was something of a blessing as our four-year-old colour telly was fucked. The colours were as fucked on it as the pile of washing Big Ev had once thrown in our twin tub on a boil wash. On our telly Liverpool in the purple shirts would have been playing the pink-shirted Borussia Moenchengladbach on a blue pitch. I thought it best all round to take up Baz's offer of watching the match at his. Baz had a shedful of ale and a seemingly endless supply of scran served up by his darling wife, Anne. Anne wasn't really into the footy so wondered what all the fuss was about but as long as she churned out the Reg Varney's that would do for me. It had been widely reported all day on the telly about how many Liverpool supporters were in Rome for the match. Some reports put it as high as 30,000. No matter how many there were all the reports came back with the facts that our contingent were extremely well behaved, were having a good laugh, a good drink and a sing song and were generally keeping both themselves and the Romans amused. When the BBC coverage of the match started half-an-hour or so before kick-off it was plain to see those reports had not been exaggerated. The Olympic Stadium, apart from one block of German fans seemed to be a sea of red and white. Chequered flags were everywhere. It seemed that every Red in Rome was bedecked in some kind of scarf or banner. One huge flag bore the sentiment:
HERE WE GO GATHERING CUPS IN MAY.

Dwarfing them all though was this monstrous one:

JOEY ATE THE FROGS LEGS
MADE THE SWISS ROLL
NOW HE'S MUNCHIN' GLADBACHS.

That is surely the greatest ever flag in the history of Liverpool FC supporters and we've had some good ones. BBC commentator Barry Davies said the sight inside the Olympic Stadium made him feel proud to be British. I knew what he meant but it made me proud to be Scouse. Davy Fairclough was again sorely upset at being left out of the starting line up. Cally stayed in the side as Bob reverted to 4-4-2 rather than the 4-3-3 he had started with so unsuccessfully at Wembley. As the players came out you could see the looks of amazement on our player's faces as they looked up at the scene that surrounded them. Phil Neal especially looked aghast at taking it all in. The Borussia players for their part looked nervous, apprehensive even. This really was an occasion when 30,000 or so of our supporters was like having an extra man on the pitch. We started well, reverting to our fluid style rather than being swamped in midfield as we had been by Man U. Another plus was that Keegan, in his last game for us, looked determined to erase his nightmare Wembley performance and was running his marker, the great Berti Vogts, a merry dance. In the 27th minute Cally carried the ball from midfield and played a pass to Steve Heighway running through the middle. Cally had carried on his run to the right taking Borussia defenders with him. Terry Mac had run unnoticed to the edge of the penalty area. With everybody expecting Stevie to play the ball back out wide to Cally he instead played a very clever ball inside to Terry Mac. Terry took what was not an easy chance to put us into the lead. That move typified the style of football we played that season: running off the ball to make space for others to run into and making it all seem so simple in the process. Of course you had to have a Manager with the tactical awareness to play that way and also the right players to make the system work. We had the perfect combination. Baz's house was shaking to its foundations as we bounced all around his living room.

"Mind the fish! Mind the fish!"

Baz was screaming about a glass fish, a rather lovely ornament I must say, that was in grave danger of being smashed into a million pieces by my manic antics.

"Don't worry Baz I won't smash it."

The songs coming out of the telly from the Olympic Stadium were being bellowed out in unison from Chez Baz. A scare when the great German midfielder Rainer Bonhof hit the post with a stunning shot was a taste of things to come in the second half. Still, we'd managed to retain our lead and were full value for it. Six minutes into the second half Jimmy Case lost the ball in midfield to Allan Simonsen who was probably the one Borussia player you would most not want to lose the ball to. Simonsen was a great player. The Dane carried the ball to the edge of the penalty area before hitting a dipping, swerving, vicious shot that gave even Clem no chance. The turning point of the game came five minutes later when Uli Stielike was clean through on goal with only Clem to beat. Even when faced with possibly the world's greatest goalkeeper you would have put money on Stielike to score. The fact he didn't was down to a truly magnificent save by Clem. That was it - Borussia had hit us with their best shots in that ten minutes or so of ascendancy - if we could weather that we could weather anything else they had to throw at us. It's my belief that because they didn't take the lead then that Borussia lost heart. Keegan was having his best ever game for us without a doubt. We were once again solid at the back after the rocky ten minutes and the midfield was functioning well. The oldest man on the pitch, Cally, was playing like the youngest. Cally's unbounded energy was winning balls for us in midfield and making space for the more creative players such as Razor and Terry Mac. In the 65th minute we won a corner on the left-hand side of the pitch. Steve Heighway ran across to take it. We didn't have any great height advantage over the German side to give us any real hope of scoring from this. Even then we weren't the most productive team ever at corners. Seemingly as soon as Stevie took the corner the ball was in the net. Baz and me were going bonkers without knowing which player had actually scored. Barry Davies gave us the answer:

"It's Tommy Smith! Would you believe it, it's Tommy Smith!"

Barry was going as mental as we were. I think Mr. Davies turned into a Liverpool supporter that night. Certainly he wanted us to win this game - no impartiality there my man!

"The fish! The fuckin' fish!"

Phew, nearly went that time! Poor Baz was nearly having a heart attack as his precious fish was on the way to being wasted Evo style.

Eight minutes from time Keegan ran Vogts one time too many for the German. Berti could do no more than chop Keegan down in the penalty area. To be honest it wasn't the clearest cut penalty I've ever seen; I've certainly seen them not given for far more serious offences but it was a measure of how much on top we were that there was not a single complaint from any Borussia player. Phil Neal stepped forward to take the kick having scored ten times from the penalty spot this season. Would his nerve hold though for this, the most important, dramatic moment of his career, possibly his life? Of course it did - Phil was made from strong stuff! His shot went unerringly into the net sending the Borussia 'keeper Kneib the wrong way.

CRASH!

"Fuckin' 'ell Evo - the fish!"

Baz's beautiful glass fish was on the floor as dead as a.....well.... a dead fish I suppose. Freddy Fish lay in a million pieces on Baz's floor.

"I've got some super glue in ours Baz. I'll glue it back tomorrow.

"'Ow the fuck are yer gonna do that? It's a fuckin' jigsaw puzzle now!"

"Big Ev's good at jigsaws. I'll get 'er to do it."

"It's not fuckin' funny!"

Fishy fun was temporarily forgotten as the final whistle blew. That was it - we'd won the European Cup. What a sweet feeling it was. The scenes on the TV screen were amazing. Joey could hardly do the lap of honour he had that many scarves and banners draped around him. We'd become the first English side to win Europe's premier trophy on foreign soil. The great Manchester United side of 1968 had won their European Cup in magnificent style against Benfica at Wembley. I don't think I was being biased in saying that this was a better triumph. The celebrations and cavorting would go on in Rome throughout the night that was for sure. For me and Baz it was off down to the newly opened Viking to get leathered.

"Baz, I'm sorry abarr yer fish mate."

"Ah, fuck the fish! **WE ARE THE EUROPEAN CHAMPIONS!**"

Baz phoned as many Evertonians as he could to wind them up. I was just content to bask in our own glory. The fact I should have been in Rome not Skem hadn't really hit me yet but I knew it was going to. When I got home well and truly laced Ev, by now having decided that going up and down the stairs too many time was NOT actually a hanging offence, told me of the celebrations on Willow Hey.

"They're a miserable shower of gets round 'ere. Me and our Ste went outside after the match an' there was nobody around. We 'ad a good laugh an' a dance though. Yer shoulda been 'ere."

I knew what she meant but I knew where I should have been and it certainly wasn't anywhere near bloody Skem!

"No I shouldn't. I shoulda been in Rome. I'm tellin' you now Ev, no matter what it takes, no matter what it costs, no matter where I get the money as long as I don't rob anybody there is no way I'm EVER gonna miss another Final. It doesn't matter where we're playin' I'm goin'."

I'm writing this 25 years on from Rome. There is only one thing I regret about my life. I've done good things in my life, I've also done quite a few bad things but life is life - you can't change it. "No regrets" is my motto but the one regret I'll always have, and it sticks with me like shit to a blanket, is that I didn't go to Rome.

The homecoming the following night was awesome. Even though most of the lads who'd been in Rome weren't back yet town, indeed all along the victory route, was choc-a-bloc with Reds

making a sea of red and white. There were also a good few Evertonians out along the route to wish us well but not so many in town. The noise and the scenes when the team took to the balcony in William Brown Street had to be heard and seen to be believed. Bob as usual was shying away from the limelight until the shoves of his players and the demands from the crowds made him give a little speech. Don't ask me what he said, nobody could understand a word of it, but it didn't matter. I don't think even Bob himself knew what he was saying. I wondered what the man who had started all this - Bill Shankly - thought of everything. I'm sure he was well pleased for everybody but there might have been just a little twinge or two of regret. Bob, later said that he hadn't touched a drop of alcohol after the win. He wanted to be able to take everything in, to savour the feeling, to get drunk on victory rather than drink. The same could definitely not be said for the players, most of who were well sauced! Especially pissed (no pun intended) was Terry Mac. Terry decided that he could wait no longer for a pee and decided to relieve himself over the side of the balcony. Unfortunately a nurse, I think of the St. John's Ambulance Brigade, was in the way of Terry's cascade. It was an unfortunate incident to say the least but I'm sure Terry didn't mean to do it on purpose as has since been claimed. Emlyn was pissed too and got a bit of stick for a song he started which he asked us all to join in with. The song had actually been sung by us for months before that so Emlyn was only asking us to sing our own song. The song was: **LIVERPOOL ARE MAGIC. EVERTON ARE TRAGIC!**
Now what's wrong with that? The Evertonians had also been singing it, obviously in reverse, for as long as we'd been singing it but they decided to take the moral high ground and roundly condemned Emlyn.
NICE ONE EMLYN!
Also looking slightly the worse for wear, although in this case not through drink, was Kevin Keegan. Kevin was sporting a black eye. Popular rumour had it that Jimmy Case had snotted Kevin after the FA Cup Final. Credit to both players that they didn't let the incident affect either of their marvellous performances in the

Olympic Stadium. Kevin had by now virtually sewn up his transfer to Hamburg. While definitely sorry to see such a great player go the record transfer fee for a British player of half-a-million pounds would be most welcome. Everybody was looking forward to the dosh being spent on a top-class, world-renowned player.

The celebrations continued the following night at Tommy Smith's Testimonial match. There were still loads of fans not yet back from Rome. Tales were coming through of broken down trains, of people sleeping on luggage racks, of trains without water or toilets. Christ, what those lads had to put up with. I'd pay a million pounds now to be able to say I put up with it too. The absence of those fans though didn't diminish the carnival atmosphere. The European Cup and League Championship trophies, an unprecedented Double, were of course on prominent display. Tommy and Emlyn even forgot their enmity for one night and ran round the ground proudly together each holding a handle of the European Cup. It might have been Emlyn kissing Tommy after Tommy's goal that did the trick. Emlyn even tried his hand in goal during the first half, swapping places with Clem. The Kop urged everybody standing to sit down and those sitting to stand up. When the Directors in their box joined in they got their own special tribute from the Kop:
WE ALL AGREE: OUR DIRECTORS ARE MAGIC!
There were all kinds of mad things going on during the match. Buckets of water were constantly produced from the dugouts to drown everybody in sight. Tosh had his great mate, Welsh Rugby Union star Gareth Edwards playing for us. They produced a sweeping downfield move that led to a marvellous goal. Well, actually it was a try as the pair of Welsh loons had carried the ball with their hands towards goal. Even Bobby Charlton, manager of our opponents that night, was moved to laughter. Great player though Bobby was he certainly wasn't a laugh a minute - more a laugh a year! The goal/try was allowed to stand by the referee who was joining in with all the fun. Alex Stepney was in goal for our opponents and was getting some unmerciful stick.

STOLEN PROPERTY. STOLEN PROPERTY. GIVE US BACK OUR FA CUP!

Alex took it all in good heart though. The BBC were filming an episode of a series fronted by Esther Rantzen called "The Big Time" that gave ordinary members of the public a chance to fulfil their dreams as long as they were at least capable of holding their own in doing what they wanted. A local amateur footballer, Lol Cottrell, had asked to play at Anfield and so was invited by Tommy to take part in his Testimonial. Lol was a good player and had risen to quite a decent standard in the amateur/semi-pro game. His chance to score was given, and I do literally mean given, to him by the referee who gave us the dodgiest of dodgy penalties - I'm sure the only time he had cheated in his life. Lol stepped forward to take the penalty. Stepney easily saved a shot my Granny wouldn't have been proud of. "RETAKE" roared the Kop so the ref acceded to our wishes. Lol was by now completely knackered and could only produce an action replay of his first effort. Stepney couldn't help but save it - it would have been crueller not to. That was enough for the ref - he'd given Lol two chances, he wasn't going to give him a third. Of course Stepney was roundly booed but again he took it well turning to the Kop and shrugging his shoulders. Esther was also getting it big time if you'll pardon the pun.

ESTHER, ESTHER, SHOW US YER TEETH!

She did too!

The players joining up with the England squad for the Home Internationals were allowed to play for just the first half. Totally missing from the proceedings though sadly was Joey. Joey would have revelled in this and made a mad night totally barmy but unfortunately the Welsh management insisted he didn't play at all in the match.

A great occasion and a great crowd had finally brought the curtain down not only on the greatest season in the history of Liverpool Football Club but also on the career of one of our finest ever players - The Anfield Iron - BORN A MAN - Tommy Smith. Let's hope he enjoyed his retirement.

CHAPTER SEVENTEEN

WHERE ONCE WE WATCHED THE KING KENNY PLAY

Summer '77 was not quite the long, hot Summer that '76 had been but it wasn't far off it. Once again I set about my unenviable task of working every hour God could send down to me to save the necessary to renew my season ticket. Once having got it I was determined not to let it go. I was wondering though why I hadn't been offered any overtime by Thursday of one particular week. I was going to have to get some in soon or I wouldn't be offered weekend overtime and that was absolutely vital! Twelve hours overtime on Saturday and Sunday was a lot of coin. I was beginning to feel exasperated not only by me being overlooked for overtime and the intense heat but also by Ev being on my back to bring some more money home. Not that Ev for one minute thought about going out and having a bash herself. Nah, she couldn't be working and bringing up kids too! Despite my exasperation I decided to approach Shift Foreman Jack Huyton in a cool, calm, collected manner.

"Jack, why haven't I been offered any ovies this week?"

"'Cus tha's been bloody late three days outta bloody four."

I couldn't argue with that so tried a different tack.

"Yeah, but Marge 'as been late this week an' yer've offered 'er overtime."

"Aye, but tha's allus bloody late."

I couldn't argue with that either but I was going to - I needed the dosh.

"Ah, come on Jack, I'm bloody skint."

"Nay, not 'til bloody timekeepin' improves."

Cool, calm, collected went out of the window as the red mist descended upon me. I really could be an angry bastard when I'd a mind.

"Well fuckin' fuck yer! YER FUCKIN' OWLD BASTARD!"

Honestly, the chair just happened to be there. I wouldn't have gone searching for it that's for sure. I probably would have lashed a load of elements at Jack instead as they were readily to hand. I picked the wooden chair up and with all the strength I could muster, which was considerable, I was a big lad (a euphemism for fat bastard), and hurled it straight at Jack. Jack, in a display of fleet-footedness never before seen in Grimwoods, managed to escape the chair which missed his head by about two milli. If the chair had hit him I'm sure I would have been on a murder charge. Well, manslaughter at least. I could have pleaded insanity, which actually wouldn't have been that far from the truth. The chair crashed into a mesh cage behind Jack's head nearly demolishing it.

"Tha bloody sin that Les. Yer bloody saw it didn't yer Les?"

Les Foster, the chargehand, totally unfazed by it all, sat steadfastly in his chair.

"I saw nowt."

Nice one Les. I should have been sacked for that. Good on Jack that he didn't report me to the high-ups for my madness but he had the last laugh anyway; I didn't get my overtime and spent the weekend looking at Sue Barker's and Chris Evert's knickers. It was a nice consolation prize I suppose but it wasn't going to get me my season ticket, nor would it get Ev off my back.

"Did yer ask in work about overtime?"

"Yeah, Jack Huyton won't let me work because I'm always late."

"Well why don't yer start gettin' in early?"

"Cos normally about ten minutes before I'm due in work you're lyin' on me dick!"

"Ah well, yer on afternoons next week so yer won't be late then will yer?"

"That's up to you. Let me go abarr 'alf-one an' I should be okay."

It's hard being a sex-god you know.

The papers were full of stories about a young Liverpool player committing a misdemeanour on Blackpool Beach. Allegedly the young centre-half signed just before the end of last season had streaked along the beach in front of a load of girls. Well this behaviour by a Liverpool player just wouldn't do! Who the hell did this lad think he was anyway? Okay, he came with a big reputation; he had represented Scotland at junior and youth level at a host of different sports: volleyball; golf; tennis; basketball and cricket to name a few. In fact the young lad supposedly could have taken up a career as a pro golfer so good was he. It seemed everything he touched turned to gold. He'd be in trouble at Anfield though with this kind of carry on. He was needed however as a replacement for the now retired Tommy Smith. This errant young Scot's name? Alan Hansen. Jocky to his mates.

What happened next? Tommy Smith decided that he wasn't going to retire after all and wants to stay on for another year. No problem Tommy says I - can never have enough good players. Young Jocky would take time to bed in anyway so experience at the back is vital. Only one small problem though - Tommy's had his Testimonial. Liverpool Football Club rules say that a player can only have a Testimonial if he has served at least ten years at the club and has retired. Nothing underhand about Tommy's way of doing things I'm sure but the club's rules had then to be rewritten to say that you only needed to have served ten years - no retirement was now necessary. A classic case of moving the goalposts if ever there was one but Tommy was happy, the fans were happy and the club was happy to have secured the services of a fine player for another year. The good of Liverpool Football Club is first and foremost in everybody's mind.

With just three days to go before the season's curtain-raiser - the FA Charity Shield at Wembley against Man U - the Keegan money was burning a big, fat hole in Uncle Bob's considerably big, fat trouser pockets. Fans were becoming impatient that we hadn't signed anybody with the money but Bob, astute buyer that he was, knew what he was doing. He was biding his time until the right player for Liverpool Football Club became available.
"Evo, we've signed Kenny Dalglish!"
"Fuck off Baz, 'ave we fuck! 'E's not gonna leave Celtic. 'E's fuckin' brilliant."

"We 'ave. Get 'ome and get yer radio on. There's a press conference now."
Sure enough Baz was right. Christ almighty, what a signing. Kenny, who had so severely embarrassed Ray Clemence in the two previous Scotland v England matches, was indeed a great player; possibly better even than Kevin Keegan but time alone would tell the tale on that one. Kenny began training with his new team-mates almost immediately. The papers, especially the Echo obviously, were full of it. Kenny wasn't great in his TV interviews though, as hardly anybody could understand a word he said but his football would do the talking for him.

After Fletcher's previous Wembley debacle I decided to chance the only slightly better Crown's for the trip to London. There seemed to be an even split of Mancs and Scousers for this one, no doubt due to the presence of our great new signing. To gauge the size and grandeur of this signing just think of Liverpool signing Pele in the '60's, Cruyff in the '70's, Maradona in the '80's, Baggio in the '90's or Ronaldo now and you have some idea of what Kenny meant to us. When the players came out for the traditional pre-match Wembley walkabout Joey was like a Prime Minister taking kids from the crowd and carrying them round the running track. There were some seriously delighted kids at Wembley that day. That was definitely one to tell the grandkids. The biggest pre-match cheer though was reserved for the first glimpse of King Kenny. The roar to greet him was absolutely huge. Dalglish's name boomed out from our end. The old St. John/Toshack chant was used for him and how good and loud it sounded. Even Kenny, who had been cheered to the rafters by crowds of over 70,000 in Celtic games seemed somewhat taken aback. The match itself was something of a non-event - both teams seemingly willing to accept the scoreless draw that would see the Shield held for six months each. Big fun was had in our end though as we mercilessly ripped into the just-departed Tommy Docherty who had been sacked by Busby for knobbing Mary Brown, wife of United physio and supposedly Docherty's best mate Laurie Brown:

WHO'S UP MARY BROWN?
WHO'S UP MARY BROWN?
TOMMY, TOMMY DOCHERTY!
TOMMY, TOMMY DOCHERTY!

'E SHOT, 'E CUM
ALL OVER MARY'S BUM
TOMMY DOC, TOMMY DOC!

Great fun!

I was reffing a friendly between Horseshoe and Almond Tree three days later. Lollipop the loon was playing for Horseshoe. There wasn't much that Lollipop couldn't do with a football. He was a greedy bastard mind - there had to be two balls on the pitch; one for Lollipop and one for the rest of the players. He was a treat to watch though. Only the fact that he was a skinny twat, couldn't get out of bed and had a liking for Guinness prevented him from making it as a pro. I was beginning to feel seriously pissed off reffing this pre-season friendly played in early evening blinding heat when Lollipop got the ball in his own half. He danced, literally, around half-a-dozen Almond Tree players before lifting the ball just far enough over the goalkeeper so that he could run around him and volley the ball into the net as it dropped. He was a cheeky bastard but he was good. He then stood in the middle of the penalty area, hands above his head and just shouted, "Ashley Grimes!" Grimes was a Man Utd player just starting to make a name for himself and was Lollipop's double - skinny, scruffy and long red hair.
"Evo, 'as tha ever sin a goal like that?"
I had to admit I hadn't but I wasn't going to tell the big-headed get that so just settled for saying, "Geet knob art!"
He bloody did too!
Back in the Ollie after the match Lollipop's goal was dissected by the Ollie players who threatened to slit his woolyback throat for having the audacity to score such a goal. Lollipop revelled in it

though - absolutely loved it. Somebody came running into the pub screaming at the top of his voice, "Elvis 'as just died!"

"Elvis who?" was my reply.

"There's only one fuckin' Elvis yer daft twat!"

Of course that was true; it was just I couldn't believe that Elvis Presley - the King of rock 'n' roll had died. I wasn't a particularly big fan of Elvis but I knew that Lollipop was. I'd been in his house where every spare inch of wall was adorned with pictures of the King. Lollipop had every Elvis record that had ever been made. When the realisation dawned on Lollipop that his great idol had indeed died he started weeping uncontrollably. That was really sad to see. I don't know of anything else that could have got Lollipop, my mate and a man with an unbounding joy of life, in such a state.

"Come on Lollipop, I'll take yer 'ome."

I've got to be honest and say I wasn't really arsed about Elvis dying, I wouldn't be holding any candle-lit vigil, but to see a mate in such a state was a sad sight indeed.

It was reasonable of me to assume that as Crown's had got me to Wembley and back safely enough then a trip to Middlesbrough for the opening League game of the season the following week wouldn't be too arduous. Wrong!

The front and middle pages of the papers were still full of stories of the King but the back pages and all the talk on our coach was of our own King - King Kenny. Chugging, farting and spluttering sounds weren't just coming from me after a Friday night in the Derby Arms but ominously also from the coach.

"Fuckin' 'ell driver, we gonna get there or what?"

"Yeah, no problem. This coach is always like this and gets us everywhere. We used it for St. Etienne, Zurich and Rome last season."

Oh that's okay then isn't it? That's a definite guarantee. I'd been on Crown coaches that had struggled to get to Burnley. This fuckin owld heap of rust had been half way round Europe in the last six months and was going to get us to Middlesbrough. I don't think so! I was right too. It was in Mexborough I think that the old rust heap finally gave up the ghost. If it wasn't Mexborough then it was definitely somewhere else in the middle of bloody nowhere. The driver assured us that we'd be there in time for the match as he was arranging for a local coach firm to send a vehicle out and it was only twelve o'clock anyway. There were forty-odd hot, frustrated lads on that coach who knew we had as much chance of seeing Kenny's League debut at Ayresome Park as there was of Elvis raising himself from his shitter and returning to life. Luckily for us we had broken down very near to a social club called, I think, the King George V or it could have been the VI, I'm not sure. I never was very good at Royals unless they'd happened to be the King of Anfield at some point, such as King Billy Shankly or King Kenny. 3 o'clock came and went with not a sign of the replacement coach. By now everybody was well sauced. Even the locals were enjoying us despite our interrupting their Saturday afternoon dominoes. News of scorelines on the first day of the season was filtering through on the radio. An almighty roar went up when it was announced that Liverpool had taken the lead at Middlesbrough. The scorer? Our new King of course!

OH OH OH KENNY, KENNY
I'D WALK A MILLION MILES FOR ONE OF YOUR GOALS
OH KENNY!

I think they must have actually heard that one at Ayresome Park. It was sickening not to have been there to see Kenny's first goal. Fuckin' Crown's! Some of the lads went into the nearest town to see if they could find any action. They found it alright returning with tales of how they'd been legged all over the place. I was content to just sit there getting merrily pissed and finish the book I was reading, "The Haunting of Toby Jugg" by the king of the occult thriller writers, Dennis Wheatley. The replacement coach arrived at four o'clock by which time I think the good people of the King George the whatever Social Club were well glad to see the back of us. Not that we hadn't entertained them royally of course. As due payment for this they gave us (well okay, not quite) about two dozen bottles of Newcy. For some obscure reason we were singing the theme tune from an advert of the time for a beer called Colt 45:

ANY TOM, JACK OR WALT
WHO LOVES THE TASTE OF MALT
WILL LOVE THE MALT IN A COLT 45!

The Elvis songs were getting belted out too. The one I was singing, a bastardised version of "The Wonder of You" was my favourite:

WHEN NO ONE ELSE CAN FUCKIN' STAND ME
WHEN EVERYTHING I DO IS WRONG
YOU GIVE ME SOAP AND CONSTIPATION

Pity I could never remember the rest of that song.

A wasted journey? Well no, not really; we'd had a good bevy or twenty, a lot of it free, and a good laugh but it did come a very poor second best to actually being at the match. The bonus was that we'd been told to get down to Crown's through the week to get our money back. They were still twats!

I made a big mistake when I got back from the matchless 'Boro trip - I went to the Viking. Not that the Viking wasn't a very equable alehouse. It was okay in a "fight-a-minute" sort of way but you'd be safe if you managed to dodge the flying chairs in a John Wayne. No, the mistake I made was that I should have realised Pat Asp was in there. Not only was he in there, he was even more pissed and spoiling for a fight than usual. Not that I was stone cold sober of course! Pat had this mad idea that he could fight. Sure, he was big and wide enough but our Ste would have given him a fight when he was pissed - Pat that is, not our Ste. Pat didn't pick a fight in the Viking - even he knew he'd get pummelled if he did that. No, the target of his ire were the Chinese waiters in King's restaurant. We'd just finished a banquet for four between the two of us.

"Come on Evo, let's do a runner."

"Fuck off Pat. I can hardly walk, never mind run so you've got no fuckin' chance!"

"Yer chicken twat!"

"Yeah, but I wouldn't mind keeping both me bollocks 'til the day I die. If we do a runner outta 'ere they'll end up being served as fuckin' Sui Meis tomorrow night!"

The waiters agreed with me. They'd heard the word "runner" and had silently surrounded us armed with fearsome looking weapons. Surely they didn't use these to cut meat?

"You pay now!"

"Fuck off yer Chinky twats. We're fuckin' payin'!"

Pat would never have got a job in the Chinese Embassy.

"Yeah, ee arr mate. Sorry about 'im 'e's pissed. 'Ere's yer dosh."

Pat then took a swing at probably the only seven foot tall Chinese waiter in the world.

For fuck sake!

Seven foot man nearly died of pneumonia from the draught incurred by Pat's haymaker but recovered sufficiently to put Pat's arm behind his back while another waiter headlocked him. Together they managed to run him out of the door without bothering to open it. Pat was soon followed by me - exited in the same way by the irate waiters.

"Yer fuckin' loon! Yer nearly got us killed!"

"Ah fuck it! Come on, let's go the One Seven."

The One Seven was a particularly dodgy place but as it was the only nightclub in Skem it attracted a lot of business. I knew it was going to spell trouble for me as by this time I was well twatted, it was turned midnight, I'd been out since seven o'clock that morning and having survived my bollocks becoming Sui Meis they were surely gonna be chopped off and hung on the line to dry by Big Ev.

"Yeah, come on Pat. Let's go an' get a bevy!"

Five minutes after setting foot in the One Seven Pat was offering two bouncers out. I managed to save Pat from having his head put in a wheely bin as I worked with one bouncer and knew the other one from playing in the Skem Sunday League.

"Evo, that bird over there fancies yer!"
Now I know I'm no Robert Redford but this bird wasn't exactly beautiful.
"Nah, fuck that Pat. I'm not interested. Yer've seen my bird. Why should I wanna turf 'er?"
"Ee arr, come on. It'll be a laugh. Walk 'er 'ome. She lives by us."
Rita Webb had this bright red jacket on, more like a blazer than anything, that made her look like a Butlin's Redcoat. Maybe she was.
"Nah, come on Pat, it's two o'clock. I'll 'ave to get 'ome. I'm gonna get fuckin' killed as it is."
"Okay, come back to ours and 'ave a bevy."
I was well up for that idea as we were walking over the bridge from the One Seven to Pat's 'til I noticed Redcoat following us and even worse gaining on us with every stride. By the time I tried to protest it was too late as we'd reached Pat's front door. Before I knew it we were inside the house with Redcoat in close attendance. Worse was to come. I'd never met Pat's missus before but had heard how she was a fanatical Jehovah's Witness.
"Marie this is Peter. Peter, this is Marie. She's a Jehovah's Witness."
"I didn't know there'd been an accident."
That old chestnut cut no fuckin' ice with Marie whatsoever.
I was quite happy necking a can of ale but I was in mood at all for the kind of necking that Redcoat had in mind. I was almost relieved when Jobo Marie asked, nay ordered, us to kneel down and say prayers. Fuckin' 'ell, the Catholic Church was loony but this lot was totally off it's fuckin' rocker! Fuckin' three o'clock in the morning and I was totally twatted with some ugly fuckin' bird who looked like she'd had her coat set on fire trying to shag me, kneeling down saying prayers to a God I knew fuck all about, a religious fuckin' nutter one side of me and a nutter, just a plain honest-to-goodness nutter but a nutter nonetheless, the other side of me. They were gonna kill me. Yeah, that was the plan. They were gonna make me close my eyes to say a prayer and then twat me on the head, tie me up, all of them shag me and then sacrifice

me. Fuck this! I made a dash for the door.

"Ee arr la! Yer'll 'ave to fuckin' walk me 'ome at least yer twat!"

Redcoat had a lovely way with words.

"Pat said yer only live round the corner."

"Nah, I live on the other side of fuckin' Digmoor."

"Well come on then, 'urry up for fuck sake!"

Anything to get outta of that fuckin' madhouse!

Ten minutes of avoiding getting the face sucked off me and we were at Redcoat's chalet.

"'Ee arr lad, come in an' 'ave a cup of fuckin' coffee."

"No ta. I'll 'ave to get off. Me missus'll fuckin' kill me."

"'Ee arr, come on, yer prick, me 'usband's in fuckin' bed! 'E won't 'ear us!"

"Yer 'usband? Fuck off yer fuckin' loonball!"

I legged it non-stop for about five minutes 'til I was sure I was well clear of the Digmoor Dingbats. Problem now was not only that I was arseholed but I had no money to even phone a cab, much less actually get one. That was fuck all though to the problems I was gonna have with Big Ev. After the long walk home I eventually arrived ay my front door right on the stroke of six o'clock. I knew that as I heard the alarm clock going off upstairs after having set it to get up for the trip to Middlesbrough. That all seemed like a century ago now never mind a day ago. Disaster heaped upon disaster - no key! I tapped as lightly on the door as I could.

"Ev. Ev. Open the door. Come on love."

I was whispering but if she could hear me she wasn't letting on. Big mistake coming up. I opened the letterbox and tried whispering through that.

"Ev, come on, let me in."

I wasn't to know that Ev was standing behind the door armed with a brush. Not for Ev the archetypal rolling pin. Mind you, she must have been mellowing, it could have been a knife she shoved through the letterbox. The top of the brush pole hit me smack in the middle of the forehead. Such was the force with which Ev had shoved it that I was propelled backwards and crashed into the wall of Linda's house.

"What was that for yer fuckin' loon?"

"It's six o'clock in the fuckin' mornin'! That's what it was for!"

Fair enough I suppose.

"Come on, just let me in. Me 'ead's fuckin' bangin' 'ere."

"Where the fuck 'ave yer been?"

"Middlesbrough."

"'Til now?"

"I went for a bevy with Pat Asp and went back to 'is later."

"That fuckin' loon?"

"Tell me abarr it!"

I couldn't tell her about Redcoat - the brush would have ended up in my arse.

"Yer've been with someone else 'aven' yer?"

"I 'aven' Ev, honest."

"What was the match like?"

"I don't know. The coach broke down on the way so we didn't even get there."

"Yer've been out for a full day and yer didn't even get to see the match? You are a fuckin' loon!"

She must have taken pity on me at that point though as she opened the door for me to seek the sanctuary of my bed - or so I thought.

"Get on the fuckin' couch an' don't speak to me for the rest of the day!"

I did as I was told and climbed on to the couch like the obedient little dog I was. Oh fuckin' marvellous! The Tremeloes treatment. Probably for about three weeks at that too. That was the least of my worries at the moment though. I just wanted to get my head down and relieve this banging headache caused not only by the ale but also by the cartoon bump appearing at the front of my head. It looked like I had a fuckin' alien growing inside there ready to burst out at any moment. Oh, how I loved these awaydays.

Kenny's opening goal was, as far as I'm aware, never shown on

TV; not even on news snippets so if anybody has it please let me have a look. I duly got my 'Boro fare returned to me by Crown's on the day of the midweek match against Newcastle. Letters were still flooding into the Echo about Kenny. One lady from Glasgow wrote: "Kenny's smile when he scores will light up Anfield."
That lady wasn't wrong either. Kenny's first Anfield goal came a minute into the second half as the Newcastle defence wilted. It was right in front of us too. Kenny ran to the Kop, his new adoring public, his face abeam with the smile the Glasgow lady had told us about. Terry Mac's goal sealed our 2-0 win.
I was waiting at the Halfway House for the bus home when Baz turned up
"Pedros Menignos! What d'yer reckon abarr Kenny?"
Why Baz should want to give me a pseudo-Spanish name I'm not quite sure but if it kept him happy that was okay by me.
"Yeah, brilliant Baz. Didn't see yer in the Kop mate."
"Nah, I was in the Anny Road. It's a boss atmosphere in there Pedros and we were gettin' into the Geordies."
"Oh were yer Baz? That's nice for yer."

Kenny opened the scoring again in the following game - a 3-0 win against West Brom. The Kop really did love him and he loved us back too, that was evident. Not for Kenny the slow start and settling in that other players had; he was absolutely made for Liverpool and we were made for him.

Happy Birthday Evo! It was too as we beat Chelsea 2-0 in the League Cup 2nd Round at Anfield. Kenny scored a brilliant chipped goal. This man could seemingly do anything. All thoughts of Keegan had now been banished. Chelsea didn't bring many fans to that match. Those they did bring were getting smacked all over Walton Breck Road after the match. I actually saved one from a certain pasting by taking him into the back of a shop owned by Mad John Hughes' father-in-law. The poor lad was absolutely shitting himself with a baying mob outside screaming for his blood. I say poor lad but he did look as if he was up for it anyway and would probably be smacking Reds all over the place at Stamford Bridge when we played them. Still, I couldn't just stand by and see him getting twatted by a dozen or so lads.

Fun time! Tommy Doc brought his Derby County team to Anfield on September 24th. He must have expected and certainly got a right roasting from the Kop. Derby came out and headed for the kick-in in front of the Kop. This normally brought howls of derision but when we kicked into all the "Mary Brown" songs Leighton James, now playing for the Rams, was creased over, doubled up laughing. It was said that the Doc was none too pleased about this, which was probably true as James played only another four games for Derby before being despatched to QPR. The 1-0 win, courtesy of a late Terry Mac goal was due reason for celebration by me and Delvesy. We were also getting warmed up for going to the night-time reception of our mate Keith Horrocks wedding. It wasn't good for our bladders though and we had to ask (in Delvesy's case, threaten) the driver to stop the bus halfway along Cunscough (which you have to be very careful how to pronounce) Lane to have a piss in the bushes. Whatever it was Delvesy had been drinking I can't remember but it was producing gallons of piss. I was back on the bus with the driver getting fed up of waiting for Delvesy's river of piss to abate.
"Ah fuck this, I'm off!"
It was funny as fuck watching Delvesy running after the bus with his flies open, piss still streaming forth. He leapt on the bus, just avoiding being killed, and was in no fit state to remonstrate with the driver. Delvesy managed to get home and clean himself up in good time for us to get to Keith's reception. It was a great do but sadly the marriage didn't last very long. Even more sadly neither did Keith. Keith was a super fit young lad who did martial arts. It was an amazing sight to see him practising with rice sticks during his dinner break at work. It was a great tragedy that such a good, fit, young lad should die so suddenly of a heart attack at 21. Evo cried.

Our great League start of five wins and two draws with Kenny scoring five of our eleven goals was brought to an abrupt halt at Old Trafford. Having missed the previous season's encounter through no fault of my own I wasn't going to miss this one. The 2-0 win kept the Mancs happy 'til the usual bombardment of bricks and bottles at Warwick Road Station. They really were a big shower of shithouses sometimes, not showing up 'til they were well out of reach. I suppose that suited me fine though as long as I could dodge the flying missiles. I could really do without mixing it with hoolies from other clubs. I got twatted enough at home (that's home as in Willow Hey rather than Anfield) without getting twatted at away footy grounds.

The treat that Tommy Rogers had promised me materialised when I refereed the Comrades versus Balcony Farm. Jimmy Wilson, young Tommy Rogers, Georgie Jones etc were all Tommy promised they would be. Also playing was Besty. I hadn't seen the madman for a while. I also hadn't realised how good a footballer he was. He had told me about once playing for Liverpool Reserves before breaking a leg but I'd thought it was the usual Besty bullshit. He also had a fair old mouth on him. It had been a fairly contentious game so Besty sought to air his opinions to me during a break in play.
"Thought that was a penalty before Peter."
"Nah, yer dived Ste."
"Peter, if I called yer a twat would yer send me off?"
"I'd 'ave to Ste, no choice."
"Yeah, but I'm yer mate aren't I?"
"Doesn't matter Ste. You call me a twat on this pitch and yer goin' off."
"Well if I was to just *think* yer a twat would yer send me off?"
"Err, no. I can't send yer off for somethin' yer thinkin'. I couldn't send anybody off for somethin' they're thinkin'. I wouldn't know yer thought I was a twat so I couldn't send yer off for that."
"So let me get it right. If I *called* yer a twat yer'd send me off?"
"That's right."

"But if I only *thought* yer were a twat yer wouldn't send me off?"
"That's right."
"Well I think yer a twat."
What could I say to that? Besty's manic laughter echoed all round Blaguegate as he ran up the field having royally taken the piss out of me.

Chelsea arrived for the League game at Anfield with their hoolies well prepared. They'd been caught on the hop in the League Cup game but it wasn't going to happen this time. They came mob-handed and were congregating around the Albert and the Park in a probable attempt to gather together and take the Kop. The bizzies got wind of it which was a good job for all concerned and after causing a bit of mayhem the hundreds of Chelsea lads were escorted to the Anny where I'm sure they received a cordial welcome. Kenny continued to weave his magic in this game. Another of his speciality exquisite chips gave us an early lead. Davy Fairclough added to the score in the second half to give us a comfortable win.

Jimmy Case's two goals gave us a 2-1 win at Leeds. Apart from me getting legged for about half a mile after the game there didn't seem to be much trouble. It was strange at Leeds if there was no trouble. You went expecting it, geared up for it even, but when it didn't materialise there was a mixture of relief and emptiness. Maybe the Leeds boys were storing it up for next time.

The defence of our European Cup started at Anfield against old foes Dynamo Dresden. I was there with the Terrible Twosome - Baz and Delvesy. On their own they were hard work - together they were bloody impossible!
"Rattle their underwear!"
"Crack their skulls!"
"Come on Reds, their arses are like the inside of an oil barrel!"
It was hard work concentrating on the match amidst all this. Not slagging the lads off like, they were a great laugh, it's just that

there was a game of football on and half the time I was bent double holding my sides. The scoring was opened by the Scottish Streaker - Alan "Jocky" Hansen. This lad was a bit gawky and not quite yet ready for a regular first team place but everybody could tell he was going to be class. Our eventual 5-1 win gave us a great base to take to East Germany for the second leg.

As was the case a couple of years earlier the Anfield Derby proved to be a totally forgettable affair. I honestly cannot tell you a single thing about it. I haven't missed a Derby at either Anfield or Goodison since 1964 but I cannot remember a single thing that happened in either of those games. Again, unsurprisingly the match ended 0-0.

I can tell you loads about what happened the following Saturday though as it was at my old stamping ground - Maine Road. I went with a couple of lads who played for Tawd Vale in the Skem League - Wilko and Bally. Wilko's Dad, Ernie, was driving so the two Road Enders had to be on their best behaviour. Sensibly, I had a ticket for the Main Stand. A little less sensibly, Wilko and Ernie were going in the Liverpool section of the Kippax. Mad arse, totally off his head, Bally was going in the City section of the Kippax. He said he couldn't get a ticket for the Liverpool section and would have to pay in the home part of the Kippax but I think Bally wanted to go in with the City lads anyway as an act of bravado. Well, it wasn't an act really - loons can't act! Wilko probably wanted to be in the mix with the City lads the same as his mate but couldn't as he was with his Dad. Even Road Enders were scared of their Dad! I found a kindred spirit in Ernie. He was in his forties and had been watching the Reds since he was a lad so regaled me with all the old, great stories of players such as Liddell that I loved so much. Ernie was a really nice guy who worked in Park Lane hospital so I suppose was on a sort of busman's holiday looking after Bally. Having found a safe parking place, if there ever was such a thing at Maine Road, we went in search of drink.

"Ee arr, Robin Hood Social Club. That looks okay. Let's go in there."

Okay, I admit, it was the first pub we came across but I was gagging for a bevy. The other lads looked a little apprehensive but trusted my judgement of watering holes. They were right to be apprehensive; hole was the operative word for this "establishment". The place was chocker with pimps, prostitutes, pot heads and drug dealers - and that was just the women! Even the couple of old Jamaican boys playing dominoes looked decidedly dodgy. We were in there now though so there wasn't much point in walking straight out. If we'd done that we'd have got our heads kicked in anyway so best to just front it and get on with drinking. The place was dark and dank with the air full of pot smoke. The atmosphere was decidedly nasty and was made worse by about forty pair of big white eyes peering at us, piercing the gloom like a knife through butter. The assorted collection of rabble that made up the clientele of the Robin Hood must have admired our cheek though as they left us alone save for a prostitute offering me a shag. I politely declined her kind invitation on three grounds: I didn't have enough money; my knob would have dropped off if I had shagged her and finally, most importantly, if Ev found out she would have cut my meat and two veg off and served it up to me for dinner the next day with her special cockroach gravy. Fuck me, I got accused of shagging around often enough - imagine if I'd actually done it! Well I'll leave you to imagine it if you don't mind. I won't bother. Things like that make me queasy. We managed to walk out of the Robin Hood with all our body parts still intact though our nerves were properly shredded. Bally was a bit upset though that he hadn't been offered a spliff. We bade each other silent farewells (loads of City lads around you see) and made our three separate ways into the ground. For once at Maine Road I was surrounded by fairly friendly people although I must admit they were more "blanket and flask" than "bricks and bottles." There was some old dear sat a couple of rows in front of me with a bell as big as Bally's head. It made as much noise too! Every time City attacked she'd give it the bells of Shannon; well, I suppose the bells of Manchester more like. Whatever, it was fuckin' loud! Fuckin' annoying too! That was 'til Davy Fairclough shut it the fuck up when he scored after half-an-hour. The goal came at the end I was nearest, North Stand, too. For the rest of the half the bell was silent. Miss (she had to be a Miss as she was damn ugly) Quasimodo was in fine form in the second half though. City just hit us with wave after wave of attacks. The inexperience of Jocky and the older legs of Emlyn were being cruelly exposed by City's three-pronged attack of Kidd, Channon and Royle. Joey at left-back was also being given a very torrid time by right-winger Peter Barnes. Barnes should have been, certainly had the potential to be, a really great player. He was fast, tricky and could cross a ball but never really made as big a mark in the game as he should have done. Unfortunately for us though he was right on blob for this particular game. It was no surprise when Kidd equalised. That was bad enough with Quasi giving it loads on the bell but it got worse when Channon put City ahead. The twat was off with that stupid fuckin' windmill celebration all over the pitch. I was getting some stick from the City fans but at least I wasn't getting pummelled. To complete my misery Joe fuckin' big 'ead Royle scored their third. Had to be him didn't it? Fuckin' ex-Evertonian! I couldn't get out of the ground quick enough at the final whistle. It was getting quite cold now too so I couldn't wait to get back to the safety, warmth and sanctuary of the car. Where the fuck was it parked? I really just didn't have a fuckin' clue. The maze that was the streets of Moss Side gave me no clues either. Every street looked the same to me. I was in trouble; no fuckin' doubt about that! There were gangs of City lads everywhere; I was surely going to get my head kicked in. I spotted a bizzy station and went in there on the premise of asking the name of a mythical street. I didn't have a fuckin' pot what the name of the street was we'd parked in; I was going to have to make one up. The object of the exercise was to keep my head attached to my shoulders 'cos if I got sussed, which I was surely going to be if I kept wandering around like a fuckin nomad, then I'd be a head missing at the end of the day.

"Excuse me officer. I can't find our car. I think we've parked in Willow Road. D'yer know where that is?"

"No Willow Road around here lad."

"Oh okay, can I just stay in 'ere for a bit then? There's loads of loons all over the place. I'm gonna get me 'ead kicked in if I go back out there now."

"No, we're busy. You'll be okay. Go and find your car."

Oh fuckin' thanks yer fuckin' Manc twat! I thought yer supposed to protect the fuckin' public, even if I am a Scouser, not send them out to almost certain death. Fuckin' wanker!

I was fucked both physically and emotionally. I'd been walking for miles. It was now a good hour after the final whistle and still no sign of Wilko and co. They'd probably gone by now.

EVERYWHERE WE GO!
EVERYWHERE WE GO!
PEOPLE WANNA KNOW!
PEOPLE WANNA KNOW!
WHO WE ARE!
WHO WE ARE!
SO WE TELL THEM!
SO WE TELL THEM!
WE ARE THE KIPPAX!
WE ARE THE KIPPAX!
THE BARMY, BARMY KIPPAX!
THE BARMY, BARMY KIPPAX!
WE HATE MAN U!
WE HATE MAN U!
WE HATE SCOUSERS TOO!
WE HATE SCOUSERS TOO!

For fuck sake, that's all I fuckin' need. I was walking straight towards about fifteen mean looking fuckers. If I tried to run back or cross the road I was in for a certain cracking. I was just gonna have to take the digs I'd get and hope I wouldn't be too badly hurt. I can't describe the stomach churning feeling I got on occasions like this. You have to be in the situation to know it. Suffice to say it felt like there was a brick in my belly with the rest of my insides all knotted up. I was very close to being physically sick. I was also very close, and I mean this - no messing, to actually pooing my pants. It really is a horrible feeling. I was sure that the first punch or kick that landed would see me both spew and shit at the same time. I could only hope that some of it landed on these twats.

Whoever it was that looked after me from on high on these occasions was certainly doing the biz for me now. I walked straight through the City lads. How the fuck they didn't suss me I'll never know. I don't look like a Manc do I? I couldn't believe my luck but I still had to work out a way of getting home in one piece. I'd left home with enough money to get me a bevy when I got back but it was nowhere near enough to cover the train fare. Even if I fancied bunking the train there was still the perilous journey to Victoria and the equally dangerous dodging of the City lads certain to be assembled there. What the fuck was I going to do? I really was very close to tears when the great Liverpool God smiled down on me. I turned the corner to see Ernie's car just about to pull away. I couldn't shout as this would have attracted the City lads I'd just avoided and we'd all get filled in. Luckily my frantic arm waving was spotted by Wilko. I couldn't thank Ernie, Wilko and Bally enough for waiting over an hour for me to get back. It would have been easier for them just to get off and leave me. It was my own stupid fuckin' fault that I couldn't find my way back to the car as I've absolutely no sense of direction. They'd risked getting their own heads kicked in to wait for me. Wilko later told me that the fifteen or so City lads I'd managed by the grace of the LFC God to dodge had attacked one lone Scouser. Even though he went down under the barrage the lad managed to give four or five of them a good crack after he got back up. Dead brave and hard them City lads aren't they? Twats!

After such a traumatic time I couldn't be arsed going straight home so it was to the Derby Arms for me. Jimmy the Singer was in there. Jimmy was a smashing little bloke who worked with me in Grimwoods. He never did anybody any harm, always had a smile on his face even though he kept himself pretty much to himself and was constantly singing, hence his nickname. I was feeling pretty shit after such a bad day but it was nothing to what Jimmy had been through.

"Hiya Peter. Lost three one didn't yer?"

"Yeah Jimmy. Fuckin' fed up. Nearly got me fuckin' 'ead kicked in too. You don't look too 'appy for once either. What's the matter?"

"Me wife's left me."

"Fuckin' 'ell Jimmy that's sad. When did that 'appen?"

"Today. I went out for a pint this afternoon. When I got back the 'ouse was empty. She took everythin', fuckin' everythin'. I 'aven' got a fuckin' stick of furniture. She even emptied the food cupboards an' the fridge. She left me a note. She's fucked off with someone else."

"Fuckin' 'ell Jimmy, that's bad mate. I'm sorry."

"Fuck all I can do abarr it now Evo. Come on, let's 'ave a pint."

"Okay. Yer can stay at mine tonight. Sort yerself out tomorrow."

By the time we left the Derby I had Jimmy singing again. I felt more sorry for him than he did for himself.

LITTLE OLD WINE DRINKER ME!

Go 'ead Jimmy lad!

We got back to mine in time for me to relive the events of the day, well those inside the ground, on Match of the Day. All you could hear was this fuckin' mad bell!

"Who's ringin' that bell?"

"Some fuckin' owld cow! I was sittin' right behind 'er. Yeah, fuckin' owld cow ringin' a fuckin' cow bell!"

That got Jimmy laughing again. He'd just been through a fuckin' horrendous experience but he wasn't one to dwell on things. He told Big Ev all about his misfortune.

"'Ah that's terrible. 'Ave yer 'ad anythin' to eat Jimmy?"

"No, nothing. She took all the food."

Ev responded by cooking Jimmy and me the biggest, fattest wagonload of chips you've ever seen in your life. There were gangs of sausages, a mountain of peas and two eggs, not even congealed, to accompany the chips.

"Fuckin' 'ell Ev, Jimmy's only a little fella. 'E doesn't know whether to eat it, climb it or fuckin' fight it!"

The Singer certainly did know though as he walloped the lot! I was very proud of my wife. Certainly we had major barnies. We were both as bad as each other for scrapping with each other, that has to be said. Sure, Ev had left me a few times and mostly for trivial reasons, or so I thought, but she always came back, even though sometimes I wasn't the best husband in the world. She had never though pulled such a shitty stunt as to fuck off with all the furniture and worse still leave me with nothing to eat. Ev was a gorgeous looking woman but above all else she had a very compassionate nature. There was no way on earth she was going to see Jimmy with nothing to eat. No wonder I loved her very much.

"Peter, thanks for the couch. Ev, thanks for the scran Ta ra. Jimmy."

Jimmy had left a note on the couch and was gone before I got up. By the time I got back into work on the Monday Jimmy was right as rain again and looking forward to refurnishing his house. Above all else though he had scran in his cupboards as Ev had made him a food parcel to take home with him. I felt good that I and more especially Ev had been able to help him in his hour of need. Top woman Ev and don't let anybody ever forget it!

CHAPTER EIGHTEEN

MEN NOT TO BE MESSED WITH

Our 5-1 win at Anfield against Dynamo Dresden proved a more than comfortable enough cushion in East Germany even though we lost the game 1-2. That was it now as far as Europe was concerned until March. We could concentrate on getting our League form back to what it should be. That was what we thought anyway 'til Villa took us apart at Anfield the following Saturday. We only lost 1-2 in the end but it could have been even more as Andy Gray and co steamed into us. I knew taunting Gray with "Andy Pandy" before and during the game wasn't a good idea. Sure enough it backfired on us. Gray scored the two goals. Enough said.

We lost again the following week 0-2 at QPR. This wasn't good. We'd now lost four games in a row. The three consecutive League games we'd lost had dropped us down to sixth place. We only half stopped the rot in the following game, struggling to get a 1-1 draw at home against Bristol City.

Filbert Street was a notoriously hard place to get points at but it was the scene of us getting back on track as we trounced Leicester 4-0. The Leicester fans were none too happy about this and tried their usual trick of throwing people in the canal but they were well fucked off by plenty of hardcases.

We were showing signs of at last taking the League Cup seriously. After beating Chelsea and Derby County our opponents in Round 4 at Anfield were Coventry. Coventry were taking it very seriously as the crowd of 33,000 contained about 10,00 of their supporters. The Anny weren't taking this lying down though and there were some mad battles going on in there. We were observing all this from the Kop. Prominent in the Coventry half of the Anny was a lad with the whitest jumper on you've ever seen. He couldn't have been more conspicuous if he'd tried. White jumper man was winding everybody up. He was not only urging the Coventry fans on during the singing and fighting but was also giving it large to the Road End on the other side of the fence. That might have been a very brave thing to do in the safety of the ground with a fence and loads of bizzies between him and the Road End loons but he might have to pay for his show of bravado after the game.

"We're gonna fuck the fella in the white," was the song coming from the Kop. I think the Anny lads had also spotted him and were making similar noises. Taking no notice of all this of course were the patrons of the Kemlyn Road. Taking no notice of course because they were all sat at fuckin' home! Coventry fans occupied the Kemlyn Road that night. The blanket and flask brigade would want their Wembley tickets though should we get to the final of the competition. Maybe they wouldn't have to bother with stuff like that though as we could only manage a 2-2 draw and the replay at Highfield Road would be decidedly tricky. I later heard that white jumper arsewipe got his just deserts.

"WHERE WERE YOU ON TUESDAY NIGHT?"
Billy Blanket, Sammy Scarf, Freddy Flask and the rest of the Kemlyn Pensioners Club were reminded of their dereliction of duty at the Coventry game before and during the 2-0 win against West Ham the following Saturday. Tommy Smith couldn't help but laugh at this as for years he'd had a turbulent relationship with the patrons of that stand.

TOMMY IS A KOPITE. TOMMY IS A KOPITE DA DA DA DA DA DA DA!

Kevin Keegan returned to Anfield with his Hamburg team for the second leg of the European Super Cup. The first game had ended 1-1 so we had high hopes of winning the trophy. Hamburg were a good side even the season before without Keegan, having won the European Cup Winners Cup. Kevin received quite a good reception from the Kop. Sure, he took a bit of stick but most of it was of the good-natured variety.

"We all agree Dalglish is better than Keegan!"

By the time Terry Mac had scored a hat trick to add to Thommo's opener the Kop asserted that even Terry was better than Keegan! The crowd were willing Kenny to score and after Davy Fairclough scored the fifth goal of the night to add to the one he'd scored in the first leg our King duly obliged two minutes from time.

"Yer shoulda stayed at Anfield!"

Kevin looked totally pissed off by the 6-0 thrashing and might have even silently agreed with us doubting the wisdom of moving from the European Champions. Kevin however took it like the man and great player that he was. Kenny was better though!

The Grimwood loon count was significantly increased with an influx of new employees. First of all there was Billy Mac. Billy was actually sound but his favourite drink was a strange brew of pale/bitter. It was like a brown/bitter but replacing the bottle of brown to pour into the half-pint of bitter was a bottle of pale. I'd never heard of that one before and certainly never heard of it since. Billy did get himself into trouble once though when another of the new loons, Wooly, was buying a round. Billy asked for a *pint* of bitter as well as the bottle of pale and was told exactly where it could be shoved. As I say, Billy was sound but he was tighter than a duck's arse. Then there was The Captain. The Captain was probably only about the same age as myself but wanted to be 60. He was forever telling us about this boat he had moored at the canal in Burscough.

"Alright Spider. I've got a boat yer know."

Quite why he used to call me Spider I didn't know but was relieved to learn later that he called everybody Spider. It was a wonder anybody could ever see him anyway as his head was always covered in plumes of shit smelling smoke emanating from the pipe he had permanently on the go. A couple of the lads actually took up his invitation one day to go and have a look at and a ride (is that the right word?) on his boat. I had no intention of going but in the end was sorry I didn't. Apparently he was unmooring (or whatever you call it) the boat but didn't get aboard

in time and ended up in the canal! I'd loved to have seen that one!
THERE'S ONLY ONE CAPTAIN BIRDS EYE!
Minto - I liked him. Minto was an ex-gravedigger (somebody's got to do it) who called everybody "Ugly." He thought it was hilariously funny when people responded to that. It was I suppose as it always made me laugh.

John the Jobo - Christ he was a whopper. Is that a mixed metaphor or something? I tried the same joke on the latest Jehovah's Witness to enter my life as I had on Pat Asp's missus Marie but was met with the same Morocco response. John was okay but was deffo away with the fairies. Billy Mac and me used to piss ourselves laughing as John ran around the factory hurdling every obstacle in his way. We pissed ourselves even more one day when John singularly failed in his attempt to hurdle a one-foot high flat rack and ended up face down. I'll never go to heaven will I? But then neither will John as I'm sure I heard him swear!

Topping everybody though in the whopper stakes like a big slam dunker was Mr. Benn. Now there was a real loonball! Mr. Benn, or John to his friends, of which I'm sure he had many, was the biggest liar since The Virgin Mary. For those of you who don't know, Mr. Benn was a Children's TV cartoon character who went into a costume shop every day and turned into the character of the costume he was wearing. Our Mr. Benn, John, had been in the Army, Navy, RAF, the Marines and the SAS. He'd been a window cleaner, a plumber and an electrician. He'd been a docker, a mountaineer and a stunt motorbike rider. He'd been a deep-sea diver, an airline pilot and a tank driver. In short, he was a fuckin' liar! He'd supposedly done all this even though he was only about mid-twenties. He must have left school when he was two! His biggest whopper though was the one he told us about when he'd lost control of his motorbike, skidded through a garden fence and then crashed through the patio windows of the house. The woman then said to him as he was lying on the floor of her living room with his bike on top of him, "Do you want a cup of tea?"

All of this, bear in mind, was done even though he only had one leg!
WHAT A FUCKIN' WHOPPER!

I didn't go to the 2-0 League Cup replay win at Coventry. Wilko and Bally went and never tire of telling me of the biggest pitched battle they've ever seen. It happened in the park you have to go through to get to Coventry station. Hundreds of lads from both sides did battle in a massive mud-heap. The bizzies just fucked off and left them to it. Apparently in the end nobody knew who was who and were probably twatting their own lads. I'm glad I wasn't at that. I would have got twatted by a Red - probably Wilko! Mind you, I think he probably would have done it on purpose as revenge for me disallowing for offside what he considered to be a perfectly good goal the previous Sunday. It didn't matter to him that he was very near having a pint with the barman in the Roundabout when the ball skidded inadvertently off his shin and past the bemused goalkeeper. The centre-half supposed to be marking Wilko was having a ciggy on the halfway line, such was the "threat" he knew Wilko would cause him. Wilko did actually score a goal I couldn't find a reason to disallow. He claims it as the greatest goal ever seen at Blaguegate but I remember it more as a case of him getting in the way of a shot which hit his knee and spun crazily into the net past the disbelieving goalkeeper. Wilko wasn't exactly a world-class marksman. I once had to stop a game to get a taxi to the Warden's Club in Lathom. The ball had ended up behind the bar there after one of Wilko's better shots!

I really wanted to go to Nottingham on Boxing Day. Brian Clough's newly promoted Forest were doing marvellously well and sitting pretty at the top of the League. We were third so it was going to be some game. I hadn't been to Forest for seven years mainly due to the fact that they'd been in the Second Division for most of that time. The last time I'd been I'd taken a couple of cracks, got legged all over the place and nearly got lashed in the Trent. I did still really desperately want to go though. Big Ev had other ideas. My darling wife had a Boxing Day night out planned in the Derby Arms. Delvesy and Mary would be there. Baz and Anne would be there too. That's a motley collection if ever I saw one. I couldn't really get out of this one. Maybe I was mellowing but we hadn't been out together for a while, we were getting on very well at the moment - we hadn't had a nark for at least a week, Ev hadn't fucked off for a while and in general it was just a better idea to keep Ev sweet. I wasn't arsed about the possibility of getting lashed in the Trent - I'd been through worse at away games but I was arsed about incurring the wrath of Ev. I settled instead for listening to the game on the radio. Steve Heighway scored our goal in the 1-1 draw. We were discussing the match in the Derby.

"Did yer listen to the match Baz?"

"Nah, I err didn't Pedros. We were err out vistin' relatives an' that."

I wondered why Baz shot a nervous glance towards Anne as he said it.

"Did you Delvesy?"

"Yeah, wish I'd been there."

"Tell me abarr it."

"Is that all you men ever talk about, bloody football?"

Mary was piping up now as she was getting slowly pissed.

"We'll talk about sex if yer want."

That was my second favourite pastime!

"Go 'way yer bloody perv!"

Anne was getting pissed too.

"'Ow's that pervin'? It's bloody natural!"

Ev smiled. She knew it wasn't just talk. She'd be getting it good style later on.

U-NI-TED!

Lollipop announced his presence. He'd been to Goodison where Man U had beaten Everton 6-2. This was gonna be good fun. Lollipop, as I've said, was a loon sober - drunk and having just watched his team win 6-2 he was gonna be a riot!

"Nah then Baz. What the bloody 'ell were tha doin' at Goodison today?"

"Errr....what d'yer errr... mean errr....like. I errrr... wasn't at Goodison."

"Tha's a lyin' bloody tuss! I sin thee comin' aht!"

Baz's kite went as crimson as the dead smart shirt he had on. He'd been well and truly copped. Time for some stick off Evo and Delvesy.

"What? Yer went to bloody Goodison?"

"Yeah, what the fuckin' 'ell's that all abarr Baz?"

"Fuck off will youse. I just fancied goin'. What the fuck's it gotta do with youse?"

"Well why d'yer say yer'd been visitin' relatives?"

"Yeah, relatives my arse!"

"'Cos I knew I'd get stick off youse fuckers!"

"Yer fuckin' deserve it! Fancy goin' to fuckin' Goodison!"

"Where about d'yer go anyway Baz?"

"Errr...in the err...Paddock like."

I had a sneaking suspicion that Baz had actually gone in with the Park End lads to have a crack at the Mancs in there but I wasn't gonna say anything in front of Anne. That wouldn't have been fair. It was okay giving a bit of stick but I didn't want to see him killed. Baz's bacon was saved by half-a-dozen Asian lads who walked in. I have to say that it was very unusual to see Asians around Skem. Not sure why but not many Asian families lived in Skem. The fact they all had turbans on made it even more unusual. Baz was well pissed by now so he it was who opened up.

"Fuckin' 'ell, it's the Bengal Lancers!"

Now I must tell you that this was meant to be in no way racist; none of us were like that in the slightest. It was meant as a joke and certainly taken that way by the Asian lads as they were laughing along with us. One of the lads went to put money in the jukebox. That was Delvesy's cue.

"Eh mate, that jukebox only takes ten pences. It doesn't take rupees."

All of us, including the Asian lads were pissin' ourselves laughing at that one. Lollipop started the singsong with a couple of Man U songs. Delvesy and me soon followed with our songs. Baz was being fairly quiet.

"Come on Baz. Giz an Everton song!"

"Fuck off Evo! An' you Delvesy!"

The night got madder when Besty graced us with his pissed up presence.

"Me missus 'as just 'ad a baby! A little girl!"

"Ah, that's nice. What 'ave yer called 'er?"

It was only a polite enquiry from Ev, just being nice and all that but she was soon to be in trouble.

"Danielle."

"Ah, that's a lovely name. Danielle. Danielle Best."

I knew what Ev was doing. She was just seeing how the name sounded. Besty saw his opportunity and seized it gratefully with both hands.

"No, Danielle fuckin' Rockefeller! What the fuck d'yer think. Fuckin' 'ell Peter, where d'yer get 'er from? She's fuckin' dead brainy 'er isn't she?"

I felt a bit sorry for Ev then. Everybody, including me, was pissin' themselves laughing and she was the butt of the joke. She took it well though. Chucking out time and I was well bladdered singing the Christmas Number One, "Mull of Kintyre." I loved that song and knew all the words so was giving it large as we were walking home. A great night out that. I was almost glad I hadn't gone to Forest. Only almost.

My hangover the following day wasn't helped by having to be at Anfield for a truly awful game against Wolves. We won it 1-0 with a Phil Neal penalty but it honestly was a terrible game.

As much as I'd wanted to go to Forest on Boxing Day I definitely did not want to go to Newcastle on New Year's Eve. It was just not my idea of fun to be traipsing up to Newcastle for an almost certain pasting when I could be enjoying the New Year's Eve celebrations. Ev came to the rescue though by arranging another night out with the same crew in the Derby Arms. Of course I told her that I'd really wanted to go to Newcastle but was sacrificing it to be going out with our friends. Another boss night out was had ending with a party at Baz's. I told everybody that would listen, and some that wouldn't, what a good lad I was for not going to Newcastle, especially in view of the fact that we won 2-0. Oh how gutted I was that I hadn't got to see that splendid victory, preferring instead to be at the side of my darling wife. Aren't I a good husband?

The catalyst for our season and in many ways for the club as a whole came in the 3rd Round of the FA Cup at Stamford Bridge. Chelsea walloped us 4-2. We desperately needed a new midfielder. Cally, for all his eagerness and willing running was now running out of gas in those ageing legs of his. Even though we were right back to form in the League, the 2-0 home win against Boro giving us our third win a row, we needed somebody to keep that drive going. Bob knew who he wanted and went out and got him. Graeme Souness arrived a few days after the Chelsea debacle. The new man's debut would be away at West Brom the following Saturday. I was deffo going to this one. I'd accrued enough Brownie points for Ev not to have a cob on about it. I wanted to see Souness' debut but also I loved going to West Brom. It was always a brilliant atmosphere at the typically old-fashioned ground. There was never much bother there, certainly not on the scale of City, United and Tottenham say. I'd missed the last four away games and the buzz that came with it so was really looking forward to getting back into the swing of things. Me and Wilko arrived at Lime Street too late to book on to one of the two specials so instead had to go on the ordinary to Birmingham. New Street was going to be fun seeing as Birmingham were at home to Leeds that day. After we left the station we were walking around to find a bus or taxi to take us to West Brom. We were soon sussed by a few Birmingham lads. Wilko had the answer.

"Take our belts off and if they have a go give the nearest one a fuckin' crack with it."

This was not a bad idea at all as the belt I was wearing had a big heavy buckle on in the shape of a huge Liverpool badge. The lads followed us for a while but as we showed no signs of running and saw that we had our belts off didn't have the nerve to have a go.

Anyway, we couldn't have run; our jeans would have fell down! We eventually found a bus that would take us to the ground. Fortunately there were a few other Liverpool lads on the bus. There were some West Brom lads on too so potential for bother. Our lot though settled for taking the piss out of one of the West Brom lads who had this big, stupid Panama hat on. As we were getting off the bus, right outside their end I might add, the hat was removed from divvy's head and found a new Scouse home. How the hell it didn't go off I'll never know. We'd arrived quite early so not many people or bizzies around which gave an ideal opportunity for bunking in the ground. There was an owld fella manning the old-fashioned low turnstile. I scrambled under and was on my toes up to the terraces with Tommy Turnstile shouting after me, "Eh, come back 'ere. Come back!"

Yeah, right, like I was gonna fuckin' go back. I fully expected a bizzy to come and collar me at any moment. The terrace was fairly empty but there was one big problem; I'd managed to bunk into the West Brom half of the segregated Smethwick End. Fuckin' divvy!

"Excuse me officer. I'm a Liverpool fan and I've come into the wrong half."

"No problem son," said the kindly officer as he opened the fence to allow me into our half. I'm a cheeky bastard! Where the fuck was Wilko though? No sign of him! If I'd managed to crawl under the turnstile with my piggy belly surely he had with his stick insect frame. The answer came about twenty minutes before kick off.

LIV-ER-POOL!

There were a few thousand Reds in our end but this chant was coming from the other end. It seemed there were a good few Reds managed to get in West Brom's end; the opposite end to us. I could just about see the little knot of Reds in that end before they were converged on by hundreds of Albion fans. The Reds were chased out and over the wall. The bizzies were escorting our lads along the running track and into our end. Fuck me, who should be walking alongside the bizzies only Wilko! Our little crew,

Road Enders obviously, nobody else would be fuckin' daft enough to expect to take the West Brom end with about twenty heads, were cheered all the way up our side of the terrace. The West Brom lads in the other side were going mad trying to get at them.

"Fuckin' 'ell Wilko, what happened to you?"

"I tried to jump over the turnstile and a bizzy gripped me. 'E saw you crawlin' under but said 'e couldn't be arsed runnin' after yer. 'E let me go an' I saw some Road End who were goin' in their end so I went with them."

"Yeah, that's about par for the course; twenty Road End trying to take the West Brom end. Yer fuckin' loonballs!"

Souness had a quiet debut in a match we won with an early David Johnson goal but the big Scot had shown enough touches of class to suggest he would become a Liverpool great. We were getting plenty of agro from the Albion lads on the way back to the station, especially from one gobby bastard. Wilko once again had the answer.

"Fuckin' shut up Stan Harvey!"

For those of you who don't know, and maybe it's best that you don't but I'm going to tell you anyway, Stan Harvey was an archetypal Brummie character in the TV series Crossroads.

"What's bloody wrong with Stan Harvey loike?" drawled Stan in his horrible Brummie accent.

"This!"

Before you could say "Amy Turtle" (don't ask; again, it's best if you don't know) Wilko well and truly shut Stan Harvey up by twatting him in his mouthy gob, if that makes any sense at all. There were a few bricks flying around while we were waiting outside the station to board the train but nothing too bad. That was until we got on the train. A massive pebble crashed through the window and landed on the table between me and Wilko.

"Fuckin' 'ell, that was close!"

"That's your fuckin' fault Wilko for upsettin' Stan!"

Fuckin' bastard Stan! I was glad his missus Jill had fucked off and shagged Adam Chance behind his back. Don't ask!

Having got over the Stan Harvey experience we settled down to discuss details of the following Tuesday night's trip to Wrexham for the League Cup Quarter-Final. Well, Wilko and a few of the other Skem lads we met on the train did anyway. There was no way I could go. It was just an away game too far for me. Not in terms of distance of course but in terms of Brownie points, money and time off work. I had now used up all the Brownie points I gained on New Year's Eve for the trip to West Brom. I'd also used up most of my money even though I had saved a few bob by bunking in. I'd deffo used up all credit with Jack Huyton after the great flying chair incident. Old Jack still hadn't properly forgiven me for that. I can't say I blamed him for that as the poor old get was probably still getting counselling for severe trauma. I was properly, well and truly gutted at having to miss Wrexham especially as Kenny scored his first hat trick for us in the 3-1 win.

My little brother Price was fast approaching his 11th birthday and as he was as red an Evo as any of us I thought it was high time I took him to his first match. He desperately wanted to see, in the flesh, this King Kenny I was always going on about and also our new signing. Price was just slightly older than I was when I went to my first match but he was to be spared the arduours of the Boys Pen; Price was to be a Kopite from minute one. By the time the day was over I was wishing I had thrown him to the lions in the Pen and bloody well left him there! The first half was bad enough as we were playing shite and I was having to feed Price a constant diet of crisps, lemonade, chocolate and sweets to not only keep him happy but also to keep him sat on his precarious perch on a crush barrier. Price didn't seem to care too much for having a numb bum but wouldn't listen to me telling him that he would have no chance of seeing anything should he stand on the terrace.
"Peter, I need a wee."
"Piss on the steps like everybody else. The men'll make room for yer."
"No, I wanna go the toilet."
I thought this was strange as Price never had a problem with

pissing in the street. He was quite a street-wise little kid (a euphemism for right little scally) so I wasn't unduly bothered at letting him go on his own. Imagine that happening now in 2002. I wouldn't let a ten-year-old kid in my care out of sight for a second! Very unfortunately that is how present day society has us all thinking. The bad guys, whilst not winning, are definitely influencing the good guys (the majority of society) thinking. Anyway, back to the plot. Where we were stood in the Kop wasn't too far away from the toilets so I'd be able to keep an eye on Price and he'd be able to find his way back quite easily. I wasn't that bothered when he hadn't turned up fifteen minutes into the second half. I was more bothered that our shite performance of the first half had now turned into a two goal deficit. Fuck me, this was bad. Perhaps Price had done what our John had done at Blackpool thirteen years earlier and robbed money out of Ma's purse to feed his face. It was just after Trevor Francis had almost completed a fuckin' miserable day for me by slotting Birmingham's third from the penalty spot when I heard the Tannoy announcement:

"Peter Etherington in the Kop please report immediately to the police room and collect your brother."

Collect my fuckin' arse! The little twat had probably been trying to rob the snack bar or the turnstile man. He could fuckin' wait 'til the end of the match. Even if we were getting beat 0-3 there was no way I was leaving before the end of the match. Thommo gave us some hope by pulling a goal back fifteen minutes from time. Razor then gave us an unlikely chance by making it 2-3 with three minutes to go. If we could get a draw out of this totally inept showing it would be the biggest miracle since that water and wine bollocks.

"Peter Etherington; please report IMMEDIATELY to the police room. Your brother is waiting for you."

"FUCK OFF!"

The bloke standing next me nearly shit himself.

"What the fuck are you lookin' at?"

"Er, nothin' mate. That your brother?"

"Yeah it is. So fuckin' what! 'E's gonna 'ave to wait."

Totally pissed off at our defeat I trudged round to the main entrance.

"I've been told to report to the police room to pick up my brother."

A bizzy came out leading little lost soul Price by the hand. Little lost soul my fuckin' arse!

"You shoulda been lookin' after yer little brother not lettin' 'im wander off on 'is own."

"What, wander off? 'E fucked off more like! Come 'ere yer fuckin' little twat!"

I was in grave danger of being arrested. My fault again eh? That makes a fuckin' change doesn't it!

"Just get 'im 'ome to yer Ma an' look after 'im properly next time."

"Next time? There won't be a fuckin' next time!"

"I'll lock yer up if yer swear again."

Fuck off!

"Sorry officer."

I felt like kicking my little bro up and down the car park but waited 'til we were out of sight of plod before berating him.

"Where the fuck did yer go?"

"I got lost cómin' back from the bog Peter so I went to see a bizzy."

"Did yer fuck get lost! Yer fuckin' just fucked off an' pretended yer were lost didn't yer?"

"Yeah. It was boss though. I saw all the players comin' back in. I saw Kenny an' that new fella. Yer should see the size of 'im Peter. An' Ronnie Moran said hiya to me."

I couldn't help but smile at the little twat. Wasn't I as much of a scally as him when I was his age? Of course I fuckin' was!

By the time we arrived back at Ma's we were laughing and joking again at the tricks Price had got up to but he was warned in no uncertain terms never to pull a fuckin' stunt like that again.

"Did 'e behave 'imself Peter? Was 'e a good lad?"

"Yeah, 'e was as good as gold Mam. Just a pity we got beat."

"Can I go the match with yer again Peter?"

"Yeah, course yer can son."
My Dad then said something to Price that he'd said to me all those years ago after I'd been to my first match:
"Yer a Red now lad. Once a Red, always a Red."

Our second defeat in a row came at Coventry so we weren't in the best of shape for the first leg of the League Cup semi-final at home to Arsenal. The Gunners brought thousands of fans for this match, much more than they'd ever brought before, and it seemed every single one of them was a nutter. There was bedlam all night before, during and after the game as they did battle with our lads. I'd been to Southport Hospital visiting our little Ste who was recovering from a very delicate operation. To put it nicely the little fella was dropping a bollock. I'd just got off the bus at the Halfway House when all hell was breaking loose and I found myself right in the middle of a load of Arsenal fans. They were getting charged by about a hundred of our lads and took to their toes. There was nothing else I could do only run with the pack. What a shit feeling being in amongst a load of opposition supporters and being legged by your own kind. If I hadn't done though I'd have been fucked one way or other. In the end I somehow managed to dodge a kicking and dive into the Halfway House which was nearly empty as the usual clientele were outside in the middle of the battle. We struggled to a 2-1 win with goals from Kenny and Razor in a game Arsenal really deserved more out of. Tommy Smith brilliantly kept our lead intact with a despairing last minute goal-line clearance from Arsenal scorer Malcolm MacDonald. The return at Highbury the following week would see fun and games alright.

I was spared the agony of making a decision whether or not to go to Highbury by Big Ev. There definitely weren't many Reds going, that was for sure. There certainly would be no safety in numbers for me in North London. I'd been kicked to fuck at Highbury six years earlier and definitely didn't fancy the idea of an almost certain repeat. I wanted to go though. This was a Semi-

Final after all. A Semi-Final at that which could see us reach the Final of this competition for the first time ever. Big Ev to the "rescue."

"We're goin' out on Tuesday."

"Are we? That's nice. What's the occasion?"

"Valentine's night."

"Yeah, I know. I was only messin' Ev, of course I knew. I was plannin' on takin' yer out anyway."

"I thought yer'd wanna go to Arsenal."

"Well I wanted to Ev but I'd rather take you out for a nice romantic night."

"Okay, I'll make it worth yer while."

"I know yer will love."

It was murder knowing the match was on the radio and not being able to listen to it but I did manage to hear the odd score flash that told me we'd drew 0-0 and so would be at Wembley for our first ever League Cup Final. Happy days! Our romantic evening was cut short by me feeling sick which was the best excuse I could think of to get home in time to watch the "highlights" such as they were, it was a bloody awful game, on the telly. I felt better when we got to bed though!

Graeme Souness had a fairly quiet first few weeks of his Liverpool career but exploded into life against Manchester United at Anfield. A brilliant volley from just outside the penalty area nearly ripped the Anfield Road net out. The goal gave us the lead five minutes before half-time and was that good it won the BBC's Goal of the Season award. We went on to win the game 3-1 with goals from Razor and Jimmy Case. It had been a magnificent team performance with Souness outstanding. Overshadowing all this though in the newspapers was possibly the most publicised act of hooliganism in this country ever at the time. Monday's Daily Mirror carried a full front page picture of a Manchester United fan, Peter Brookes, with a dart in his nose. The picture really was horrific as the dart was stuck in the bone of his nose very close to his eye. This incident showed just how low relations between our fans and those of Manchester United had become. The intense rivalry that had been there for years had now turned to blind, unadulterated hatred. There was fault on both sides for that of course; I had very painful experience of that. It could well have been one of our fans who ended up with a Jim Pike in his grid. Indeed I had seen may horrific injuries to Scousers, including my own, after matches at Old Trafford but to go to a football match and end up being nearly blinded, not to say killed is something I wouldn't wish on anybody. As I've said before, I recount these incidents not to glamorise, much less to condone, acts of hooliganism but just to make people aware that they happened. It's no use trying to pretend they didn't. In subsequent home games T-shirts and badges appeared bearing the legend "Anny Road Darts Team." Funny or sick? Make your own mind up. I have.

CHAPTER NINETEEN

EUROPEAN CUP - AT THE DOUBLE!

Form was still patchy going into the League Cup Final. After the victory against Man U we'd lost at Chelsea (walloped again) and at Derby before a 1-0 home win over Leeds. We had however also completed a marvellous 6-2 aggregate victory over the Portuguese champions Benfica to put us into the European Cup Semi-Final where we would face old foes Borussia Moenchengladbach. The Nottingham Forest side we would face in the Football League Final were fairly romping away with the League title. Nobody was mounting a serious challenge to them although ourselves and Everton were going well. It was just that Clough's new boys were very consistent. Not since Ipswich in the early sixties had a team been promoted from the Second Division and won the Football League Championship in their first season but Forest were well on the way to doing just that. People said their style of football wasn't always pretty to watch but as that accusation had also been levelled at us by green-eyed goons in seasons when we had won the League I did have some sympathy for them. They were pretty much unloved though because of their abrasive managerial pairing of Clough and Peter Taylor. Forest had won four of their first five League games but it was the one they lost, 0-3 at Arsenal, that decided Clough he needed a new goalkeeper. Clough went out and bought the second best 'keeper around (I still think Clemence was better) and certainly the best one available. Peter Shilton came from Stoke having to live up to Clough's billing that the brilliant 'keeper would win Forest ten points a season. For once Clough wasn't talking out of his arse and Shilton more than lived up to those huge expectations. The good news for us was that Shilton couldn't play in the Final; one of his few games for Stoke at the start of the season had been in the League Cup so he was Cup-tied. Happy days! Things would be inestimably easier for us without the massive presence of Shilton to contend with. Or so we thought! Shilton's replacement was 18-year-old Chris Woods, yet to play a League game. Woods was tremendous, keeping out everything we could throw at him. Defences in general dominated what was a turgid game. The 0-0 draw meant the Cup would be decided at Old Trafford the following Wednesday. Both sets of fans got the usual "welcome" from those loveable Mancunians. Coaches had to dodge a seemingly unending barrage of bricks and bottles on the way in to Old Trafford. The match itself was not much better than the Wembley affair. The destiny of the League Cup was decided in the 53rd minute when John O'Hare was about to shoot at goal from just outside the penalty area. Thommo tripped O'Hare, no doubt about that, outside the area. Referee Pat Partridge pointed to the spot. What the fuckin' 'ell? He can't be giving that! He fuckin' has! Even from our vantage point in the Stretford End we could tell that the foul at the other end of the pitch was clearly outside the area. A massive error by Partridge, no doubt, but he did only get one look at it and no benefit of slow motion TV action replays. John Robertson despatched the resultant kick with consummate ease. He might have been a fat bastard but he was a good player and couldn't half take a penalty! The decision later in the game to disallow a Terry Mac "goal" for handball was also debatable but probably right as the linesman on that side of the pitch had also seen Terry bring the ball down high on his chest/arm. These things happen in football though; no use bleating about them. No conspiracy theories from us! Referees make wrong decisions but in general they are made in all honesty; you just have to live with it. What I couldn't live with in this match though was the fact that Cally was booked. Cally was a real gentleman of the game evidenced by the fact this was his first ever booking in a career spanning the best part of 20 years and 850 games. Cally has probably forgiven Partridge for that but I haven't. Thommo got himself into a load of trouble when being interviewed straight after the match. Thommo, still in a high state of excitement and naturally feeling peeved at the perceived injustice of the penalty awarded against him, admitted that he had deliberately tripped O'Hare to prevent him scoring but that he had made sure he fouled the Forest man outside the area. So the term "professional foul" was born. Thommo's contribution to football jargon did not go down well with the FA and was harshly punished by a ban.

I made the "show of defiance" trip to Wolves the following Saturday courtesy of the good people of the Southport branch of the Supporters Club. They very kindly came through Skem to pick me up on their coach. Our players were in the same defiant mood as the fans. They wouldn't let the small matter of a Cup Final defeat get them down for long. We walloped Wolves 3-1 with goals from Jimmy Case and two from Kenny. It was at this game I first heard what has become, apart from "You'll Never Walk Alone" our most famous song: "Poor Scouser Tommy."
Now I don't wish to preach and pontificate here but for Christ' sake (where did he come into it Evo?) why the fuck do people insist on singing their own words to it? We've only been singing it for 25 fuckin' years for fuck sake, you'd think people would know the words by now! As if getting the words wrong isn't bad enough people are even putting their own tune to it now! The tune is "Red River Rock" sometimes also known as "Red River Valley." Okay, I'm no Pavarotti but at least I do know and sing the proper tune. Topping all that though is the fact that it now gets sung in the Kop like people's arses are on fire! What the fuck's all that about? The song is meant to be, should be, best sung and sounds better when it's belted out as it originally was - very slow. Listen sometimes to people singing it slowly in say the Albert or the Blob Shop and it makes your bloody hair stand on end. Well mine doesn't 'cos I ain't bloody got any but you know what I mean. You see I can put up with people singing about a HIGHER division when it should be HIGHLAND. Think about it; the song is about a young lad who is sent off to fight in the Second World War so it's HIGHLAND, as in a Scottish regiment, not HIGHER as in a higher division of the Football League for fuck sake! I can also put up with PLAYS IN RED when it should be DRESSED IN RED. I can even put up with I GO THERE QUITE A LOT

when it should be I GET THROWN OUT QUITE A LOT as in creating that much racket etc that the bizzies have to lash you out. What I definitely can't put up with though is the bloody fuckin' awful 128,000 miles per hour version. It sounds like people can't wait to get it over with. Imagine if this song was sung properly and slow in the Kop by everybody. I tell you, visiting teams would shit themselves. Such a pity that what should be our flagship song has been ruined in this way. Anyway, here's how I remember it sung at Wolves that day. Not saying it was the first time it had ever been sung, just the first time I heard it.

LET ME TELL YOU A STORY OF A POOR BOY
WHO WAS SENT FAR AWAY FROM HIS HOME
TO FIGHT FOR HIS KING AND HIS COUNTRY
AND ALSO THE OLD FOLKS BACK HOME.
SO THEY PUT HIM IN A HIGHLAND DIVISION
SENT HIM OFF TO A FAR, FAR FOREIGN LAND
WHERE THE FLIES SWARM AROUND IN THEIR THOUSANDS
AND THERE'S NOTHING TO SEE BUT THE SAND.
WHEN THE BATTLE IT STARTED NEXT MORNING
UNDER THE ARABIAN SUN
I REMEMBER THAT POOR SCOUSER TOMMY
HE WAS SHOT BY AN OLD NAZI GUN
AS HE LAY ON THE BATTLEFIELD DYIN'
WITH THE BLOOD GUSHIN' OUT OF 'IS 'EAD
AS HE LAY ON THE BATTLEFIELD DYIN' THESE
WERE THE LAST WORDS HE SAID......

Then comes the second part to the tune of "The sash my father wore" which was originally sung in the sixties but sounds good and is obviously very appropriate added to PST:

OH I AM A LIVERPUDLIAN AND I COME FROM THE SPION KOP.
I LIKE TO SING, I LIKE TO SHOUT, I GET THROWN OUT QUITE A LOT (EVERY WEEK)!
WE SUPPORT A TEAM THAT'S DRESSED IN RED, IT'S A TEAM THAT YOU ALL KNOW.

IT'S A TEAM THAT WE CALL LIV-ER-POOL AND TO GLORY WE WILL GO.
WE'VE WON THE LEAGUE, WE'VE WON THE CUP AND WE'VE BEEN TO EUROPE TOO
AND WE'VE PLAYED THE TOFFEES FOR A LAUGH AND WE'VE LEFT THEM FEELIN' BLUE.
The "1-2, 1-2-3, 1-2-3-4, 5-0" is, I feel optional. We did sing that in the sixties, recalling our 5-0 win over the Blues on September 25th 1965 but it's now used also with reference to the 5-0 win at Goodison in November '82 - hence the "Rush scored one etc." I also feel the Rush bit makes people want to get there more quickly. Also the "Dyin' dyin'" and "Of 'is 'ead" repeated bits add to the speed of the song. Sorry for ranting boys and girls but come on, let's get it right.

The first leg of the European Cup Semi-Final was played in Dusseldorf as Borussia's ground was considered to be too small. Hannes gave Borussia an early lead. The usual scenes of bedlam in the Evo household when Elton Welsby screamed out the news that David Johnson had equalised with just two minutes to go were short-lived. Rainer Bonhof who had beaten Clem all ends up with a free-kick when West Germany had played England earlier in the year repeated the trick. This time though Bonhof had a lot of luck as the ball was about to be safely collected by Clem. The ball hit the crouching Clem's shoulder and reared up over him into the net. That was a cruel twist of fate we didn't deserve. Borussia weren't the side they'd been the season before though so hopes were high of overturning the deficit in the return, especially with the bonus of an away goal.

Derby night at Goodison was fun. We went into that game on the back of a marvellous 3-0 win at Villa. Johnno scored the only goal of the game in the 13th minute but the fun and games came later on. Bob Latchford, a big man himself, squared up to Tommy Smith. I don't know what possessed Big Bob to think that would be a good idea but he must have instantly regretted it. Tommy grabbed Latchford by the throat and after shaking him like a rag doll for a few seconds then literally threw him away.

WE ALL AGREE, TOMMY IS 'ARDER THAN LATCHFORD!

That incident must have inspired Tommy's goalscoring talents as he scored an unlikely brace in the 3-2 win against Leicester in the next match. Little Sammy Lee, who looked more suited to ballboy rather than first team duties, scored the other goal in an impressive debut.

The assertion that Borussia Moenchengladbach were not quite the team we'd beaten in the previous season's Final proved to be correct as we easily overturned the deficit from the match in Dusseldorf. Razor, Kenny and Jimmy Case all scored in a resounding 3-0 win. Problem now I thought would be getting a ticket for the Wembley final against other old adversaries, Bruges, who had done marvellously well to defeat Juventus in their Semi-Final. Actually that turned out to be not so much of a problem at all, for me at any rate. Although we were only given 20,00 tickets for the 92,00 capacity stadium (8,000 had to be taken off the capacity for floodlit games) most Season Ticket holders qualified.

We still had work to do in the League. Forest duly and deservedly won the League, clinching the title with a 0-0 draw at Coventry with four games to spare. A virtuoso performance by Kenny in the penultimate League game of the season against Manchester City saw him score a magnificent hat trick in the 4-0 win. Kenny really was awesome. He'd had a brilliant first season in England and proved himself to be a truly world class player. Defenders kicked lumps out of him in every game but he almost always managed to rise above it, in fact he seemed to thrive on it. Kenny had the heart of a lion and the touch of an angel. Kenny's crowning glory to the season was yet to come.

The final League game of the season saw Champions Forest force a 0-0 draw. They didn't quite receive the reception Leeds had when actually clinching the title at Anfield nine years earlier but were a fine side and good luck to them. We couldn't do any more than gain the same 57 points we had when winning the League the previous season. We'd remained unbeaten in our last twelve games, drawing three and winning nine but Forest were just too good for everybody that season. It hurt that we'd lost our title but we'd be going for it back hell for leather next season.

Everybody from Skem going to Wembley were doing their own thing. Baz had this huge Union Jack bearing the legend: "LIVERPOOL EUROPEAN CHAMPIONS" which took two huge poles either side to keep it upright. It really was something else and I wanted to go with him but he went by train with another lad from work. I was going by coach from the trusty old Lawrenson's in Bootle. Luckily there were a good few Bootle lads on there I knew from when I was kid. One of them was Jimmy Limb. Christ, could that man drink? The coach was full of Stella; well, we had to pay tribute to our Belgian guests didn't we? You could do things like that, take loads of ale on footy coaches, then. Such a pity that 25 years on the few have spoilt it for the many, unless you go on Barnes' Happy Al's coaches that is where it seems you can't get on if you HAVEN'T got any ale! Happy Al's are always good for a bit of mind expanding too! We were all well and truly Stellatised by the time we neared Wembley. Most of the coaches were carrying Liverpool supporters. The few Bruges supporters that passed us seemed mostly friendly folk. It seemed they were going to enjoy themselves more than anything else. One of them outdid us in the robbing stakes though. A Bruges coach was right alongside ours. One of the lads on our coach had a flag fluttering out of a window. A Bruges supporter jumped off their coach, dragged the flag out of the window and took his booty aboard. The Bruges supporters were laughing like fuck at us as they sped away. The lad who had his flag robbed was doing his fuckin' nut but everybody else was pissing themselves laughing. A new song was being given an almighty airing to the tune of Lily Marlene:

UNDERNEATH THE FLOODLIGHTS DOWN IN DUSSELDORF
ALL THE KOPITES SINGIN', BEVVIED UP OF COURSE.
WE'VE BEEN TO LISBON AND TO ROME
AND OUR TEAM NEVER WALKS ALONE
WE'RE GOIN' BACK TO WEMBLEY TO WIN THE CUP
AT HOME.

Great song that; one of my favourites. Once inside the stadium it became clear that even though we'd only been given 20,000 tickets there were at least 80,000 Reds present. Apart from about 10,000, at the most, Bruges supporters at the opposite end to where I was the rest of Wembley Stadium was a sea of red. I think this was possibly the start of our out of town support, in a big way anyway. I'd seen people from different parts of the country following our team before but never on this big a scale. I was made up that Davy Fairclough was in the starting eleven. He had been so disappointed at being left out of the team for last season's Final. The same could also be said of course for different reasons about Thommo. He had missed out in Rome because of injury so there was nobody more determined to retain our European Cup. Also missing was Tommy Smith. The end to the Anfield Iron's career came in ignominious fashion when he sustained a freak accident at home dropping a pickaxe on his foot. He must have been getting soft in his old age as in his younger days he probably would have volleyed it over the garden wall. Tommy's place was taken by young Jocky. The Bruges players seemed to take the match in the same vein as their supporters - just happy to be there. They certainly didn't put up much of a fight. The game plan for them seemed to be to keep the score down. Maybe you couldn't blame them as playing at Wembley that night was virtually like a home game for us. Our two best players combined to give us the lead after 65 minutes. Graeme Souness, a big bear of a man with the touch of a violinist, played an exquisite pass into the path of King Kenny. Kenny waited for the Bruges 'keeper Jensen to commit himself by going down at his feet before delicately lifting the ball over the 'keeper, using the space he'd created by his audacity. The ball seemed to take an eternity to reach the net. Davy Fairclough following up Kenny's shot might even have got a touch on it himself if he'd been half a second or so quicker. There was no taking this goal away from Kenny though. Bedlam all over Wembley! Kenny vaulted the advertising hoardings to run to the crowd and very nearly ended up on the terraces with us. It takes great players to win massive games like this. It also takes equally great players to save these games. Kenny and Thommo were certainly in that category. With just a couple of minutes left to play a terribly misplaced back pass by Jocky was collected by Simoen. Simoen rounded Clem and rolled the ball towards the seemingly empty net. Thommo appeared as if from nowhere and managed to stretch one of his long, skinny legs just enough to knock the ball off the line and out for a corner. That was Bruges' only chance of the night. We had achieved what no other British team had and retained the European Cup. Okay, it was a poor game and we hadn't done it in the grand manner as we had in Rome but it was still joyful all the same. Wearing the biggest smile of the night was King Kenny.

EVERY OTHER SATDEE ON ME 'ALF DAY OFF
IT'S OFF TO THE MATCH I GO.
WE'LL ALL GO WALKIN' DOWN THE ANFIELD ROAD
ME AND ME OL' PAL JOE.
WE LOVE TO SEE THE LASSIES WITH THEIR RED
SCARVES ON
WE LOVE TO HEAR THE KOPITES ROAR
BUT I DON'T 'AVE TO TELL YER BOYS THAT BEST OF
ALL WE LOVE TO SEE THE LIVERPOOL SCORE!
WE'VE WON THE ENGLISH LEAGUE ABARR A
MILLION TIMES; UEFA WAS A SIMPLE THING.
WE GAVE SOME EXHIBITIONS IN THE FA CUP
WE'VE 'AD OUR WEMBLEY VISITS TOO
BUT WHEN WE THE EUROPEAN CUP IN ROME LIKE
WE SHOULDA DONE YEARS BEFORE

WE GATHERED DOWN AT ANFIELD ROAD A HUNDRED THOUSAND STRONG TO GIVE THE BOYS A WELCOME HOME.
OH OH OH KENNY, OH OH OH KENNY I'D WALK A MILLION MILES FOR ONE OF YOUR GOALS OH KENNY!